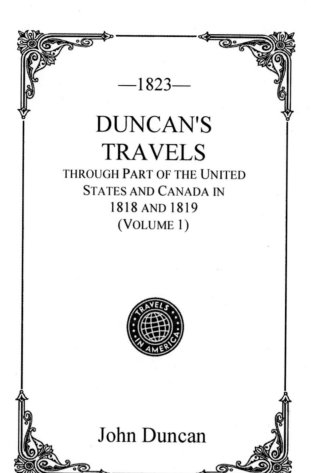

—1823—

DUNCAN'S TRAVELS

THROUGH PART OF THE UNITED
STATES AND CANADA IN
1818 AND 1819
(VOLUME 1)

John Duncan

Volume 40a

APPLEWOOD BOOKS
Carlisle, Massachusetts

First Edition

ISBN: 1-4290-0097-X (Paperback)

For a free copy of our current print catalog, write to:
Applewood Books
PO Box 365
Bedford, MA 01730

For more complete listings,
visit us on the web at:
awb.com

TRAVELS IN AMERICA.

"There is a people who will one day be very great:—I mean the Americans. One stain only obscures the perfect splendour of reason which vivifies that country—slavery still subsists in the southern provinces; but when the Congress shall have found a remedy for that evil, how shall we be able to refuse the most profound respect to the institutions of the United States?"

MADAME DE STAËL.

TRAVELS

THROUGH PART OF

THE UNITED STATES

AND

CANADA

IN

1818 AND 1819.

By JOHN M. DUNCAN, A. B.

IN TWO VOLUMES.

VOL. I.

GLASGOW:

Printed at the University Press,

FOR HURST, ROBINSON, & COMPANY, LONDON;

OLIVER & BOYD, EDINBURGH;

AND WARDLAW & CUNNINGHAME, GLASGOW.

1823.

GLASGOW:
ANDREW & JOHN M. DUNCAN,
Printers to the University.

TO

BENJAMIN SILLIMAN Esquire

PROFESSOR OF CHEMISTRY AND NATURAL HISTORY

IN YALE COLLEGE

&c. &c. &c.

THE FOLLOWING PAGES

ARE

AFFECTIONATELY AND VERY RESPECTFULLY

INSCRIBED

BY THE AUTHOR.

PREFACE.

So much has been written within these few years
respecting North America, that it may not be unnecessary, in introducing the succeeding pages to
the reader's notice, to state the grounds on which
the author ventures to solicit for them a favourable
reception.

In the numerous works which have been published, both on the United States and Canada,
comparatively little has been said as to the moral
condition of the inhabitants, their literary and religious characteristics;—on these, certainly the
most important features in the American character,
the writer is persuaded that much misapprehen-
sion prevails in his native country, and he would

gladly be instrumental in removing a part of it. He does not indeed pretend to have given any of these subjects a systematic discussion; but they have been steadily kept in view as particularly deserving of attention, and he hopes that he has succeeded in bringing together a good deal of information, on matters of permanent interest and importance, without altogether excluding topics of a lighter kind, on which a traveller is generally permitted to be somewhat loquacious.

It may be asked, why so long an interval has been allowed to elapse, between the date of the travels and the period of their publication? He can only reply that the resolution to publish, was formed and abandoned oftener than once; and after the composition was begun, various interruptions occurred to retard its progress. He is persuaded, however, that the work has suffered nothing from this delay; on the contrary, that however defective it may now be, it would have been still more so, had the compilation been completed any considerable time sooner.

The interesting author of the ' Diary of an Invalid,' remarks, that "no one but he who has tried the experiment, knows how difficult it is to be accurate;—a book of travels must always be more or less a volume of inaccuracies." / Perfectly assured, from his own experience, of the truth of these positions; the author bespeaks the indulgence of the reader, both to the materials of his book, and to its execution. On matters of opinion, he must expect that many will think him in error; on those of fact and observation, he trusts, that, although he may have sometimes gone wrong, he will not in general be found unworthy of confidence.

University Press, Glasgow,
    October 25th, 1823.

CONTENTS

OF

VOLUME FIRST.

9

LETTER I.

LETTER I.

Fayal, one of the Azores,
March 14th, 1818.

WHEN the Fanny's topsails were loosed on the 2d of February, and the anchor weighed by which she had been riding, I anticipated no landing place between Greenock and New York; but here we are amidst the orange groves of Fayal, after six weeks' tossing upon the boisterous ocean.

The wind was unfavourable when we sailed, and has continued so with very little intermission, till within the last two days; sleet and rain poured on us almost incessantly for four weeks; while heavy gales, and even hurricanes, succeeded each other for the same period, with a frequency and violence which our Captain says he never before experienced, in about thirty passages across the Atlantic. Our vessel bears the sad tokens of the hardships of a winter voyage; the greater part of the bulwarks have been stove in, our sprit-sail

yard is gone, twice the jib boom has been carried
away, the billet head is lashed with ropes, or it
would have long since left us, and on one occasion,
while lying too under a new main-stay-sail, the
canvass burst with a tremendous report, and a great
part of it was blown to rags before it was possible
to haul it down.   To complete the detail, we have
beat about from near the 58th degree of latitude,
to our present position, close by the 38th, without a
possibility of getting any farther to the westward.[1]

During the last fortnight, we have been in
smoother waters and a warmer climate; but the
winds continuing to baffle us, we are compelled to
take refuge here, and glad indeed to attain it, that
we might procure a supply of water and provisions.
The delay is somewhat mortifying, yet I scarcely
regret that it has occurred, since it has been the
means of bringing us among these orange clad isles,
blooming in the verdure of perpetual spring, which
I should probably never otherwise have had an opportunity of visiting.

Four days ago we first descried land; but then,
by inexperienced eyes, scarcely to be distinguished

[1] Soon after our arrival in New York, tidings were received of the
loss of several vessels which had sailed from Liverpool for America,
a few days after we left Greenock, and had encountered on the coast,
the same gales which we had with difficulty weathered at sea.   Some
were dismasted, some cast ashore and totally wrecked; others were
never heard of after leaving the port, and of course, must have found-
ered at sea.   Thus it is, in the mysterious operations of Divine
Providence, that " one is taken and another left."

from a dim cloud hovering on the verge of the horizon. Next morning we were within a few miles
of St. Michael's. The sky was cloudless and se-
rene, the fishing boats of the natives were rowing
about, land birds were sweeping in airy circles
around us, and the eye rested, with a hitherto unknown delight, upon the green verdure of the
swelling eminences which receded from the rocky
shore.

St. Michael's, the largest of the Azores, or Hawk
islands, as the name signifies, bears like the others,
every appearance of a volcanic origin. The shore
is most generally bold and precipitous; and in many
places around it huge and shapeless rocks start
abruptly out of the water; some of them broad and
square, showing patches of vegetation, others bare
and splintered, and at a distance resembling somewhat the dilapidated columns of an ancient temple.
Backwards from the rocky shore the ground heaves
with graceful undulations, between which may be
sometimes seen scattered cottages and inclosures,
but I could discover few trees of any considerable
size. These hills terminate in a bare rocky ridge,
which appeared to us to traverse the greater part of
the island.

Doubling the northern point, and gaining sight
of the principal town and harbour, we tacked and
stood in. A westerly breeze would now for the
first time have favoured us, but during the preceding night it had shifted to the eastward, and we

soon found that it would be difficult to make the port. Unwilling to lose entirely the benefit of the change, our captain determined to abandon the attempt, and to make rather for Fayal, about three degrees of longitude farther in our direct course for America. The vessel was therefore put about, the yards were squared, the studding sails for the first time spread before the breeze, and now

> " Merrily, merrily goes the bark,
> Before the gale she bounds ;
> So starts the dolphin from the shark,
> Or the stag before the hounds."

But disappointment reigned on board. We had assured ourselves of setting foot on dry land, the steward's shoe brushes had been busy in the morning, we were all rigged out in our best, and now our eager anticipations were baffled, by what we least expected, a fair wind. The waves were curling their white tops behind us, and the vessel driving gaily along at the rate of seven or eight knots an hour, but we could not help gazing wistfully over the stern, at the rapidly receding shores of St. Michael's.

The following day was cloudy, but the wind continued fair, and early in the forenoon we descried the conical summit of the Peak of Pico, resting in solitary magnificence above a throne of clouds. The height of this mountain is estimated at 9000 feet; in fine weather it is seen at a distance of 25 leagues, and now its lofty apex was a land mark in our view, long before we could discover the base of the island. Gradually it enlarged at our approach, and in a few hours we entered the narrow channel between Pico and Fayal.

Villa Orta, the principal town in Fayal, is built in the form of a crescent, in the hollow of a little bay towards the middle of the island, and, from the water, has rather an imposing appearance. The ground slopes up pretty abruptly from the shore, and the houses, which are almost universally white washed, with black mouldings and projections, overtop each other as they recede; several churches and other large buildings relieve the eye at intervals, and some inconsiderable fortifications skirt the beach. The deep toned peal of church and convent bells floated through the air as we passed, and we felt gratified at the prospect of mingling again in the busy hum of men."

Except in this little bay there is no anchorage ground; the shore everywhere else is as steep and rocky as that of St. Michael's, and the water of great depth. The wind, however, blew so strong that the Captain thought it dangerous to enter, and it was not till the following day, after having made the circuit of the island, that we had the satisfaction of letting go the anchor; we were now within a quarter of a mile of the shore, and yet found 21 fathoms water. In a short time we were visited by the health boat, and after a few pre-

liminary ceremonies, we received permission to go
on shore.

I accompanied the captain to the office of Mr.
D——, the American consul, and after the necessary orders had been given for the supplies which
we required, we were invited by the consul to
accompany him home.

The residence of this gentleman is in a beautiful
situation at a short distance from the town; the
house fronts the sea, and commands a view of Pico.
The garden with which it is surrounded, is such
as cannot be seen in our inhospitable clime. Skirting the upper part of it, was a hedge composed
entirely of geraniums, about six feet high, containing every variety of leaf and flower, and blooming
with all the luxuriance of summer. Scattered in
the richest profusion along the walks, were orange,
lemon, and citron trees, covered with blossoms and
fruit in every stage of advancement; and thus they
appear the whole year round, with only this exception, that the principal crop is ripe about
the month of December or January, at which
period the fruit is exported. Roses fully blown
were shedding their fragrance, the peach tree and
the acacia were covered with blossoms, and around
were the sugar cane, the tea and coffee shrubs,
the almond tree, and the fig. All these were in
full verdure, the vines alone were bare. We saw
also the dark green shrub, from which it is said

that the island takes its name; its buds, however, had not then burst.

We returned in the evening to the vessel, with a large basket of the most delicious oranges, a present from Mr. D——, and an invitation to the cabin passengers to spend the following day with his family. We found on board a number of the natives, spreading out on the deck various articles of merchandise, among which were little red baskets of very delicate workmanship, some of which I secured as a memorial of my visit.

At breakfast next morning, I remarked the want of a fire place in the parlour where we sat; but fire places, except in the kitchen, are here unknown. The thermometer ranges from 52° to 80° Fahr., consequently the islanders know nothing either of cold or of excessive heat. Vegetation never ceases. To counterbalance these advantages, the whole of the Azores are liable to frequent earthquakes, and even to occasional volcanic eruptions.

To occupy a part of the forenoon, a visit was proposed to some of the churches, where the ceremonies of Lent were going forward. Under the patronage of Mr. D——'s son, we found ready access by a private passage to one of the largest; and were permitted to stand within a few yards of the altar, apart from the congregation, where we were recognised as mere spectators of what was going forward.

The scene which presented itself was of the most

gorgeous description.   The walls and roof were
profusely adorned with painting and gilding; the
altar was decked with crucifixes, large candle-
sticks, chalices, and salvers, most of which were
gilt, and boquets of beautiful flowers.   Behind
the altar was a sloping platform of very considerable extent, rising as it receded into a deep oval
recess, and covered with a multitude of lighted
candles.   Pyramids of candles were fixed here and
there over the walls, as well as on an iron railing
which crossed at the bottom of the platform, to
separate it from the body of the church.   The
officiating priests were three in number, attired in
splendid robes of richly figured and embossed
silk, of a primrose colour, with massy cords and
tassels hanging over their shoulders.   Portions of
the dress of the principal priest were occasionally
changed by his colleagues, and one of them at
intervals, removed the spectacles from his nose,
with the most ridiculous solemnity.   Their persons, of the goodliest diameter, and their round
rosy cheeks, contrasted most wonderfully with the
scarecrow congregation below the railing.   Their
smooth shining bullet heads were surrounded with
a ring of hair, and one of them resembled strongly
the portrait of Louis the 18th.   Two or three assistants in white robes attended beside them, and
at one corner of the platform, stood a young man
closely habited in black, with a candle larger than
a walking stick in his hand, bowing, muttering,

and crossing himself, during the whole of the ceremony.

The service was high mass, that is, mass accompanied with singing; and however disgusting in other respects, the vocal music, with the accompaniment of the organ, was exceedingly fine. The melodious voices of a body of females rose from the lower end of the church, where, as I afterwards learned, were the nuns of an adjoining convent, shrouded behind a grating.

After consecrating the wine, in a gilt cup, the senior priest carried it down from the altar, one of the attendants then expanded over his head a large silk umbrella, of a similar texture to the robes, the other two priests followed behind him, and around were the whole body of assistants, carrying enormous wax candles.   In this order the wine was paraded down to the bottom of the church, and back again, through the kneeling ranks of the congregation, who crossed themselves most zealously as it passed.   By and by the same form was repeated with the wafers, and part of them administered through the iron grating to the abbess and the nuns.   At intervals, silver censers filled with glowing embers were handed to the priests, and clouds of incense were offered before the altar.

I could not help remarking that the priests with all their assumed solemnity and devotion, seemed somewhat at a loss to keep it up.   One of them eyed us askance with considerable intentness dur-

ing the greater part of the time, and both of the
less active ones whispered occasionally to each
other, and to the assistants, in a trifling and irre-
verent manner.   The ceremonial itself was far too
stiff and fidgetting to be at all imposing; a priest
pulling spectacles off another's nose, marching
within doors under an umbrella, and shifting from
one side to another like an awkward dancer in a
minuet, seems a very probable means of exciting
disgust, but a very improbable one of cherishing
devotion.   An indescribable sensation of uneasiness
pervaded my mind, during all the time that we
continued in this temple of superstition; and I was
happy to escape from the sickening smell of the
incense, and the smoky glimmering of the candles,
to the freshness of the open air and the pure light
of heaven. ·   ·

We were next conducted to a nunnery; but a
wrinkled portress, who answered our summons at
the porch, told us that no strangers could be admitted during Lent.   If all the nuns within resembled her, I thought there was but little need to be
very careful in locking them up.   By the side of
the nunnery door was a kind of small barrel, filling
an opening in the wall, and whirling round upon
pivots at top and bottom; this is open at one side
and fitted with shelves, so that an article may be
conveyed out or in by turning it round, without
the parties being seen by each other, and some
mendicants were waiting in the porch to receive

alms from within, by means of this machine. The old lady before sending us away, gave us to understand, that the sisters made some fine artificial flowers, of which they would be happy to sell us a few.

Mr. D—— informed us, that seclusion in these nunneries was, in many cases, by no means a voluntary act; but parents who had several daughters, were often accustomed to force one or two of them to take the veil, that they might thus be enabled to give the others a more handsome marriage portion. The daughters of our northern isle may, perhaps, envy the natives of Fayal their ignorance of frost and snow, and all the rigours of our ungenial climate; but how grateful ought they to be, that they enjoy the far greater blessings of personal and religious freedom, and that we have been rescued from the unrelenting tyranny of so demoniacal a superstition.

Villa Orta, although of a showy appearance from the water, is in reality a confused and dirty town. The streets are narrow, crooked, and ill paved, the houses low and gloomy. The buildings are of stone, covered with tiles, and except the churches, in general but one story in height. The windows are covered externally by a projecting lattice, of crossed slips of wood, painted of a dark green colour, which conceals effectually those within. They are, however, capable of being opened outwards on hinges, and we frequently saw the inmates peeping at us from behind them. One of the largest buildings, consisting of several stories, was formerly the Jesuits' college, but is now occupied by our kind entertainer, Mr. D——, as a wine cellar, in which trade he is extensively engaged.

The only carriages which I saw, were small clumsy carts drawn by two oxen. These singular machines consist of a bottom of solid boards, tapering out in front into a single shaft, with a few rude pins stuck into it to serve in place of sides; the wheels are each of a single piece of solid wood with a thin outer edge, and have heavy iron nails hammered into the circumference, as a substitute for rings; they are fixed immovably to the axle, which revolves along with them, within a small box passing under the cart. No mercy is shown to the poor animals which drag them; we saw them urged with heavy blows and loud vociferations, while the wretched cart went wriggling through deep ruts, under the most disproportioned loads.

The Azores are subject to Portugal, and the language of that country is universally spoken. The natives are slender, but well made. The men wear cotton jackets and trowsers, and some who had come from the country with cattle for sale, carried a long staff or pole in their hands. The women are more fantastically attired. Some are completely shrouded in large blue cloaks, somewhat resembling in shape, the *red duffles* of our native country, but much more ample in their folds;

the hood is very large, and is gathered close by
the hand at the mouth, so as completely to conceal
the features; the upper part projects forward, and
no more is left open than is barely sufficient to
enable the lady to pilot her way. These are most
convenient dresses for those who court concealment, for a husband cannot recognise his wife on
the street, unless some peculiarity of gait or figure
betrays her. Others wear a man's great coat; a
large gay shawl over the shoulders, and a smaller
one falling from the crown of the head to the back
of the neck, surmounted by a man's hat; a white
handkerchief round the throat, and a staff in the
hand.

Externally the natives are amazingly polite, and
universally salute you in the street, with their hand
to their hat, but in the little intercourse which we
had with them, we found them avaricious, crafty,
and malignant. The soldiers and sailors of the
health boat importuned us for money in the presence of their officers; the prices which they
asked for their baskets and other commodities,
were most exorbitant, and they often accepted a
fourth of their first demand; but what was worse,
one of them having disagreed with one of our
steerage passengers, about the price of a pig, drew
out a large knife and threatened to stab him.

The white wine, which is made in considerable
quantities at Fayal, is, to my taste, a very poor
article; it is, however, very potent, and some of

our steerage passengers got prodigiously loquacious
under its influence.   The grapes are chiefly the produce of Pico, where there are few inhabitants except those who are employed in the culture of the
vines.   Fayal produces wheat, Indian corn, oranges and lemons.   The lemons are I suspect of
rather an inferior quality, but the oranges, as is
well known, are of the most delicious richness ; the
skin is thin and tender, and they contain few seeds.
When allowed to ripen on the tree, however, they
attain to a perfection which is never found in the
exported fruit, which must necessarily be gathered
when hard, or it could not endure the voyage.
Fayal oranges, as well as those from all the other
islands, bear the general name of St. Michael's,
when in the European market.

Our arrival here has been exceedingly opportune
as regards our intercourse with Mr. D——'s family, for this happens to be his eldest son's birth day.
We have had in consequence an opportunity of
being guests at the birth day dinner, and of mingling our congratulations on this happy occasion,
with thanks for the polite attention which has been
paid to us.   The back of the chair in which Mr.
D——, Junior, sàt, was adorned with a profusion
of the most beautiful flowers and fruit blossoms ;
a voluntary expression of regard and good wishes
from the servants of the family.   After dinner, two
of Mr. D——'s daughters, very interesting young
ladies favoured us with some fine music upon the

piano forte, and you can easily imagine with what feelings of homeward attraction I listened to the " Blue bells of Scotland," on this little fairy island in the middle of the vast Atlantic.

I could with great pleasure have spent a few days here, to have had an opportunity of climbing the vast Peak of Pico, and of enlarging my acquaintance with the general aspect of Fayal, but our captain has attained the object of his visit, and has summoned us on board, in the hope, as the wind is still fair, that the latter part of our voyage will be more pleasant and more propitious than its commencement.

B

LETTER II.

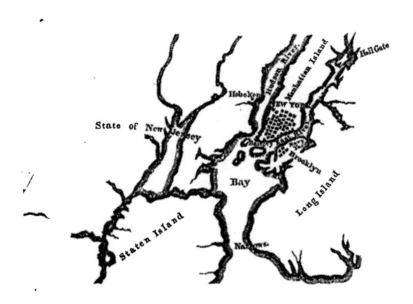

LETTER II.

New York, May, 1818.

AFTER leaving Fayal we enjoyed in general fair
winds and pleasant weather, till near the banks of
Newfoundland, where we experienced the usual
fogs and a thunderstorm. Excepting the phenomena of the Gulf stream, we met with nothing
very deserving of notice during the second portion
of our voyage. This singular current is so called
in consequence of having its source in the Gulf of
Mexico from which it issues between Florida and
the island of Cuba, and flows in a north-easterly
course, skirting for a time the shore of America
and then losing itself in the vast Atlantic. Its velocity near its source is about four knots an hour,
which gradually decreases, as the distance from
the source and the centre of the current becomes
greater, but its most remarkable characteristic is
the very high temperature which it retains even at

B 3

a distance of fifteen hundred to two thousand miles from the Gulf. Intelligent shipmasters are accustomed to observe the comparative state of the thermometer in the water and in the air, as an important assistance in ascertaining their course; and in going out to America they keep as much as possible to the north of the stream, to avoid its powerful obstruction. For several days we found the water from ten to fifteen degrees warmer than the air, and on one occasion the variation was as much as twenty-two; we were then at no great distance from the southern extremity of Nova Scotia, when the thermometer stood in the air at 45° and in the water at 67° Fahr.

On the seventeenth day after losing sight of Fayal, we made Sandy Hook, and had the pleasure of taking an American pilot on board. The boat in which he came out to us particularly attracted my notice, by its neatness of appearance and great rapidity of sailing. It was a small decked vessel, schooner-rigged, and very sharp in the bows. At a great distance we observed its peaked sails skimming over the water, and bearing down upon us with the utmost precision and velocity; when a short way off, its foresail was backed for a moment, and a small two oared yawl lowered over the side, which brought the pilot to our vessel, and returning, was instantly hoisted on board; the sails were again trimmed, and it darted away, as if to display its superior speed and mock our tardy motion; it

stretched across our bows, and dashed alternately
to windward and leeward, sweeping round our vessel like a sea gull round a rock.

The progress of our ship up the river was prevented by a strong head wind, but the passengers
were eager to get to New York, rather more than
twenty miles distant, and we chartered the pilot
boat to convey us: to her the head wind was a
matter of little consequence, and in four hours we
were safely landed at the wharf. Before getting
ashore, which was about nine o'clock at night, we
were boarded by the emissaries of two morning
newspapers, who extracted from us the principal
occurrences of the voyage, with the names of the
passengers, and next morning by six the whole was
served out to the public from both offices.

The custom house regulations of the United
States relative to passengers, are very liberal,—
all their personal luggage, and even implements of
trade and husbandry for their own use, being ex-
empted from duty; and I found the officer who
was put on board the vessel to examine our trunks,
perfectly civil and accommodating. His appearance bespoke him a man of habits and taste very
superior to a large proportion of those whom we
find performing similar duties at home, and one
whom no one would be disposed to insult with the
offer of those paltry gratuities, to give them no worse
name, for which excuses are so frequently discovered. I had been solicited to take charge of some

B 4

volumes as presents from persons at home to their
friends here, and as they could not be included in
the entry which I was required to make, under the
sanction of an oath, respecting my own luggage, I
showed them to the searching officer, and at once
obtained his permission to send them ashore.   All
that he detained was a selection from a bundle of
tracts, which he begged me to give him with a view
to their being reprinted here;—few persons in the
same profession at home would have been likely to
prefer such a request.

I have now spent several weeks in New York,
but shall postpone for the present any remarks
upon the social, moral, or political characteristics
of its inhabitants, in the hope that I shall hereafter
have abundant opportunities of more extensive observation; the remaining pages of this letter shall
rather be devoted to brief notices of the more remarkable peculiarities of their city.

New York is built upon the southern point of
Manhattan island, and enjoys a situation in every
respect admirably suited for commercial purposes.
The Hudson, or North River, passes it upon the one
side; a narrow part of Long Island Sound, familiarly
termed the East River, washes it upon the other ;
while in front is a noble bay, expanding between
the shores of Long Island and New Jersey, in
which the united navies of the world might spread
their canvass.   Below the bay are the Narrows,
facilitating the defence of the harbour, and at va-

rious points above and below them are forts of
such imposing strength, that it seems impossible
that any naval armament can ever reach the city,
unless in consequence of the co-operating exertions
of a powerful land force. Ice very rarely, now,
obstructs the navigation, and about twenty miles
from the city the Atlantic opens to the vessels,
without a rock or island thereafter to annoy them.
With the eastern coast of America, there is a convenient and safe communication through Long
Island Sound; and the Hudson, having its source
in the upper part of the state, affords an inland
navigation, even for large vessels, of more than a
hundred and fifty miles.

Extensive as the commerce of the Hudson already is, the great canals which are now in progress, between Lake Erie on the one side and
Lake Champlain on the other, must operate powerfully to augment it. New York will thus become
the concentrating point, for the greater part of
the commerce of the great lakes on the left,
and the state of Vermont on the right; and the
stimulus which is already to a considerable degree
felt from steam navigation, must, from the nature
of the country, operate more powerfully in this
district than in any other of this vast continent.
The population of the upland country will now
advance more rapidly than ever, and not a tree
will be felled which does not necessarily operate to
increase the trade and riches of New York.

The harbour of New York is one of the best in
the country, and is capable of almost unlimited ex-
tension. The wharfs skirt both sides of the island,
and piers project at right angles into the stream,
leaving intermediate slips, which have many of the
advantages of wet docks and are free from several of
their inconveniences. The tides rise and fall about
six feet, but there is always water enough abreast
of the piers to float the largest merchantmen.
They do not however enjoy the advantage of dry
docks, for the tide does not ebb sufficiently to empty
them and mechanical means have not yet been resorted to; but vessels which need repair are hove
down in shallow water, first upon the one side and
then upon the other.

With such accumulated advantages, in possession and in prospect, it is not surprising that New
York has been hitherto the commercial capital of
the United States, and the principal point of communication between North America and Europe;
it is probable indeed that it will long retain this
pre-eminence. Masts surround the city like reeds
on the margin of a pool; and when one passes
along the wharfs, and witnesses the never ceasing
operations of loading and discharging, warping out
and hauling in, vessels of every description arriving
and sailing with every breeze that blows, together
with the bustling of shippers, custom-house officers,
sailors, and carmen, he cannot but be impressed
with the great extent of the commerce, which can

supply such extensive means with such unceasing employment.

The streets in the lower and older portion of the city are very narrow and crooked, and what is more immediately inexcusable, kept in very bad order. Garbage and litter of almost every kind are thrown out upon the pavement, where a multitude of hogs of all ages riot in abundance. The foot walks are encumbered with projecting steps and cellar doors, lamp posts, pump wells, and occasionally poplar trees; and where any open space occurs, barrels, packing-boxes, and wheelbarrows, are not unfrequently piled up. The citizens could not, I think, do better than import half a dozen of our Glasgow police officers, to make a reform in their street regulations, and instruct them in the mysteries of common-sewers and gutters. No town affords greater facilities for subterraneous drains, for the ground slopes on both sides from the centre to the water, and no town that ever I saw stands so much in need of them. The more modern streets are greatly superior in every respect; they are in general wide and straight, and the footwalks comparatively free of projections and encumbrances. The city is throughout very indifferently lighted, and in many places the feeble glimmerings of a solitary oil lamp, must struggle past two stately trees, which stand like sentinels to defend it.

Broadway, the Trongate of New York, passes longitudinally through the centre of the city, and occupies in general the highest part of the ground; it is wide and straight, and pretty compactly built for nearly two miles. It contains a great many well built houses of brick, but there is still a considerable intermixture of paltry wooden ones; a few scattered poplars skirt each side, but I cannot think them any improvement; their bareness in winter increases the dreariness of the prospect, and they are too ragged and dusty in summer to be at all beautiful.

The early Dutch settlers, with a pertinacious but characteristic adherence to national customs, imported bricks from Holland to construct their dwellings, and a few of these houses still remain; they are one story in height, with the gable end to the street and a little iron weathercock perched upon the top of it. The British settlers, however, of more innovating dispositions, laid the surrounding forests under contribution for building materials, and a considerable proportion of the older part of the city is still constructed of wood. Frequent and destructive fires were the natural consequence of this system, and these are still every winter grubbing out a few of the remaining wooden tenements. The erection of wooden houses is now prohibited, and the brick ones which succeed them are built with a neatness which is unknown in houses of a similar material at home. The bricks are made of a very fine clay, which affords a very close and smooth grain, and the buildings are always showily painted, either of a bright red with white lines upon the seams, or of a clean looking yellow. In many of the more recent ones, the lintels and steps are of marble. Stone buildings are very rare.

Except the City Hall there is scarcely a public building deserving of notice. This is a splendid edifice, almost entirely of white marble; the architecture however is unfortunately very faulty, so that the very reverse of Ovid's description, " materiam superabat opus," is in this case applicable. Internal convenience seems to have been the presiding principle in its design, and a republican propensity to saving, exhibited in constructing the basement story of red free stone, and the dome of painted wood, has still farther injured its appearance.

The building is an oblong square with projecting wings, two stories in height besides the basement; with a portico of half the height between the wings, and a kind of lantern dome, supporting a figure of Justice. The portico consists of sixteen Ionic columns, springing from a handsome flight of steps, but unhappily surmounted by a balustraded balcony, in place of a pediment. In the front there are no less than between sixty and seventy windows; some of them flat and others arched, and a few with intervening Corinthian pilasters. The prevailing defect is the absence of simplicity and grandeur. The portico, in relation

to the building, is exceedingly dwarfish, and the
windows with their minute ornaments break down
the whole into too much detail; the injudicious
use of red stone also, in the basement story, materially diminishes the apparent height. The principal entrance is by the portico in front; within
is a handsome lobby, with a marble stair of elegant
proportions leading to the second story, and from
a circular railed gallery at the landing place, ten
marble columns arise, supporting the dome. The
apartments of the building, are appropriated to the
use of the Common Council of the city, and the
different Courts of Law. The chair occupied by
the Mayor in the Council Room, is the same in
which Washington sat, when presiding at the first
Congress of the United States; and a full length
portrait of this great man, with those of some
others of the Revolutionary chiefs, adorns the walls.
In the other rooms there is a profusion of portraits
of officers who distinguished themselves during
the recent conflict. It is remarkable, that in this
building there is no room at all adapted for the
purposes of a popular meeting; we may well wonder at this omission in the principal city of a republican state, where every Act of the Legislature
is introduced by the proud preamble, " WE THE
PEOPLE OF THE STATE OF NEW YORK, BY THE
GRACE OF GOD, FREE AND INDEPENDENT."

A very few of the churches are of stone, but
their architecture in general presents glaring speci-

mens of bad taste.[2]   The steeples are in some cases
lofty, but always of wood, and though as gay as
white paint and a gilt weathercock can make them,
have to one from the *old country* an air of paltri-
ness and insecurity ; one of them is so exceedingly
slender that it might not, inaptly be likened to an
enormous darning needle.   In one of the principal
churches, the architect, wishing to avoid the incongruity of a steeple rising above a Grecian portico,
has placed it at the other end of the building ; in

[2] After the above remarks on the general style of New York architecture were written, a number of the North American Review
reached me, (a work to which I shall hereafter have frequent occasion
to refer) containing extracts from 'Letters on the Eastern States,'
published anonymously at New York in 1820, from which I select
the following corroborative testimony.

" How few buildings in this country, either public or private, are
constructed with a due regard to the principles of beauty, or a wise
distribution as to convenience for the occupants.   How often are they
left to mere mechanics, who erect them with the aid of the ' Builder's
Assistant,' with about the same degree of success that would be obtained in a correspondence guided by the ' Complete Letter Writer.'
—There are in Boston, Providence, and in some other towns, places
of public worship that are not destitute of merit, but it is united with
great defects.   It would be an invidious task to point out all these,
but there are two cases where bad taste has operated to destroy a good
effect where it might have been produced, that may be mentioned as
examples.   A church was built a few years since in Boston, for
which the original design was very handsome.   It was intended to
be a parallelogram, with a Doric portico ; the walls were plain with
large windows, making only one story, and built of a beautiful white
granite.   Thus far the original design ; but the plans of an architect
have to pass through the hands of a committee.   The first thing that
was done was to add a steeple ; a very pretty one ; and this though a

this there is of course only a choice of difficulties, but the result is in the present case not happy, for the awkward position suggests to the spectator the idea of a tail.

In front of the City Hall is a triangular grass plot of half an acre or so, intersected with gravel walks, and skirted on two sides with a few poplars, which is dignified with the rather inappropriate name of the Park. Green turf however is scarce within the precincts of the city, and the natives may be

sort of monster in architecture, is justifiable from the agreeable effect it produces at a distance : no church indeed ought to be built without one ; a village spire is always picturesque, and awakens pleasing emotions ; and the effect of steeples and domes, in giving an air of animation and grandeur to a town, may be judged of nega- tively, by seeing what a dull, lifeless, unmeaning aspect, Philadelphia presents to the observer without, though it is such a handsome city within. The next alteration was to change the form to an octagon, a figure which is appropriate enough for a crystal, but is an absurdity in architecture. The portico was Doric, but these columns, though made of wood, were with an Ionic proportion ! thus mutilating and destroying its whole beauty. To remedy this glaring fault, an ad- dition which does not belong to the order was put on at the bottom, to diminish their dyspeptic appearance, that only increased the dis- order. If it had been proposed to paint one red, one green, one blue, one yellow, it would have been scoffed at as absurd ; and yet it would have been a less grievous blunder than has been committed now, for it is not uncommon in Italy to see columns of different coloured marbles in the same edifice, where the proportions are all alike. Fortunately these deformed columns are of wood, and must soon grow shabby. They will then perhaps be replaced by columns of the Nova Scotia freestone, which is easily worked, and is now getting into use here for every thing where the chisel is required."
Vide North American Review, No. XXVIII. Pp. 86—88.

excused although they overrate a little what they possess. The only other portions are the Bowling Green, and the Battery. The Bowling Green is a small oval enclosure, at the lower end of Broadway, in the centre of which once stood a leaden statue of our good old king; but when the natives threw off their allegiance to George the Third, they turned his representative into bullets, and fired them at his troops. The Battery is a stripe of ground at the southern extremity of the island, about a quarter of a mile in length, which in the days of the Dutch governors was the site of an earthen breast work, over which a few pieces of cannon presented themselves to the vessels coming up the bay; but the embankment has long been levelled and the guns thrown aside. It is now covered with a verdant turf, and shaded by the branching foliage of numerous trees; with a modern stone fort, of great strength, projecting from one corner of it into the water.

In a summer evening the battery is a deservedly favourite promenade, and the prospect which it affords is very rarely to be equalled. The noble bay expands before it; bounded, on the left by the sloping hills and valleys of Long Island, in front by the Narrows about ten miles off, and on the right by the shores of New Jersey. Two or three forts appear, upon as many islands, and vessels of every size, from the seventy-four gun ship, to the sloop, at anchor or under sail. The cliffs of some stately mountain are almost all that could be desired to complete the landscape. A native of New York listens with impatience to the praises of the bay of Naples, and it is said that some who have seen both, have expressed some hesitation as to which deserves the palm. I suspect that Vesuvius is more than sufficient to turn the balance.

Long Island is a favourite summer resort of the inhabitants of New York, the climate is salubrious, and there are numerous villages at short distances along the shore. Among these is Rockaway, for some time the residence of Mrs. Graham. As yet I have only visited Brooklyn, a rapidly growing little town immediately opposite to New York, with which a steam ferry-boat affords the means of easy communication. The ground upon which it stands, with all around it, was long the patrimonial inheritance of a race of contented Dutchmen, who, hating innovation and restlessness, peacefully gathered apples or drove their cows to grass, where there forefathers had done the same. At last one, more adventurous than his fellows, perhaps from an intermixture of New England blood which is now forgotten, ventured to break up a portion of his farm for building ground, in despite of shrewd shakings of the head, and ominous prognostications of disaster. Now streets after streets cross each other, and a populous suburb is shooting up apace; while a little above it the United States have established a navy yard, and are building ships of war.

The navy yard is most conveniently placed upon the bank of a commodious little bay, opening into the Sound, where vessels of the largest class may float in safety. Here lies the famous steam frigate, ' Fulton the First', dismantled and roofed in; which through the kind offices of a friend I have had an opportunity of visiting. On the stocks in the yard is a seventy-four gun ship, to be larger than any of that class that have yet been launched; she will carry at least 90 guns, and it is said that they are to be all forty-two pounders.[3]

' Fulton the First' is a most singular machine; in shape pretty nearly an oblong octagon, rounded off a little at the corners. A most tortoise-looking man of war. We entered by a gun port upon her principal deck, and carefully explored every nook to which we could find admittance. Since visiting her I have had an opportunity of reading an official description, by the commissioners who superintended her while building, and the following combines what I saw, with the information which that document affords;[4] the accuracy of the details may, I believe, be relied on.

The steam frigate is a double boat, resting upon two keels, with an intervening space, 156 feet long and 15 feet wide, in which the paddle wheel revolves; this is carefully covered in, so as to be as

[3] She has since been launched and is named the Ohio.

[4] This is to be found in one of the early numbers of Constable's Magazine, but I cannot at present ascertain which.

C 2

much as possible unapproachable by shot. The
wheel has a free motion both ways upon its axis,
so that it can propel the vessel with either end
foremost: for this purpose each individual boat has
two rudders, one at each end, which are also carefully defended ; each pair acts simultaneously, and
when the pair at one end is in operation, the other
is secured so as to offer no obstruction to the vessel's progress.   She carries two bowsprits and two
masts, which are intended to bear what are called
latteen sails.[5]   The rigging formed no part of the
original design, but was added at the suggestion of
Captain Porter who had been appointed to her
command.   The sides are four feet ten inches
thick, composed of four thicknesses of oak timber, alternately vertical and horizontal.   Her gun
ports, thirty in number, are all on the principal
deck, and go completely round both ends of the
vessel, so that if necessary her shot can fly simultaneously at every angle like radii from the
centre of a circle.   She carries thirty-two pounders, some of which are in the carriages; with these
she is intended to throw red hot shot, for preparing which she is amply provided with furnaces.
Fulton also intended that she should carry upon
her upper deck four Columbiads, as they are called,
enormous guns capable of discharging a ball of a

---

[5] Three cornered sails, bent upon a long yard, which crosses the
mast angularly, and common in small vessels about the Mediter-
ranean.

hundred pounds weight, into an enemy's vessel, under the water mark. At present however her upper deck is without any armament, but sur- rounded with a strong bulwark. The officers' cabins are in the centre of the vessel, on the main deck. The steam boilers are contained in the one boat, and the engine in the other, but of their appearance or that of the paddle wheel, I can say nothing, as the whole were completely shut up.

Room is left for a machine which Fulton purposed to add, capable of discharging with great force an incessant stream of water either hot or cold, which it was anticipated would completely inundate an enemy's armament and ammunition, if it did not also destroy the men. Our newspapers, copying the marvellous reports which were afloat respecting her, assured their readers that this nondescript man of war was to brandish along its sides some hundreds of cutlasses and boarding pikes, and vomit boiling pitch on her unfortunate antagonists; these however are poetical exaggerations. Her machinery impels her at the rate of five and a half knots an hour, and her inventor felt confident that in a calm, or light breeze, no seventy-four would be a match for her. It was even hoped, that she might have been able to raise the blockade of New London, which was long carefully watched by a British squadron, could her energies have been brought into timely operation.

The commissioners were harassed with numer-

C 3

ous obstacles in getting her constructed, and their
difficulties give a pretty lively idea of the distress
which generally prevailed throughout the country.
Our vessels kept the whole of the sea coast in a
state of close blockade, and it was with the greatest
difficulty that building materials could be got for
her. Timber, copper, iron, lead, and coal, required
to be imported from distant parts of the Union, or
from foreign countries, and the vigilance of our
cruisers allowed so little to escape, that they were
all scarce and enormously expensive.   Ship carpenters had been sent off in such numbers to the
lakes, and so many stragglers had volunteered into
the army and navy, that workmen could scarcely be
procured, and only for very high wages.   When
she was launched, no artillery of a suitable description was to be found in New York; but a British prize was opportunely brought into Philadelphia, and twenty of her guns were dragged round
through the deep roads of New Jersey.   The state
of public credit was another source of embarrass-
ment.   The commissioners were supplied by government with treasury notes, which were then at
a considerable discount, but which they were posi-
tively forbidden to pay away under par.   Even this
depreciated paper was occasionally so long withheld, that they had in some cases to pledge their
private credit, and in spite of all their efforts, the
men at one time actually broke off from working;
while those who had furnished building materials

were discontented and importunate. These interruptions were chiefly felt in the latter part of 1814,
and they continued till winter made it impossible
for the vessel to act, even had she been finished.
Peace, which was concluded early next year,
rendered her for the present useless, and it was
thought unnecessary to furnish her with a full
equipment; but the commissioners persevered in
completing her construction, and in June she made
the first trial of her machinery. On a subsequent
occasion she made a trip to Sandy Hook, with a
considerable part of her artillery and stores on
board, saluting the forts as she passed them; and
the last occasion on which her powers were put in
requisition, was when the present President, Mr.
Munroe, made an official tour through the Union.

I have endeavoured to ascertain whether as much
confidence is reposed in her powers as to realize
the anticipations of her projector, and to justify
the panegyrics of the newspapers; but I am led to
think, that considerable doubt prevails as to the
possibility of working her, so as to make her efficient against an enemy's vessel. Fulton died before her engine was put on board; had he lived to
superintend its complete adjustment, it is impossible to say to what degree of perfection he might
have brought it, but his biographer acknowledges
that there are, at present, great and obvious defects
in her machinery. During the trial voyages various inconveniences were experienced, one of these

was the heat of the furnaces, which is so insupportable, that the engine-men cannot remain beside them for more than a minute or two at a time. In the confusion and bustle of an action it would probably be found extremely difficult, if not impossible, to regulate, with deliberation and coolness, the many complicated operations which would be necessary in such a machine; and where so much internal combustion is going forward, the slightest inattention or accident in managing the powder, might be instantaneously fatal to all on board. Should they succeed in overcoming these difficulties, and acquire that expertness in her management which practice alone can be expected to produce, we can scarcely imagine for a bay or harbour, a more powerful instrument of attack or defence. Independent of wind or tide, she could plough her way under an enemy's stern, or across his bows, and vomit forth her flaming balls, wherever the foe was most vulnerable; while the reverting of the paddle wheel would instantly relieve her from a wrong position, without the delay of working round, and the enormous thickness of her sides would render any but the largest guns inefficient upon her timbers.

The commissioners in their last report recommended, that, notwithstanding the peace, she should be commissioned and sent to sea, that officers and men might be trained to her management, and that defects in her construction, might be discovered and obviated; but this recommendation could only have been complied with at an expense which would ill agree with American ideas of economy, and here she lies, slumbering in ignoble indolence and security. I would add with all my heart, *Requiescat in pace!*

LETTER III.

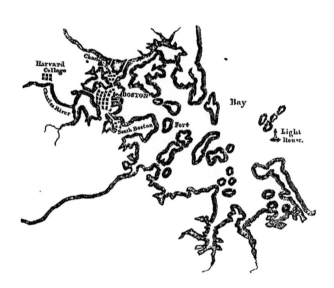

LETTER III.

Boston, July, 1818.

DURING the period which has elapsed since the
date of my former letter, I have traversed several
hundred miles of this western continent, and after
visiting both Upper and Lower Canada have arrived by a circuitous route in Boston; I delay
however, for the present, giving any account of my
Canadian travels, as it is probable that a better
opportunity will afterwards occur, and proceed
rather to make you somewhat acquainted with the
ancient capital of New England.

Boston occupies a small peninsula in Massachusetts bay, and possesses a safe and commodious
harbour, strongly defended from maritime attacks.
The commerce of Boston is very considerable;
probably in this respect it ranks as the fourth city
in the United States, for New York, Philadelphia,
and I believe New Orleans, are before it.

The town has outgrown the limits of the position
which it occupies, and Charlestown upon an opposite peninsula, and South Boston upon the main
land, may be regarded as integral parts of the city.
Circumscribed, however, as they are, the citizens
have had the good taste to reserve a park of up--
wards of forty acres, upon which no buildings have
been allowed to encroach.   The Mall, as this is
called, is surrounded with spreading elms, and is the
finest that is to be found within the limits of any
considerable town in the United States.   It would
be needless to remark how much it contributes to
the beauty of the town, and the comfort of the inhabitants, were it not that so simple and so obvious
an ornament is strangely overlooked in the larger
American cities, notwithstanding the abundance of
elbow room which all of them enjoy.

Boston has much more of the appearance of a
British town than New York.   Many of the buildings are of a fine white granite, and most of the
others are of brick ; the streets are very compactly
built, and although many are narrow and crooked,
all exhibit a degree of order and cleanliness which
will in vain be looked for in New York.   On a
finely rising ground at the upper part of the Mall,
stands the State House, a building of humbler pre-
tensions as to size and materials than the New
York City Hall, but in situation and architectural
outline greatly superior.   It is nearly square ; in
front is a lofty projecting colonnade of the Corin-

thian order, twelve columns in length, springing
from a piazza of rusticated arches, but unhappily
bearing only a balustrade, over which rises a small
attic story with a pediment; and overtopping all
is a large circular dome terminated by a small
square lantern. From the lantern of the State
House a most commanding view is obtained of the
surrounding country. In front is Boston bay,
studded with nearly forty islands, with fortifications
and a light house; the shores which surround its
ample basin, advancing and receding with most
capricious irregularity, and forming numerous
capes and peninsulas, on one of the largest of which
is the city. The vast amphitheatre around the bay
exhibits a country richly variegated with hill and
valley, immense forests and cultivated ground; and
sprinkled with about twenty little towns of snowy
whiteness, among which a dozen of spires may be
counted.

The celebration of the Fourth of July, the anniversary of the national independence, took place
since my arrival here; but the public demonstra-
tions of joy were, in most respects, so similar to those
with which we hail our king's birth day that a very
minute detail of them is unnecessary. In the
morning the national banner was displayed from
all the public buildings, and from the masts of
the vessels in the harbour. The Independence of
seventy-four guns, and the Guerriere of forty-four,
were both at anchor in the bay; the former of

which was profusely decorated with colours, and
each, at noon, fired a salute of twenty guns. In the
Mall were numerous booths, where refreshments of
various kinds found ready customers, but I thought
this system of punch-drinking little calculated
to sustain the dignity of the festival. The militia
and volunteers of the city and neighbourhood paraded in the forenoon and fired a *feu de joie.* The
volunteers resembled very much those at home,
excepting that in place of being collected into one
respectable battalion they consisted entirely of independent companies of fifty or sixty men; each
company had a different uniform, blue, red, or
white, and no way remarkable for neatness of
make or decoration. It seems strange that they
should choose a system of training, which prevents
them from ever acquiring a knowledge of battalion
movements, and could in the event of active service produce nothing but confusion. The Governor of Massachusetts received the congratulations of the various public functionaries, and distinguished citizens, and sat down, with above four
hundred persons, to a cold collation which was .
served up in the principal room of the State House.
The apartment was decorated with banners of various kinds, disposed in tasteful festoons upon the
walls; and the pillars which support the roof were
encircled by a double row of muskets and bayonets,
the upper ones inverted and the bayonet points
meeting each other. The whole had a very im-

posing effect. After the entertainment the Governor
and his guests walked in procession from the hall,
and the chaplain for the day, a Baptist minister,
walked conspicuously by himself dressed in full
canonicals.

In the forenoon an oration was pronounced, in
accordance with annual custom, on the subject
of the national independence, and the causes which
led to it. This is in every point of view well calculated to perpetuate those principles of liberty,
to which the nation owes its existence; to fan
the spark of patriotism, and foster that love of
country, which has been the theme of the poet and
the orator in all ages. . I unfortunately did not
hear of this oration, until after it had been delivered; I have however lost only the effect produced
by it on the audience, for the speech itself has been
published.

The orator was a Mr. Gray, and his address is
more characterised by plain good sense, than by
declamatory brilliancy. It has the merit of being
free from that vituperative abuse of Great Britain,
in which mere mob orators in the United States
are prone to indulge, and which, I am afraid, is
sometimes a cheap substitute for purity of principle
and good citizenship. America has undoubtedly
been wronged by Great Britain, at many times,
and in many ways, but these wrongs have been
productive upon the whole of only temporary evil,
while the benefits which she has derived from the

same source pervade her whole system; give sinews
to her strength, wisdom to her councils, intelligence
to her people, and dignity to her national character.
But for these she could never have either achieved or
maintained her independence, and were it possible
to separate from her population, all that has been
derived from the laws, institutions, and literature
of my native country, personal liberty, security of
property, freedom of thinking and of speech, and
last of all, true and vital religion, with all the moral
effects which have flowed from these, would vanish
like a dream, and an American contemplating the
dreary void, would have good reason to sigh,
" *Fuimus Troes!*"   Few, probably, of sober reflection and impartiality will be found to deny the
truth of these positions; then why should Britain
be hated by an American?—why should he not
rather overlook a little of that feeling towards
the United States, which was scarcely separable
from the circumstances in which the two countries
were placed by the revolution, and was too long
kept alive by errors in the conduct of both governments, towards each other; but the inveteracy of
which is now, I trust, rapidly decreasing, and will
soon be remembered only as a subject of regret,
and a powerful reason for future kindliness and
friendship.   It is the characteristic of noble minds
to forgive injuries; and with all our faults, there is
confessedly so much in our national character deserving of respect, and even of imitation, that

Americans must certainly be themselves in no small degree of error, if they do not feel a warmth of affection towards their parent country.

Mr. Gray's speech is probably rather a favourable specimen of the anniversary orations of the Fourth of July, and a specimen or two of its contents may not be uninteresting.

" This," says the orator in commencement, " is a glorious but a solemn day. Set apart for the celebration of independence, a common object of enjoyment and solicitude to us all, it ought not to be disturbed by controversy, nor wasted in mere exultation. It should remind us of our high responsibility, as well as our distinguished blessings; and direct our attention to the origin of the national privilege now commemorated, since this, like others, can neither be appreciated nor preserved, without a knowledge of the principles on which it is founded, and the means by which it was established. This duty of recurring frequently to the establishment of our independence, fortunately perhaps for its performance, is also a triumph; for there is not on record a revolution more sound in principle, more temperate in conduct, more beneficial in result.

" The encroachments of the British government on the liberty of the Colonists were the commencement of our revolution. But these cannot be assigned as its cause; oppression not being of itself sufficient to produce liberty. Many nations have

borne a heavier yoke than that which it was attempted to impose on this, and uttered no murmur;
some have had the impatience to complain, without
the courage to resist; while a few have been goaded
into desperation, only to waste their strength in ill-
directed and ineffectual struggles, and to fall at
last feebler victims. Nor are we indebted for independence to the peculiar talents of the individuals, illustrious as they were, who placed themselves
in the front of danger, as the guides and leaders
of the people.   Men determined to be free, will
never want a leader to freedom, and those willing
to endure despotism will never follow one.   Ex-
hortations to resist, as well as commands to obey,
are dependent for their effect, on the temper and
character of those to whom they are addressed.
It is undoubtedly the conviction of this truth,
which has induced you to select for the topic of
the orations annually pronounced before you, not
the injustice of your enemies, not the talents and
virtues of the great men who occupied the posts of
danger and of glory, during the struggle for the
establishment of independence; but the feelings,
manners, and principles, which led to that event."

He then traces the origin of the feelings which
led the Colonists to declare themselves independent, to that spirit of reformation which pervaded Europe when their forefathers emigrated
from its shores; and more especially to the self-
devoted enthusiasm of the Puritans, which led them

7

to abandon home with all its endearing ties and recollections, that they might enjoy the yet dearer treasure, unfettered liberty of conscience. These principles regulated the system of government which they adopted on landing in the American wilds, and produced that simplicity of manners, general diffusion of education, equal distribution of property, and persevering firmness of purpose, which characterized the early settlers; while these peculiarities, in their turn, all tended directly to cherish the spirit of manly independence.

He next states the grand principle of all representative governments, that the people is the source of legitimate power;—shows how this was disregarded by the supreme government in its conduct towards the colonies, and alludes to the discontent, disobedience, and resistance, which successively arose from it. He then notices in terms of glowing commendation the moderation, firmness, and prudence of their forefathers, and reminds them of the high responsibility under which their children lie, to preserve what they had won, and to profit by the enjoyment of it.

The means by which this is to be effected, are next adverted to by the orator, and he calls upon them to foster their religious and literary institutions, and carefully to protect their political system. " Let your constitution," says he, " be scrupulously respected and preserved; touch it not rashly and irreverently even for a good purpose. Let it

be a holy thing; a common object of universal
attachment; something fixed and stable, to be a
rallying point in every disturbance, and to concentrate at all times the affections of the people.   Rather than accustom yourselves to trifling innova-
tions in it, submit to slight and temporary inconvenience.   It is the part of wisdom to render even
our prejudices, for men will have prejudices, conducive to our happiness.   If it should not be
lightly altered, still less should it be made the
mere tool of convenience and expediency by forced
constructions.   This would expose it to contempt;
and when it ceases to be respected, how can it be
obeyed?   It is your duty not only to preserve the
form of your political institutions, but to maintain
their spirit, and to watch over their administration.
The example of your ancestors will teach you to
intrust the direction of public affairs, not to the
men who prefer your pleasure to your interest, and
their own aggrandizement to both; who rush into
the front rank of popular impetuosity, that they
may seem to be its leaders; and rise highest in the
whirlwind of passion, that they may have the glory
of appearing to direct the storm; but to those who
seek to enlighten, not to inflame, who merit confidence by their integrity, and wisdom, and experience, in public service; who respect the opinions,
and the very prejudices of the people, but disdain
to flatter either their passions or their vanity, or
to make public duty subservient to private interest

7

or ambition; who do not court office, nor solicit
honour, but avoid no task, and shrink from no
responsibility, properly imposed on them." These
you must do, much more you may do. " Spare no
exertions to improve the. arts, and extend .the
sciences, and polish the literature of. America."
Keep free from the political broils of other nations.
" The conviction that the security of a free government is to be sought only in the situation, habits,
and temper of the community, will deter you from
the chimerical idea of liberating other countries
by force; and teach you that the subversion of a
throne, is not necessarily the establishment of a
republic; that a nation trained up to servitude cannot be made free by breaking the bonds of government, nor derive lasting benefit from any revolution which does not begin in the character of the
people; and that the true deliverers of men suffering under long established despotism, are those
who instruct them." The knowledge of this truth,
he remarks, will prevent needless apprehensions.
Republican governments are not without their inconveniences and imperfections;—their rulers may
be guilty of errors or of crimes;—but there is in-
herent vigour to survive the effects of these, and
they must and will happen without either their
liberties being lost or their constitution subverted.
" Would you know," says he in conclusion, " when
you may despair? When the institutions of your
ancestors are neglected, their example forgotten,

their sentiments abandoned, their manners perverted, their principles betrayed; when religion and learning are ridiculed and despised; when all independence of sentiment is lost, and the rich trample on the rights of others from pride, or the poor from rapacity; when you dread the voice of truth, and have no ear but for your own praises; when men distinguished by talents, moderation, and integrity, are objects of suspicion; when disunion renders you a military people, and thus prepares you to submit to the dominion of force; or luxury bows your necks to the still more degrading yoke of corruption; then is your liberty destroyed, then are your constitutions a dead letter, then is the nation ruined. But I trust in God, that neither you nor your children will behold that day."

Such is the republican oration of Mr. Gray, and I see little in it which even a monarchist could brand as political heresy. While we regard only human means, there can I think be little doubt that kingdoms as well as republics will be stable or insecure, in proportion as its sentiments are respected or disregarded.

The evening of this national anniversary closed with another salute from the two ships of war, and a few voluntary rockets and other fire works. I saw no rioting or tumult in the streets, nor did I hear of any giving scope and illustration to their democratic patriotism, by breaking lamps and windows, or insulting peaceable inhabitants.

The naval events of the last unhappy rupture between the nations made me desirous of seeing an American ship of war, and I have had this desire gratified in a visit to the Independence of seventy-four guns. The Guerriere, which is anchored beside her, was built as you may guess from the name to commemorate one of our losses during last war; she is a fine looking vessel and is about to carry out Mr. Campbell, the American Ambassador, to Russia. My conductor in this visit was an American army officer, and probably to his acquaintance with the officers of the Independence we were indebted for the honour of being taken on board in a twelve-oared boat. A marine on duty at the gangway carried arms when we stepped on deck, and the boatswain greeted us with his whistle. The Independence, like all the other American ships of war, has no poop deck, but is perfectly level fore and aft;—this though less convenient to the officers, so far as regards their cabin accommodations, is thought to give advantages in working the vessel, and imparts to the deck an appearance of amplitude and neatness. The eye without difficulty runs along the graceful slope, and takes in at one glance the various objects which present themselves;—the bulwarks and hammock nettings, the guns lashed to the sides, the wheel, the capstan stuck full of cutlasses, the masts, the windlass, and the hatchways; all are seen and their relations at once understood, while every thing seems arranged

so as best to secure rapidity and regularity in a storm
or an engagement.   On the upper deck of the Independence is the Captain's cabin, but Commodore
Bainbridge her commander was not on board during
our visit.   On the lower deck are those of the
Lieutenants, which as in our own vessels are merely
temporary erections along the sides of the ship, and
are cleared away in preparing for action.   Here is
also the tiller, a long and heavy bar of hammered
iron, fitted with tackling and blocks which communicate with the quarter deck, and are put in
motion by a large double wheel.   Towards the
centre of this deck are the pumps, which are
wrought like our fire engines.   While we walked
along, we saw the starboard mess at dinner; the
seats and tables are planks suspended from the
roof at right angles to the ship's sides.   On one
of these I noticed two Bibles with the stamp of
the American Bible Society, which bore evident
tokens of having been perused.   The sick births
are in the bows, the cots are slung from the roof,
and neatly hung with curtains.   Lower still, and
under the level of the water is the cockpit where
is the Surgeon's station in an engagement, and
towards the stern of the vessel the Midshipmen's
births; we saw some of them busy by lamp light at
their nautical calculations.   On the same deck we
saw the stores of the Gunner, Sailmaker, Carpenter,
Painter, &c.   The extreme neatness, cleanliness,
and systematic arrangement which prevail in a ship

of war, make it an object deserving of examination, apart from every consideration as to the purposes of its construction; and so far as my limited knowledge of nautical affairs could carry me, every thing on board this vessel appeared to be of the first rate order. A certain class of our writers affect to undervalue the American navy, but I am persuaded that were another war unhappily to take place between us, there is not an officer in the British service who would prepare for action with an American ship, without

" That stern delight which warriors feel
In foemen worthy of their steel."

The Independence although rated as a seventy-four, actually carries ninety-two guns; those on her quarter deck and forecastle, are 32 pound Carronades; on the upper deck, long 24 pounders; and on the lower deck, long 32 pounders. She was intended to have carried thirty-two pounders upon all her decks, but it was found that they sunk her too low in the water. She measures about two thousand three hundred tons, and her full complement of men is eleven hundred.

Negro slavery, that bane of American prosperity, has been for a considerable time abolished in Massachusetts, and the blacks commemorate its abolition by an annual procession which I have had the pleasure of witnessing. The appearance of their long array was rather grotesque, and afforded a good

deal of merriment to the Boston wags; and some
printer, to turn the joke to account, has published
a caricature of it with a mock account of the subsequent dinner.   The older blacks who headed the
procession carried short batoons, some of them wore
cocked hats, cockades, epaulets, silk sashes, and top
boots;—after them a party of younger ones followed
bearing formidable pikes with tin heads, and a few
flags; several bands of music were placed at intervals along the line, and it was closed by a multitude
of black boys, two and two, in their gayest apparel.
A great number of female blacks lined the side
walks.   In this order the whole proceeded to
church where they heard sermon; the men afterwards dined together, elected office-bearers for the
following year, and according to custom on such
occasions "spent the evening in the utmost convi-
viality and good humour."

. It was gratifying to witness the happy looks, and
fantastic dresses of these free blacks, and to think
of the event commemorated by their holiday procession.   Melancholy reflections however were suggested by the remembrance, that though they could
no longer be bought and sold, like the inferior animals or a mass of inanimate matter, yet chains of a
stronger kind still manacled their limbs, from which
no legislative act could free them; a mental and
moral subordination and inferiority, to which tyrant
custom has here subjected all the sons and daughters of Africa.   I shall not at present enlarge upon

the condition of this unfortunate race, there will be but too frequent opportunities of recurring to the subject.

There is building in the neighbourhood of Boston an asylum for Lunatics, which is in an advanced state of preparation. America has been hitherto deficient in retreats for those unfortunate individuals, whom God has in his providence visited with mental alienation. It is not indeed surprising that where population has advanced with such rapid strides, the proportionate provision should scarcely have been made for that most afflictive of all temporal calamities; much however has been done, and much more is doing, to vindicate Americans from any imputation of insensibility to the sorrows of their suffering fellow creatures.

The Lunatic Hospital, as it is called, is a mile and a half from Boston, and the direct approach to it is by one of the many wooden bridges " which with their wearisome but needful length," connect the town with the surrounding country. The situation is exceedingly well chosen ; the buildings crown the brow of a rising ground, which swells gradually from the water, commanding a very fine view of the city and the bay, and enjoying a free circulation of the purest air. The effect of such a situation must be tranquillizing to the mind of the convalescent, and cheering by its variety to the drooping and despondent. Ten acres of ground which, with an ancient mansion house, were formerly

the property of an opulent merchant, are appropriated to this benevolent institution.   The recent
proprietor is no longer a sharer in sublunary things,
and his house, which has been one of elegance in
its day, is undergoing some alterations to render it
a convenient residence for the keeper and his assistants.   This is the centre building of the Hospital
and communicates by low galleries with two new
ones, containing rooms for the patients, which have
been erected at right angles to the first, so as to
form three sides of a court.   In their size and internal arrangement the two sides are exactly alike;
they are three stories high, a lobby runs through
the centre of each story, and on both sides of it are
six apartments, forming a total of seventy two in
the two wings.   Over the door of each apartment
is an opening of about a foot square; the two
centre rooms on each side of the lobbies are to be
supplied in winter with heated air, by flues from an
air furnace in the ground story, the other rooms
have fire places.   None of the rooms are yet quite
finished, so that it must be left for future travellers
to report as to the details of the internal arrangement, and the treatment of the patients.

Civil communities sooner feel the need of recep-
tacles for evil doers, than for the sick or insane, and
with this Boston has been long provided.   The
Penitentiary, or State Prison, is constructed and regulated exactly on the present plan of the one in
Philadelphia, which has been so long celebrated.

The system adopted there must be universally commended as a humane effort to restrain the wickedness of men, without that profuse application of capital punishments which characterize the more sanguinary codes of Europe; and as a most interesting experiment on the possibility of preventing crime rather than punishing it, and reforming criminals rather than extirpating them.

The Boston State Prison consists of a range of buildings of granite, containing numerous apartments for lodging the prisoners, and extensive work shops for carrying on various handicraft arts, with a spacious open court which affords a free circulation of air to the whole establishment. The prison is surrounded by a high wall, with turrets and platforms at the four corners, on which sentinels keep guard with loaded muskets. On approaching the prison we found a keeper overlooking a number of the delinquents, who were repairing a strong palisade fence which forms part of the outer works. The men were dressed in party coloured clothes, with each half of their jacket and trowsers of a different colour; one arm was of red, the other of blue, one leg green, the other gray. This was intended to facilitate the apprehension of any that might happen to escape, for they would thus carry about with them, till they found means to change their apparel, a most conspicuous badge of the society from which they had absconded.

In the keeper's office, a general explanation was

given me of the system of management.   All the
prisoners except those condemned to a solitary cell
are employed in some manual art; if they have
been previously taught one which can be practised
within the prison walls they are of course set to it,
if not, as most frequently happens, they are instructed in one.   Part of them are kept in regular
employment by tradesmen who provide them with
work; the rest are variously employed on behalf of
the establishment.   Of their earnings, the greater
part, along with the profit on manufactured articles,
is appropriated to the expenses of the prison; a
small proportion is allowed to accumulate for the
benefit of the prisoner, that he may be stimulated
to good behaviour and industry, and if disposed to
lead an honest life when his term of punishment
expires, have a little money with which to make a
commencement.   The expenses of the establishment however have always exceeded its receipts,
and the deficiency is provided for by an annual vote
of the State Legislature.   In the keeper's office is
a supply of arms and accoutrements, to equip his
household and assistants in the event of any attempt at outrage on the part of the prisoners; of
these weapons however I believe they have never
yet had occasion to avail themselves.

Going out into the court yard, we found in it a
great number employed in hewing blocks of granite
into graduated sizes and shapes for building.   This
is a staple commodity in the prison, and a stock of

building stone is kept constantly on sale. In the work shops we saw the prisoners variously engaged, as bakers, weavers, shoemakers, tailors, carpenters, turners, brush makers, nailers, wool-combers, spinners, &c. &c. All seemed to be as busy and as attentive to their work, as if it had been their chosen and voluntary employment; and the workmanship which they produced seemed not only good, so far as I could judge, but some of it even of a superior finish and appearance. The clothes of some of the workmen were not of that party-coloured kind which I remarked on most of them, and the keeper informed me that this was an indulgence granted to those whose conduct was exemplary; it had been recently introduced and had been found to have considerable influence upon the prisoners, giving them the idea that some degree of confidence was reposed in those who were so distinguished, and that they had thus made one step of approximation towards the character of honest men and good citizens.

The prisoners are not allowed to utter a word in the presence of strangers, and at all times quietness and decorum are rigidly enforced. The female delinquents are confined in a separate part of the prison, and are employed in cooking, washing, and sewing for the establishment, as well as in other branches of female industry.

During the whole year the prisoners are required

to rise half an hour before the sun.[1] They commence labour at sunrise; at eight o'clock they are allowed fifteen minutes for breakfast, at noon half an hour for dinner; they leave off work at half an hour before sunset, are allowed fifteen minutes for supper, and at sunset are locked up. Their food consists of rye and Indian corn bread, cocoa, molasses, soup, vegetables, and occasionally meat. A sermon is preached to them every Sabbath, and I believe the more ignorant are instructed in reading.

Prisoners who are disorderly are punished by privations of various kinds, and sometimes by solitary confinement, when they are not allowed to converse even with the man who brings them their food; some I observed with a clog of wood chained to one foot, which they were obliged to carry in their arms when moving from place to place; this is the only species of corporal punishment which is allowed. As we passed along, a mulatto boy distinguished by this *order of merit* came up to the conductor, and begged hard to be released from it; this however was decidedly and somewhat sternly refused, and the keeper told me that it would not have been asked, but that they expect to find him more easily mollified in the presence of strangers, for the sake of thus acquiring the character of kindness and humanity. I

---

[1] It must be recollected here that an American summer day is considerably shorter than ours.

observed that a very considerable proportion of the prisoners were men of colour. It is but too obvious that these unfortunate people are in a great measure outcasts from society; they are too often left without education when young, and treated with distrust when older, till they become gradually and almost necessarily not trust-worthy; and having no character to lose, they feel little scruple, when honourable means of support fail, in having recourse to those of another kind.

I was next conducted to their sleeping apartments, which are at the opposite side of the court-yard, and have every appearance of being both comfortable and secure. A gallery runs along each floor between two ranges of small rooms, in each of which are wooden bed frames for four, consisting of two upper and two under births, but both on the same side. Two narrow openings in the wall admit air and light; the walls are white washed and every thing perfectly clean. Under the sleeping apartments are the solitary cells, and above is an hospital for the sick; we found few in it, and all of them in the way of recovery.

The building is every where of very great strength; many of the blocks of granite of which it is built are twelve feet long, and in the sleeping rooms and galleries those forming the floors and roofs in all cases reach from wall to wall. The doors on the sleeping rooms are of iron, some of them solid and others grated; a strong iron

door also terminates each gallery, so that the
escape of the prisoners seems altogether hopeless.
The keeper indeed said that none had ever effected
their escape by force, although one or two had
succeeded by false keys.   An Irishman had on
one occasion got out in this way from one of the
solitary cells, but being unable to reach the pad-
lock which is fastened outside of the door at the
end of the gallery, he concealed himself till sunset, when they happened to bring in another prisoner, and managed to slip out unobserved while
they were lodging him in his cell; the sentinels
had just been removed from the walls, as they always are after the prisoners have been locked up,
and Paddy was never more heard of.   There are
at present in confinement 369 persons, and I was
happy to learn, that among all these there is but
one Scotsman.

   Of the efficacy of the penitentiary system, as at
present administered, the keeper appears to be very
doubtful; and it is unquestionable that an opinion
prevails, in the larger cities, that for the purpose
of either deterring from crime or reforming the
criminal, the penitentiaries are at present in a great
measure inefficient.   The prisoners are in many
respects too comfortable to feel their confinement as
a very severe punishment, for although the depriva-
tion of personal liberty is in itself a great hardship,
it may to very many be compensated for by a
degree of comfort in clothing and habitation, to

which they are elsewhere unaccustomed. It cannot be doubted that in America they have now gone to the extreme of leniency, in their criminal code, as we have to the extreme of severity; theirs is undoubtedly the side on which all humane persons would wish to err, but too much mercy to rogues is cruelty to society at large, and is therefore to be avoided if we would wish to attain to a perfect criminal system. Much may be done however to improve the prison discipline of the American penitentiaries, without properly speaking increasing the severity of the treatment.

In the one which I have just described there was not, so far as I could discover, any thorough classification. The males and females were indeed separated, a most essential point, but there appeared to be no farther distribution of the prisoners, excepting that which arose from the different arts at which they were employed. All those of one occupation were together, without any regard to whether they were young or old offenders, whether their term of imprisonment was short or long, whether the crimes which they had committed were trifling or enormous. Of mere boys or girls indeed I saw none, but I saw many who although not boys were very young men, and who ought by all means to have been subjected to a different course of discipline from that which was suitable for older transgressors.

There was also far too much facility for com-

munication between one division of the establishment and another. There may be rules for aught
I know to prevent criminals going about from their
own department, but there were no doors to shut
them up. The doors from the court to the different workshops were all open; so also were the
windows, and there seemed to be nothing to prevent the occupants from free intercourse with each
other. In this way each sees and hears so many
around him, engaged exactly like himself, that
even although there should not be a very great
deal of communication, they cannot be said, during the working hours at least, to feel the confinement more than the workmen in our larger
manufactories; and they are so constantly employed
that they have not time for sober reflection, on their
past life or future prospects. An equally obvious
defect is the practice of allowing four of them to pass
the night in the same apartment. The average time
of their being employed is not much above twelve
hours a day, and there cannot be a doubt that
there is time during the other twelve for a great
deal of useless, probably pernicious, conversation,
without materially interfering with the hours of
sleep. Were they kept completely apart, and left
to the secret suggestions of their own consciences,
it might be expected that while some would relent
and probably amend their ways, all would feel much
more severely the restraint upon their liberty and
comforts.

Another obstacle to the efficacy of the present system, is the lavish profusion with which pardons are granted. I believe that want of accommodation sometimes renders this necessary, since but for pardoning the older criminals, room could scarcely be found in the present buildings to accommodate the new ones; but whatever may be the cause, it is certain that be the term of imprisonment what it may, ten years, twenty years, or life, a criminal may almost count with certainty on being released in three, four, or five years, if he behave with any moderate degree of propriety. I have no document beside me stating the number of pardons granted annually in Boston, but from a printed account of the New York State Prison, it appears that the total number of prisoners in the year 1814 was 709; of which 29 died in the course of the year, 10 were discharged in consequence of the expiration of their sentences, and no less than 176 were pardoned. It is obvious that this system must be ruinous in its consequences, and that there must be some capital defect in the criminal discipline of the community where such a practice prevails. It sometimes happens that the same individual is imprisoned and pardoned several times over, for crimes which in Britain would at once send him either to Botany Bay or to the gallows, and thus rid society of him altogether. I do not think by any means that ours is the only alternative, nor do I suppose it possible by any expedient completely to prevent

E 4

the repetition of crimes by the same individual;
but certainly to let loose upon society rogues who
have been frequently guilty of flagrant outrages, and
to have no means of intimidation powerful enough
to deter them from a pretty frequent repetition of
their crimes, proves that something yet remains to
be done ere the criminal code of the United States
can be considered perfect. While you divest yourself however of all thoughts as to the drawbacks
connected with the Penitentiary system, as at present
conducted, you certainly cannot contemplate the
interior of this great manufactory without emotions
of peculiar satisfaction. To see so many hands
which were formerly active only in crime, now
taught to be equally active in some useful art; to
think of the humanity of the system as contrasted
with that of Britain; and to witness the cleanliness,
order, and regularity, which pervade the whole establishment, make you almost forget that you are in
a receptacle for knaves or fondly believe that they
are so no longer, and internally exclaim, ‘ This must
be a noble institution.’²

---

² In all that has of late been written by benevolent individuals on
the criminal code and jail economy of our native country, particular
reference has been made to the penitentiaries of America, especially
that of Philadelphia. A little additional information, therefore, to
what has been communicated above, cannot be out of place here.

“ The penitentiary system,” says an intelligent and candid writer
in the North American Review, “ proposes to reform the criminal
and restore him to society, penitent and useful. It proceeds upon
an hypothesis favourable to human virtue, and to the effect of moral

The state of Academical education in the United States is a matter respecting which much ignorance prevails in our native country. I hope hereafter to transmit a detailed account of the discipline of Yale College, in New Haven, in the mean time I am enabled to communicate a few particulars

intelligence. It rests for its efficacy upon the truth of the proposition, that reformation may be brought about by discipline and instruction; and that if the motives to an honest life are properly exhibited and enforced, there is good reason to expect that they will influence the conduct.—It cannot be denied that in respect to general design, the latter of these two systems (*the European and the American*) has greatly the preference. They have however both their respective advantages, nor is either without its peculiar disadvantages. Judging by the effects produced, neither of them has answered its original design. In England the sanguinary system of punishment has not diminished the number of criminals, and has begun to excite a disgust, which prevents its enforcement; while in the United States the practical operation of the penitentiary system has cooled the ardour of its friends, and excited doubts of its permanent utility. The warmest advocates of these institutions will probably admit that they have not in all respects corresponded to their wishes, but whoever contends that they have been wholly unproductive of benefit must surely be very little acquainted with their history.—The great source of disappointment is unreasonable expectation. More benefit has been anticipated than it was prudent to propose. The advocates of this improvement in humanity have been too ardent and sanguine. They have promised themselves too much, and injured their cause by the disappointment which has followed.—We do not believe in the empiricism which pretends, by a certain specific, to cure every possible evil. But we maintain that the regimen of the prison is, with the blessing of heaven, a mean of destroying a great mass of moral corruption, and diminishing those seeds of vice, from which spring the greatest harvest of misery. In the walls of the penitentiary will be found not only the incorrigible offender, but the inexperienced

respecting that at Cambridge, about three miles from Boston.

Harvard University is the most ancient and most amply endowed classical establishment in the United States; it was founded in 1638, in pursuance of the will of a clergyman of the name of

culprit.—Should such persons as the latter be whipped and discharged into the same scenes, the same company, the same misery, and the same temptations, and the almost inevitable renewal of their crime and their punishment! Will you convert a single error into an irreparable crime! Or will you not rather place the miserable patient where, by a kindness he will regard, and a discipline he must feel, he will become sensible of his wickedness, and be removed from the dangerous connexions in which it originated. Among such unfortunate criminals there is hope of amendment. From this great and growing class, many may be preserved from ruin, the living witnesses of the excellence of the institutions by which they have been restored to society. That our State Prisons have answered this valuable though moderate expectation, is abundantly proved by an inspection of their records. In the early period of the Philadelphia penitentiary, when it was conducted with indefatigable attention by its philanthropic founders, ‘ the prison was a school of reformation, and a place of public labour, and of the many who received the Governor's pardon, not one returned a convict.’ At a later period out of nearly two hundred persons, who had been recommended to and pardoned by the Governor, only four had returned ; the roads in the vicinity of the city so constantly infested with robbers were seldom disturbed by those dangerous characters ; the houses, shops, and vessels, so perpetually robbed, no longer experienced those alarming evils. There had been but two instances of burglaries in the city and county for nearly two years.—The early history of the New York State Prison gives the same result, and its recent and present failure to meet the public expectation can be accounted for, without controverting the grounds on which this mode of punishment is justified. In Massachusetts, from the opening of the State Prison in December 1805,

Harvard, who bequeathed for this purpose the half of his property, amounting to about £800 Sterling. Various Governors of the State, and other individuals, have been its subsequent benefactors, and under the fostering care of the local government it has enjoyed uninterrupted prosperity, and

to 15th April 1817, there were received 918 convicts, of whom 79 were afterwards returned, 305 were then in custody, 38 had died, and the remaining 496 had never been brought again within the prison limits. During the same period 155 had been pardoned, of whom 11 had proved themselves unworthy of the favour, but 144 had not been known to be again the subjects of criminal law. Of those who were liberated, many are known to the officers of that institution to have become industrious and useful citizens. These facts prove the utility of the institution in certain cases, and in a proportion which is gratifying to its advocates; while the farther fact that five convicts had been returned four times each, and one five times, proves also that to expect reformation in every convict is altogether idle. The prescription will not suit every patient, and moral as well as physical disease will sometimes baffle the efforts of human wisdom."

Thus far this judicious writer proves to us the reasonableness and the practicability of the system; he then asserts that these institutions have not accomplished all that might reasonably have been expected of them, and that some of them after having for a time done well, fell into a state of inefficiency and disorganization.

The first cause of their failure was the expense of supporting them. The public had too hastily adopted the idea that a penitentiary should in a great measure support itself, and when a vote was required to defray expenses, and supply deficiencies, the people grumbled and the money was with difficulty obtained. "This expense is a charge upon the public; and to render it as small as possible, the penitentiary character of the establishment is made a secondary consideration. It is no longer a place merely of moral improvement, where industry is enforced as a part of necessary discipline, but it becomes a great workshop, in which every man is labour-

has gradually advanced in wealth and literary respectability. The University consists of two departments, the Literary, and the Medical; the latter of which, although an integral part of the institution, occupies buildings in Boston, for the greater convenience of medical students.

ing for the public, and obliged to add as much as possible to the capital stock. The effect is seen in a variety of indulgences granted to the convicts, and to the superior importance which is attached to profit over manners. The institutions themselves are contrived with regard to economy, and as the prisoners increase in numbers a separation becomes impossible, they mingle together in the workshops, are crowded in the cells, and have opportunity by injudicious intercourse to confirm each other's bad habits, and to combine against the natural tendency of their punishment."

" Another cause exceedingly injurious to the moral effect of these institutions is the character attached in public estimation to the unfortunate inmate even after he quits the walls.—The charitable Quakers who commenced these institutions, did not leave the poor man at the threshold of the prison door, exposed to the wants of poverty, and thrown among the temptations of the world with no safeguard but his unconfirmed moral feelings. They procured employment for him, gave him countenance and character, watched over him with assiduity, and prevented any backward step, by holding out allurements and motives to honesty. The case is now changed, little or no provision is made for the discharged prisoner. The cares of the government do not extend beyond the prison walls. Society marks a man who has once been in confinement with a jealous eye.— Honest men avoid him. The police keep an eye upon his motions. Is a robbery committed, he is the first person suspected. Is labour wanted, he is the last person employed. In fact by the general public sentiment he is driven into the haunts of profligacy and crime.— Whenever these remarks apply, and the discharged convict under the influence of the evils that surround him, is forced upon the commission of new offences, the blame is laid to the nature of his former

The buildings at Cambridge are eight in number, erected in an enclosed plain of fourteen acres, sheltered on three sides by forest trees, and in the immediate vicinity of an extensive common. Three of the buildings contain the lecture-rooms, chapel, library, laboratory, &c. the remainder consist of

punishment, and not, as it ought to be, to the incomplete performance of the duty which the public had assumed. First make the system perfect; establish all the parts of which it is composed and then ascertain the result." *North American Review, No. XXVII. Pp.* 235—248.

In a more recent number of the same journal the subject has been resumed, and I transcribe the following additional observations on the deterioration which has taken place in the administration and efficiency of the American penitentiaries.

" If our State Prisons have not produced all the good effects that have been expected, it is not owing to the nature of these institutions, but to the improvidence of the several legislatures in not preparing adequate room for the number of convicts. The prison of Philadelphia was not originally constructed for this purpose; yet it was successfully administered, until the increase of criminals, and the refusal of the legislature to build another prison, so accumulated the convicts, that all possibility of classification and separation was destroyed. It was worse in New York—the prison, originally intended for three hundred, afterwards contained more than double that number, and when we visited it a few years since, a large part of the convicts could not be employed for want of room, and some of the best of them were ' pardoned out' every month, for no other reason than to make way for new convicts, that the course of justice might not be impeded by the want of room to execute its decrees. This is now remedied in New York, by the establishment of an extensive bridewell, and the erection of a new prison in the western district of the State. Pennsylvania is building a larger prison, expressly adapted to the purposes both of labour, and seclusion." *North American Review, No. XXXIII. Pp.* 419, 420.

8

apartments for the students, who here as in the
English Universities reside within the walls.   The
largest building is of fine white granite and was
erected in 1814; it is said to have cost nearly
seventeen thousand pounds sterling : the rest are
of brick, and some of the larger ones cost from five
to six thousand pounds sterling.

It will be obvious from the above extracts, which convey a very
accurate idea of the present state of prison discipline in the United
States, that the Penitentiary system has while properly administered
answered in a high degree the purposes at once of punishment and
reformation ; but it is equally obvious that at present the penitentiaries are in a state of partial, if not total inefficiency, arising solely
from inattention to the most obvious suggestions of common sense and
experience in regard to their management.   So universal has been
the outcry of the public on this subject, that means have already been
taken in some of the States to reform and invigorate the system ; and
in the last Session of Congress, a Committee was appointed to investigate and report respecting the general state of the penitentiaries
throughout the Union.   Their report, which is prodigiously long
although upon the whole judicious, is concluded by the following
" broad positions :" " *First*, That the penitentiary system, as it now
exists in the United States, with all its defects, is preferable to the
former systems of punishment in this country. *Secondly*, That it is
capable of being so improved as to become the most judicious and
effective system of punishment ever known in ancient or modern
times. *Thirdly*, That where it has been properly administered, as
it formerly was in Pennsylvania and New York, it has succeeded and
answered the expectations of its early friends. *Fourthly*, That
solitary confinement by night and by day, combined with other regulations suggested in this Report, will remedy all existing evils.
Fifthly, That it is the duty of the different States of the Union to
proceed without delay to its improvement and perfection. *Lastly*,
That corporal punishments, and the infliction of death, would not

The library, which is rapidly increasing, contains already upwards of seventeen thousand volumes, many of them of great rarity and value. I saw in it a large paper copy of Walton's Polyglot, said to have been the presentation copy, and a very beautiful manuscript of the Aphorisms of Hippocrates, executed for Dr. Mead by an English schoolmaster, and by the Doctor's son presented to this University. This manuscript is quite a gem. It possesses indeed none of the mouldy charms of

prove congenial to the moral sentiments and feelings of the American people ; and that the transportation of convicts is visionary, impracticable, and would not prevent crimes and offences, even if it were adopted in our penal statutes. The Committee hope and trust, that enlightened, humane, and public spirited individuals of the different States in the Union, will feel the responsibility that rests upon this country, in relation to the system of which we have so fully spoken." Vide " The Investigator," No. XI. January, 1823, P. 168.

One remark more shall close this long note. It can scarcely fail to occur to all who have ever taken part in the direction of any institution, intended to alleviate either the physical or the moral maladies of our species, that however indispensable general rules of management and classification are, it is also absolutely necessary to give them full efficacy, that zealous and conscientious individuals should devote their time and their energies to the good work, not from mercenary considerations, but from that hearty desire to do good for which the projectors of the Philadelphia penitentiary were so distinguished. Few such institutions are successful, however unexceptionable their rules, without some portion of ardour, perhaps enthusiasm, in the managers; and few are altogether unsuccessful where this *enthusiasm* is found, even although the economy of the system should be in some degree erroneous. Some information respecting the new Philadelphia penitentiary will be found in Letter Seventh.

8

extreme antiquity, nor can it be appealed to as
authority for settling a doubtful reading, but the
execution is in every respect most beautiful. The
paper is of the finest fabric, the binding and case
which contains it are both of rich Morocco, but
above all, the Greek characters are formed with
the most exquisite symmetry and elegance. Enclosed with it is a history of the volume in the autograph of the donor. Among the philosophical
apparatus are many instruments by the best London makers. I saw also a collection of wax models
of the human body, and some of its principal
portions, used in popular lectures on anatomy
which form part of the academical course. They
seemed to be prepared and coloured with great
delicacy and correctness; part of them had been
imported from Florence, and others were the workmanship of an Italian emigrant.

The academical course is completed in four
years; students are termed successively, Freshmen,
Sophomores, Junior, and Senior, Sophisters. At
the conclusion of the course, candidates for the
degree of Bachelor in Arts undergo rigid examination by the various Professors; after being three
years Bachelor they receive the degree of Master,
without any farther examination, provided that
there has been nothing in their conduct to dis-
honour the profession of letters. There are three
terms in the year, and the vacations amount together to about three months. The expense of

board and education cannot be reduced, with the utmost attention to economy, below four hundred and fifty, to five hundred dollars, or about one hundred guineas a year; in most cases students expend a great deal more.

The literary and scientific reputation of Harvard University stands very high; and except Yale College, none in this country can contest with it the pre-eminence. It has upwards of twenty Professorships,[s] and between three and four hundred students. There is one feature however in its character which excites the most melancholy reflections; its theological creed is undisguised Socinianism, and it is said that nearly all the professors are of these sentiments. This must be, to a parent of

---

[s] The following I believe to be a pretty accurate list of the present Faculty of Harvard University. (February, 1823.)

JOHN THORNTON KIRKLAND, D. D., LL. D., President.

Dr. Aaron Dexter, Professor of Chemistry.
Dr. Henry Ware, Hollis Professor of Divinity.
John Farrar, Hollis Professor of Mathematics and Natural Philosophy.
Sidney Willard, Professor of Languages. *(Particularly the Oriental.)*
Dr. John Popkin, Professor of Greek. *(Reading of the Classics.)*
Levi Hedge, Professor of Logic and Metaphysics.
Edward Everett, Elliot Professor of Greek Literature. *(Philosophy of the Language.)*
Edward Channing, Boylston Professor of Rhetoric and Oratory.
Andrews Norton, Professor of Sacred Literature and Biblical Criticism.
Hon. Isaac Parker, Royall Professor of Law. *(Chief Justice of Massachusetts.)*

VOL. I.   F

scriptural sentiments, a powerful reason for sending his sons elsewhere for their College education; for what are literary or scientific attainments, even of the highest order, when weighed in the balance with purity of religious faith? It is asserted indeed on behalf of the University that no attempt is made to proselyte its students, and that they are allowed to attend worship with whatever denomination. they or their friends may choose. All this may be true so far as regards active and open endeavours to inculcate doctrinal sentiments, but what is to be the young enquirer's defence from that subtile leaven which is necessarily infused into almost every lecture upon morals and philosophy; which affects the essentials of the system, and

Hon. Ashbel Stearns, Professor of Law.
Hon. Joseph Story, Professor of Commercial Law.
(Vacant.). , Professor of Moral Philosophy.
Thomas Nuttall, Massachusetts Professor of Natural History.
—— Ticknor, Smith Professor of Spanish and Italian.
F. Sales, Professor of French.
Two Tutors of Latin, one of Greek, two of Mathematics.

MEDICAL DEPARTMENT.

Dr. Jacob Bigelow, Rumford Professor and Lecturer on Materia Medica and Botany.
Joseph G. Cogswell, Professor of Mineralogy.
Dr. John C. Warren, Hersey Professor of Anatomy and Surgery.
Dr. James Jackson, Hersey Professor of the Theory and Practice of Physic.
Dr. John Gorham, Professor of Chemistry.
Dr. J. F. Dana, Chemical Assistant.
Dr. Walter Channing, Lecturer on Obstetrics.

therefore all its ramified details; and which tinctures every conversation on a religious topic which meets his ear? Although he were safe from the influence of the lectures, who will warrant him against the ridicule and the sophistry of his fellow students; by far the greater part of whom are of Unitarian families, and who have been accustomed from their infancy to laugh at every distinguishing principle of that belief to which they deny the character of *rationality?* Four years' exclusive intercourse with Socinians, spent in acquiring ideas upon every subject of speculative and experimental truth, is an ordeal to which no Christian parent ought to expose his son, however great his confidence in the correctness of his principles, and the vigour of his mind.

From Harvard University press issues the North American Review, beyond all comparison the first literary journal in the United States. The reputed editor is Professor Everett, and it evinces in him and his coadjutors talents and acquirements, literary and philosophical, of a very superior order. Would that its theological opinions were from a purer source!—happily they are but seldom obtruded.

At Boston I visited another collection of anatomical preparations in wax, by a Dr. Williams. A full length figure, modelled from the body of a criminal, exhibits the exterior muscles; and various other models represent portions of the interior mechanism of the human frame, and the different stages of some of its most important functions; they were beautifully executed, but I am not qualified to pronounce upon their anatomical accuracy.

Boston is rich in public libraries, and among these the Athenæum claims pre-eminence. This institution contains a library of about 20,000 volumes. The regulations prevent the books from being taken out of the rooms, but there are reading desks for the subscribers, and strangers introduced by them, at which in the most perfect silence they extract the mental nourishment which the volumes afford. A copy of Bowyers' edition of Hume's History of England was pointed out to me; I observed also many of the best editions of the ancient classics, and some splendid volumes of engravings, and works on natural history. The librarian informed me that to one London bookseller alone, they had paid for books upwards of twelve thousand dollars; £2700 sterling. In works on American history, the collection is said to be quite unrivalled. The Athenæum, although richest in the literary department, is intended to be also a depository for curious specimens of natural and artificial productions. It possesses a considerable number of Tassie's casts from antique gems, with a few busts, and a valuable collection of coins and medals.

The Athenæum was incorporated in 1807, and a stock subscribed in shares of 150 dollars, to the

8

amount of about ten thousand pounds sterling. To attempt such an institution was highly honourable to Boston, and to succeed in it was still more so; it marks a greatly advanced state of society, in respect of taste and intellectual refinement, and is of itself a sufficient answer to much of the coarse abuse with which the American character has been assailed.[4]

Boston is by many reputed the most hospitable of all the large cities in the United States. It becomes not a wanderer who has experienced kindness and attention wherever he has gone to exalt one city at the expense of others, but I can with safety say, that I have met with nothing in Boston which is not perfectly in harmony with such a reputation. Let me however record an act of the citizens still more honourable than the ordinary deeds of hospitality. In the winter of 1816 a

[4] The American newspapers have recently announced a splendid instance of individual liberality to this institution. A Mr. James Perkins of Boston, of the house of Messrs. J. & T. H. Perkins, has presented to the Athenæum, for the better accommodation of its treasures, a spacious building valued at 20,000 dollars; £4500 sterling. Amid all the patronage which has been bestowed on literature in our native country, I question whether we could point to an instance of equal generosity among our living commercial men. Some people become liberal in the distribution of their property when death is at hand and they can hold it no longer, but Mr. Perkins gives his townsmen the benefit of his commercial prosperity while he is still among them. Mr. Perkins, as might indeed be inferred from the character of his gift, is said to be a person of distinguished literary attainments. (1822.)

most destructive fire desolated a great part of the
town of St. John's, in Newfoundland.   When the
tidings reached Boston, the sensations of sympathy
and commiseration were instantaneous and powerful.   They did not however exhaust themselves
in unavailing expressions of regret; the townsmen
determined that their kindly feelings should be
felt as well as heard of. Forgetful that the year
before the two countries had been enemies to each
other, forgetful of every mercantile jealousy, and
the contested right to fishing on the banks which
America was eager to claim and Britain reluctant
to concede—they recollected only, that hundreds
of their fellow creatures had been burned out of
their homes, amid the frosts, and fogs, and snows,
of a Newfoundland winter, and that a great part
of their winter provisions had perished in the
flames.   That very day a vessel was chartered,
and a full cargo of flour, meat, and other provisions, industriously collected and put on board;
I believe that even the porters and carmen on the
wharfs laboured gratuitously; and on the third
day the vessel left the harbour, to brave the hardships and the dangers of a winter passage to that
inhospitable shore.   HE who prompted the act of
humanity, watched over the means employed to
accomplish it; the vessel reached Newfoundland in
safety, entered the port, discharged her cargo, and
returned, with the overflowing thanks and benedic-
tions of many a grateful heart.

The state of religion in the capital of New England is far from cheering. Whether the contagious influence spread from Harvard University to Boston, or from Boston to it, I know not, but though both were once distinguished for evangelical sentiments, both are now alike characterized by the lamentable predominance of Socinianism.

There are in the town about twenty-five churches, in more than a half of which these sentiments are avowedly or disguisedly promulgated; of these one is episcopalian in its ecclesiastical system, and uses a prayer book which has been altered in accommodation to these sentiments. It is distressing to think that the descendants of the Puritans, whose conscientious adherance to the most important religious truths drove them from their native land, should have departed so widely from adherance to those doctrines which are the only foundation of a sinner's hope.

The other churches in Boston are, three Episcopalian, four Baptist, one of which is entirely of blacks, two Congregational, two Methodist, two Universalist, and one Romish.

I have heard five discourses in Boston; two of them in a Congregational church, from men of very considerable talent and determined zeal for evangelical sentiments. One of them illustrated the answer to Pilate's question, " What is truth ?" and combated with much earnestness and ability the

F 4

doctrines of that large class who in Boston so vehemently oppose it.

The other two discourses were by the Baptist minister who was so conspicuous in the procession on the Fourth of July ; they were respectable in talent and unexceptionable in doctrine.   Between sermons on the Sabbath I saw him baptize two persons, in presence of two or three hundred spectators.   In the afternoon he dispensed the ordinance of the supper to a large congregation, as he is accustomed to do once a month, and took occasion to remark that it was twenty eight years, that very day, since he had first presided among them on a similar occasion. . The males and females of the congregation occupied different pews, and the latter were by far the more numerous.

The mode of conducting worship in both these churches was similar.   The psalms and hymns used are chiefly those of Dr. Watts, and the singing is left entirely to a choir, perched in front of the gallery with their music books before them, and aided by instruments.   This is a cold and very spiritless substitute for the united worship of the congregation.   It was in fact a mere musical parade, for while the singers rose and performed every one else kept his seat in silence, and the scene was nothing calculated to awaken or sustain the fervour of grateful devotional feeling.   How inconsistent with every right idea of social worship, to see a man after the service was over unscrewing a clarionet, putting the pieces into a leathern bag, and with the utmost indifference and unconcern stuffing the whole into his pocket !

There are several Sabbath Schools in Boston, one of which I visited. It was conducted in the English style; there were six teachers present, and they informed me that there were about one hundred scholars on their list, but not a half of that number were in attendance.

Within the last three weeks I have begun to experience the heat of an American Summer. The Thermometer at mid-day has ranged generally from 80 to 90 Degrees, and on last Sabbath, which was the hottest day of all, it stood thus; at half past Six A. M. 81^0, at Ten 90^0, at Noon 93^0, half past Two P. M. 96$\frac{1}{2}$^{0}, Five 94^0, Ten 82^0.

You have read Miss Edgeworth's tale of "Tomorrow," and will recollect the incident of the "Frog Concert." Since my arrival in America I have had frequent opportunities of listening to these performances. Marshes and ponds are filled with shoals of the Bull Frog, an animal four or five times as large as any of our hopping countrymen, who whistles away almost without intermission. Some of the frogs, probably the younger ones, have a pretty shrill note, others a deeper tone, and some tickle the auditory organ by a perpetual *trill*. The combination of these various strains produces an effect not altogether unmusical, and the distance to which the sound reaches is very great; sometimes

more than a mile. At first I enjoyed it pretty
much, but the perpetuity with which it is continued
makes it exceedingly tiresome, and to be kept
awake during the night by their monotonous tune
makes one very apt to lose temper at such untimely
serenades.

Let me introduce you to another of my American acquaintances, the Firefly; more engaging in
its manners than the other. Myriads of this brilliant little insect float through the air in the summer evening. The spark of light which they emit
is of vivid brightness, and from the fluttering of
their wings twinkles incessantly. Moore in one of
his songs, has made a pleasing allusion to these
meteoric atoms—

> " She is gone to the Lake of the Dismal Swamp,
> Where all night long by her Firefly lamp,
>   She paddles her white canoe."

Unlike the Mosquito, which is a great annoyance
here, the Firefly neither sings nor bites; it flutters
and sparkles its little hour, and passes away—an
apt emblem of many a thoughtless son and daugh-
ter of the human race.

LETTER IV.

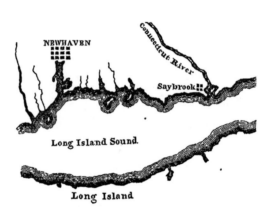

LETTER IV.

New Haven, Connecticut, July, 1818.

THERE is nothing in Britain that bears any resemblance to a New England town, and it is not easy to convey to you an adequate idea of its singular neatness.

The houses are generally of wood, painted white, and decorated with Venetian blinds of a brilliant green. The solid frame work of the walls is covered externally with thin planks, called by Americans clapboards, which overlap each other from the eaves downward, and serve effectually to exclude rain. The roof is covered with shingles, which are thin slips of wood put on like slates, and painted of a dark blue. The buildings are in general about two stories in height; the door is decorated with a neat portico, and very frequently a projecting piazza, most grateful in hot weather, with benches under it, extends along the whole front of the house.   Mouldings and minute decorations of various kinds are carried round the principal projections.   A garden is not unfrequent behind, and a neat wooden railing in- front, enclosing a grass plot and a few trees.   Such houses would soon look rusty and weather beaten, were they in our climate, but they enjoy here a purer atmosphere, and the smoke of coal fires is unknown. The painting is renewed about once a year, which serves to preserve the wood for a long time.

The churches, or meeting houses as they are more generally called, are in the smaller towns also of wood, and with the addition of a steeple and a gilt weathercock, resemble very much the other buildings.   In the large towns they are of brick or stone, but retain in almost all cases the green Venetian blinds upon the windows.

The streets are wide and generally run off, at right angles to each other, from a large open square covered with green turf, in the centre of the town; the churches, town-house, and an inn or two, not unfrequently front this green.   Gravel walks skirt many of the streets, and occasionally rows of limes, or poplars.   The agreeable succession of gardens, grass plots, trees, foot walks, and buildings, gives an air of rural quietness to the town; and the open space which frequently intervenes between one house and another, prevents much of the danger which would otherwise arise from fire. Every thing betokens an unusual share of homely simplicity and comfort, and the absence at once of great riches and of great poverty.

New Haven possesses most of the distinctive peculiarities which I have now noticed, but combines with them much of the compactness, durability, and bustle, which we usually consider inseparable from a town. The churches and a great many of the dwelling houses are of brick, a few even of stone, and two or three of the streets are very closely built. The numerous buildings also of Yale College, all of brick, and constructed with regularity and neatness, complete its claims to superiority. The population of New Haven is about 7000.

· The country around New Haven is very picturesque. Behind the town, at a distance of about two miles, is an amphitheatre of rugged hills, not unlike some of our Scotish scenery; in front is an inlet from Long Island Sound affording a safe and commodious harbour; to the right and left a richly cultivated country relieved by patches of forest, and in wide expanse before it the blue waves of the sea rolling in magnificence. Two bare precipices called East and West Rock, 400 feet high and about two miles apart, form part of the semicircular range; they are prominent features in the landscape, and events in the annals of our native country with which they are associated, impart to them that traditional charm which is so often

wanting in American scenery.   In the fastnesses of
these rocks some of the regicides of Charles 1st
found shelter from their pursuers, when the agents
of his profligate son ·hunted them for their lives.
Their story is so interesting that I cannot forbear
transcribing a portion of it from an early number
of the Quarterly Review.[1]   The event with which it
is introduced took place during a war between the
New · England Settlers and the Indians, which
ended in the utter extermination of the aboriginal
tribe,[2] by which the Eastern coast of the United
States had been previously possessed.—

   " The most impressive circumstance in the
course of this war occurred at Hadley: the Indians
having laid Deersfield in ashes, surprised Hadley
during the time of public worship.   The men of
the town had long been in the habit of taking their
arms with them when they attended divine service,
—they were however panic-stricken and confused,
and in all human probability not a soul would have
escaped alive, had not an old and venerable man,
whose dress was different from that of the inhabitants, and whom no one had seen before, suddenly
appeared among them; he rallied them, put himself at their head, gave his orders like one accustomed to battle, led them on, routed the enemy,

---

[1] Vide Quarterly Review, Vol. II. P. 324.

[2] The tragical death of their high minded but unfortunate chief,
" PHILIP of POKANOKET," forms the subject of one of Mr. Irving's
affecting papers in the second volume of the SKETCH BOOK.

and when the victory was complete, was no where
to be found. . This deliverer, whom the people
thus preserved from .death and torments long believed to.be an angel, was General Goffe, one of
the men who sat in judgment upon Charles 1st.
His adventures in America are deeply interesting.
He and his father-in-law General Whalley, another
of the King's judges, left England a few days before
the Restoration; they landed at Boston, waited on
Endicot the Governor, to inform him who they
were, took up their residence in a neighbouring
village, and were greatly respected, till the hue and
cry followed them. from Barbadoes. . They were
then warned to make their escape, and accordingly
they removed to New Haven, a place about a hundred and fifty miles distant.   Here they owed their
lives to the intrepidity of the minister John Davenport, who when their pursuers arrived preached to
the people from this text.   'Take counsel, execute
judgment, make thy shadow as the night in the
midst of the noon day, hide the outcasts, bewray
not him that .wandereth.   Let mine outcasts dwell
with thee, Moab,—be thou a covert to : them from
the face of the spoiler.'[3]   Large rewards were offered for their apprehension, or for any information
which might lead to it.   Davenport was threatened,
for it was known that he had harboured them:—
upon hearing that he was in danger, they offered

[3] Isaiah xvi. 3, 4.

to deliver themselves up, and actually gave notice
to the Deputy Governor, of the place of their concealment; but their friend had not preached in
vain, and the magistrate took no other notice than
to let them be advised not to betray themselves.
Their hiding-place was a cave on the top of West
Rock, some two or three miles from the town.
Once, when they ventured out for provisions, they
hid themselves under a bridge while their pursuers
passed over it:—once they met the sheriff who had
the warrant for their apprehension in his pocket,—
but they fought for their lives, and before he could
procure help escaped into the woods. After lurk-
ing two or three years in the cave, or in the houses
of their friends, they found it necessary to remove,
and were received at Hadley by Russell, the minister of the place, with whom they were concealed
fifteen or sixteen years. Whalley died at Hadley
in 1688, and about a year afterwards all tradition
of Goffe is lost;—one is willing to hope that he returned to England. Colonel Dixwell, another of
the King's judges, found shelter also in America;—
he visited his fellow exiles in their concealment,
and being himself unknown, settled and married at
New Haven under the name of James Davids.
By that name he signed his will, but there he adds
to it his own, and his tomb-stone is shown at New
Haven with only the initials ' J. D. Esq. deceased
March 18, in the 82d year of his age, 1688'. Another stone with the initials ' E. W. Esq.' is tradi-

8

tionally supposed to mark the grave of Whalley:
—if it be so, his bones must have been removed
there by Dixwell; an affecting act of pious friendship."

I have seen both the grave stones which are here
alluded to; they still stand in the old burying
ground behind one of the churches. The inscription on the first is in rude characters, and is thus
arranged;

I . D Esqr.

Deceased March ẙ

18 in ẙ 82d year of

his age 1688⁹.

The other stone, which has been supposed to
commemorate Whalley,[4] must have been erected
over some other person whose name and history
have been lost, for the date which has been generally read 1688, is in reality 1658. The mistake has
arisen from a slight injury which the stone has in
some former day received, and which has imparted

---

[4] President Dwight, in his Travels, which have been recently reprinted in this country, communicates some additional information
respecting these interesting men. Whalley had been secretly buried
by his kind protector Mr. Russell, and his bones were many years
after found within a rude tomb of mason work, covered with hewn
flags, outside of Mr. Russell's cellar wall. The bones were discovered
by a Mr. Gaylord, who had pulled down the house to rebuild it; he
was personally known to Dr. Dwight and communicated to him
this information. "After Whalley's decease," adds Dr. Dwight,
"Goffe quited Hadley, went into Connecticut, and afterwards, according to tradition, to the neighbourhood of New York. There he
is said to have lived some time, and the better to disguise himself, to

G 2

to the figure 5, something of the shape of an 8, although it is still quite possible to decipher its original form.   It is thus arranged :

1658

E. W.

None of these relics will long survive, unless prompt measures are adopted for their preservation. The ancient burying ground is no longer used, the fence around it has gone to decay, and the moss-grown grave stones are rapidly disappearing under the dilapidating attacks of idlers, who are daily defacing these frail memorials of the dust which sleeps below.   Many of them have been transferred to the new burying place, and although this destroys completely the charm of associated locality, it is better that they should be preserved any where, than destroyed altogether.[5]

The new cemetery which has sprung from the ashes of the old one, in simplicity of arrangement and elegance of monumental decoration, leaves at a

---

have carried vegetables at times to market.   It is said that being discovered here, he retired secretly to the colony of Rhode Island, and there lived with a son of Whalley during the remainder of his life. "—There is an obscure and very doubtful tradition that he was buried at Hadley.   *President Dwight's Travels, Vol. I. p. 353. American Edition.*

[5] An attentive and valuable correspondent writes me, that the whole of the old grave stones have now been removed to the new burying ground, with the exception of the two which are above alluded to. The ground has been levelled and sown with grass, and a marble slab affixed on the wall of the church, records the use to which it was

great distance all others that I have any where seen. It is in shape an oblong square, divided by a regular succession of avenues, crossing each other at right angles and skirted by rows of Lombardy poplars. The divisions which are thus formed are subdivided into spaces sufficient for family burying places, which are surrounded by a neat wooden railing painted white. There is scarcely a grave which has not a monument of one kind or other, and with the exception of those transferred from the old burying ground, they are almost universally of white or green marble. Some of those of white marble were executed in Italy; the green marble is found in abundance about two miles off, and is thought by some to bear a close resemblance to the Verd Antique. The monuments consist of obelisks, tables, and upright slabs at the head and foot of the grave; the obelisks are ranged in the centre of the principal subdivisions, in parallel rows, and at right angles to each other. The inscriptions which are cut on the white marble are generally painted black, those on the green are gilt and have a very rich effect.

While the monuments in the old burying ground seem devoted to ruin, those in the new one although accessible to every passenger are treated

formerly appropriated. I am afraid that the good taste which dictated the exception in favour of these supposed memorials of King Charles' judges, will not long avail them, if as I suppose the stones are left altogether without protection. (1822)

with the most scrupulous respect. A neat fence
surrounds the cemetery but openings are left at regular intervals, from which numerous foot walks
cross the ground. The soil is composed of a light
sand, and shoots from the poplars are springing up
so· numerously that they threaten to overrun it.
Except the slight wooden railing there is no kind
of fence around the ·graves; they are altogether
free from those unsightly cages of cast iron by which
our burying grounds in Glasgow are disfigured,[6]
and the enclosures are not defaced by those quaint
emblems of mortality and grief, which so often
with us betray the bad taste of thè proprietors. A
becoming respect is shown to the memory of the
departed; and an air of impressive solemnity pervades the whole enclosure, which is not counter-
acted by any of those lugubrious and not unfre-
quently· ludicrous allegorical devices, and misap-
plied quotations from scripture, which meet us at
every step in our more ancient repositories of the
dead. I have visited every shrine in Westminster
Abbey, and have heard the marble-hearted verger
dole out, in monotonous cadence, the dreary catalogue of names which are entombed and commemorated there; the damp of the long drawn aisles
chilled me to the heart, and I trod upon the ashes
of Monarchs, Barons, and Crusading Knights,

[6] The Medical·School connected with Yale College, is under a
bond to the State Legislature that no bodies shall be taken from the
New Haven burying ground, for anatomical purposes.

whose sculptured figures, scattered around, were covered with the mutilations and dust of many generations; yet I doubt whether sympathy with my kindred dust were as strongly excited there, as in the burying ground at New Haven. It seems, as if the walls of the Gothic Cathedral had been intended to commemorate, that the departed were the great and the honourable of the earth, rather than that the great and the honourable as well as the lowly and obscure are doomed to be the prey of the spoiler. It comes more closely home to my feelings and circumstances, to read on the tablets of the more humble burying ground—

> " Here rests his head upon a lap of earth,
> A youth, to fortune and to fame unknown."

It shows good sense and right feeling, that this cemetery is left open to the foot of the fortuitous passenger;—levity may here be taught to reflect, inconsiderate youth to ponder the path which is before him, and perchance he who has been reft of those who were the dearest companions of his earthly pilgrimage, may be soothed by being reminded that a few light-winged years, at most, are all that intervene between him and the world of disembodied spirits. Happy for him and them if they " die the death of the righteous," that their latter end may be like his.

Were I to venture a criticism upon this burying

ground, I should say that it is of too unvarying a
level, the arrangement too precisely angular, and
the numerous poplars too stiff and formal;—where
there is so much to admire however it is unreasonable to search minutely for deficiencies, and no one
can walk through it without the spontaneous ac-
knowledgment, that it is highly creditable to the
taste and the feelings of the inhabitants of New
Haven.

It has been my lot to make one in the ranks of
a funeral procession, which followed to this ground
the remains of an amiable young man, cut short in
the morning of his days and the full bloom of
health, by a sudden and afflicting accident.

The company which assembled to this funeral
was of both sexes and very numerous; none however wore mourning, except those who were closely
related to the family. Special invitations to a
funeral are unknown; all are expected to be present
who feel any interest in the family of the deceased.
When all were within doors who could be conveniently admitted, a clergyman offered up a pretty
long and very impressive prayer; after which the
funeral procession was arranged. The deceased
was at the period of his death a student of Yale
College, and his late class-fellows with crape
upon their hats and arms walked first in order.
The Professors followed them. Next came the
Body, drawn on a small car or hearse, and attended by six students as pall bearers. The coffin

was of plain mahogany; the upper part of the lid hinged, and bearing a silvered plate inscribed with the initials and the age of the deceased. The family followed the body in a coach. To them succeeded the other relatives in coaches and gigs; then a few individuals on foot who were in habits of particular intimacy with the family; the procession was closed by a multitude walking two and two, and a promiscuous attendance on the side walks who did not link themselves to the ranks.

On arriving at the burying ground, all left their carriages. The father and mother, brothers and sisters, of the departed youth, stood at the upper end of the grave, the clergyman and the near relatives beside them, and the pall bearers lowered the coffin into its narrow abode. After a little earth had been thrown in, the clergyman, addressing himself to the surrounding company, thanked them in the name of the family for the tokens of sympathy which the melancholy event had drawn from them, and concluded by a short but solemn address on the subjects of Death and Eternity. During the clergyman's address all stood uncovered and profoundly attentive, the relations then returned to their carriages, and the rest of the assembly dispersed.

The attendance of the Professors and students on this occasion, arose from the peculiar circumstances of the event; in other respects the funeral was conducted according to customary form.

Education, which prevails much more universally throughout the New England States than in any other portion of the Union, and is frequently accompanied with religious instruction, has given to the natives a very decided cast of national char-- acter, resembling in many respects that for which the Scots among Europeans have long been dis- tinguished. The kind of education also in the two countries is remarkably similar; it is more general than accurate, and more useful than ele- gant; imparted by means of district or parochial schools, and in this country almost entirely without expense to those who receive it.

The characteristics of a New Englander are in- telligence, sobriety, enterprise, perseverance; and when he finds his range at home too limited to admit of a sufficiently successful application of these qualities, he betakes himself to distant re- gions, and traverses one State after another, till he finds some nook in which he can establish himself with advantage.

In the Southern and Western States many of the most successful merchants, the most industrious farmers, the most money-making land speculators, are natives of New England; and scarcely is there a station in society or a mode of obtaining a live- lihood, in which there will not be found a full pro- portion of them. If you meet a waggon in some remote country road with a cheerful looking family, and a tall slender figure whistling along with an

axe over his shoulder—it is a Yankee[7] backwoods-
man, on his march for the wilderness of Illinois
or Tennessee, where he will build a log house,
clear a few acres of land, sell the whole at a profit
to the next comer, and start with the waggon a
second time, to penetrate some hundreds of miles
farther into the woods, and repeat the process. If
you see at the turnpike gate of a country town a
light carriage, resembling a British taxed cart,
built up all round with a pile of assorted packing
boxes and trunks—it is the travelling store of a
New England pedlar, who is marketing his wares,
swopping, or selling, or buying, as he and his customers can agree about it, *guessing* away with every
one he meets, but turning all to good account in
the end. In all those bye ways of getting on in
the world, for which America affords unexampled
facilities, none are found to succeed like the natives
of New England.

The consequence of this adventurous spirit is,
that they enjoy along with their prosperity a considerable share of the envy and ill will which successful rivalry generally excites. Perhaps there
are instances in which cunning, rather than hon-

---

[7] The term Yankee which we apply indiscriminately, as a nickname,
to all the natives of America, is here restricted in its application to the
natives of the New England States, who in general consider it as
by no means a reproachful appellation. I have seen an advertisement, in a Baltimore Newspaper, commencing, " A YANKEE recently arrived in Baltimore wishes a situation," &c.

esty, has characterized their enterprises; but among so many adventurers it is not surprising that some should be unprincipled, and of course a well educated and ingenious rogue has a fearful advantage over ignorant and stupid ones. From whatever cause it may have arisen, it is certain that in the south there is a strong prejudice against them; and it is very customary there to say many hard things of the Yankees, which are true only of a small number, and those the very worst of them.

The New England character is very favourably exhibited in New Haven, for the simplicity and sincerity of the ancient Puritans may be still seen strongly marked in their descendants. Plain and frugal in their domestic habits, they exhibit little of that artificial polish which, like varnish, frequently disguises very worthless materials; and a stranger is not mortified by professions without services, and show without substance. At some of their homely but pleasant evening parties, I have found myself invested with no small degree of temporary importance; for whoever can talk from personal knowledge of Loch Katrine, the Troshachs, and Stirling Castle, or the other classic spots immortalized in Scott's Poems and the " Tales of my Landlord," is listened to by old and young with open-mouthed attention, and his national vanity may almost lead him to imagine that he is for the time the accredited representative of " the Great Unknown." Should he ask the transatlantic admirers of the Antiquary and Rob Roy, to translate to him some of the wise *saws* of Edie Ochiltree and Bailie Jarvie,[8] which they quote with such rapture, he cannot fail to be amused at the good humoured simplicity with which they take Scotish wit upon trust, and contrive to be amused with what they do not half understand.

The district schools of Connecticut are supported by what is termed the School Fund, whose origin was as follows.   By the charter of Charles the Second, the colony of Connecticut extended completely across the continent to the Pacific ocean, within the parallels of latitude which now bound it; of course it included a large portion of the present States of Pennsylvania and Ohio. About ten years after the revolution, the claim to the portion of Pennsylvania was by compromise abandoned, but a vast tract beyond the limits of that State was sold by Connecticut, and the proceeds 1,200,000 dollars, £270,000 sterling, for ever appropriated to the support of free schools within the State.   This fund has increased to about 1,700,000 dollars, £382,500 sterling, the

[8] Incorporated trades are altogether unknown here, and there are no Deacons among them but those of the congregational churches, who are always designated, even in the ordinary affairs of life, by their official title; the consequence is, that the Bailie's " father the Deacon, honest man !" in place of being regarded as president of the craft of weavers, is supposed to have been a very staid and demure elder of the venerable Kirk, and of course a very pious and very worthy man, which readily accounts for the Bailie's respect for his

annual income of which, upwards of 80,000 dollars, above £18,000 sterling, is distributed a-
mong a population of about 270,000 persons.
This presents, as was remarked to me, the singular spectacle of a larger sum of money being
paid out of the public treasury for the education
of the people, than all the amount that is received
by it in taxes and contributions of every kind;—a
state of things certainly no where else ever known
in the world.

In the schools which are thus established, every
citizen has a legal claim to have his children educated, and all are compellable by law to send them.
In most districts however, the funds are not sufficient to support the schools for more than a half
or two thirds of the year; in many of them the
school is shut when the fund is exhausted, in
others the inhabitants assess themselves to support
it during the interval.   English, writing, accounts,
and occasionally a little mathematics, are the
branches taught, and I believe that it is next to impossible to discover in the State a white native
who cannot read and write.[9]

memory. Some of the deacons of our Trades' House would, I
suspect, find themselves rather awkwardly beset, if called upon to
exchange situations and duties with those of a similar title in New
Haven.

  [9] The early settlers of Connecticut showed a zeal for the instruction of the rising generation, equally remarkable and honourable.
" In the year 1677, to render the existing law respecting schools

It is cause of regret that this large sum of money is entirely absorbed by these elementary schools, and that no part of it is devoted to literary institutions of a higher order. A very unaccountable but general prejudice prevails against any such appropriation, and Yale College, in many respects the first in the Union, and an honour to the country, is left to rely entirely on its own resources, while it is in the power of the people greatly to augment its efficiency and prosperity by a comparatively trifling donation from this ample fund.

There is a Grammar School in New Haven, endowed from a legacy by one of the Governors of the State named Hopkins, in which youths are prepared for college, and which enjoys a respectable reputation; there are also two other seminaries of a superior kind to the district schools. Of the minor schools the teachers of about three-

---

more effectual, it was enacted ' that every town by the said law ordered to keep a school, that shall neglect the same three months in the year, shall forfeit Five Pounds for every defect.' " In the year 1690 an additional statute was passed, " which after reciting in the preamble that there were still ' persons unable to read the English tongue, and thereby incapable to read the holy word of God, or the good laws of this colony,' among other provisions contains the following; ' that the grand jurymen in each town, do once in a year, at least, visit each family they suspect to neglect this order, [to teach their children and servants to ' read distinctly the English tongue'] and satisfy themselves whether all children under age, and servants in such suspected families can read the English tongue, or

fourths are females, according to the ancient English custom. Even the poor blacks participate in
the prevalent taste for education, for there are two
schools in New Haven appropriated to them.
Many of them, I am assured, are able to read,
write, and keep accounts, and are in their own
sphere of life, useful and respectable members of
society.[10]

Yale College, which completes the provision
made for education in Connecticut, is too important
to be passed over with a slight notice, and shall
form the subject of a separate communication.

The inhabitants of the eastern district of the
Union have been known from the earliest periods
of their history as a religious people. In the wilds
of America they sought that liberty of conscience,
and of worship, which was refused them at home;
and although it is true, that they did not always
concede to others, the toleration which they them-

be in a good procedure to learn the same or not; and if they find
any such children and servants not taught, as their years are capable
of, they shall return the names of the parents or masters of the said
children or servants to the next county court,' &c. The penalty is
twenty shillings ' for each child or servant whose teaching is or shall
be neglected, contrary to this order.' " *Vide North American Review, No. XXXIX. pp.* 382, 3. in an article containing much
interesting information relative to the state of education in Connecticut.

[10] In building Long Wharf, two black men were contractors for
executing a considerable part of the work, where the water is 16
feet deep. *Vide Pres. Dwight's Statistical Account of New Haven.*

selves claimed, this inconsistency between principle and practice was, unfortunately, common to the early reformers of almost every nation. Popery had so long exercised its torpedo influence upon the thinking faculties of man, that it was only by slow degrees that those who found its principles intolerable in some of their applications, were brought to see them unjust, and therefore inexpedient, in all. A good deal there is in the conduct of the early settlers, of which it would be vain to attempt a justification ; but, taking them as a body, they were distinguished above most men then living, by their attachment to pure doctrine and upright practice. This purity of doctrine, as has been already noticed, has been in part of the country lost in Socinianism ; but the State of Connecticut is, as yet, free from this contamination. There are in New Haven seven places of public worship ; the College chapel, in which there is stated service, three Congregational, one Episcopalian, one Methodist,[11] and one Baptist chapel. The Episcopalian congregation was formed in 1755, that of the Methodists in 1807. The Episcopalians have here a flourishing theological academy.

The Congregational form of church government, which prevails so universally in this part

---

[11] This Methodist chapel was blown down during a tremendous hurricane on the 21st of September 1821, but was immediately rebuilt.

of the country is of a peculiar kind, and par-
takes very considerably of the presbyterian character. The following sketch of its origin and
features, I extract from a manuscript account,
politely drawn up for me by a gentleman of this
State.

In 1708 an assembly of clerical and lay delegates,
convened at Saybrook[12] in Connecticut by order
of the colonial government, drew up articles of
doctrine and an ecclesiastical system which was
thereafter denominated the ' Saybrook Platform.'
This standard being sanctioned by the colonial
legislature, became in effect the established form
of religion. Most of the churches and congregations voluntarily adopted it ; none however were

---

[12] This town is connected with a very remarkable incident in English History ; it is the place to which Oliver Cromwell would have
emigrated, when yet a private country gentleman, had not Charles
1st interfered to prevent him. I quote the following from the
Quarterly Review.

" Lord Brooke, Lord Say and Sele, and his sons, Pym, and other
distinguished men of the same sentiments, were about to remove to
a settlement in New England, where the name of Saybrook, in honour of the two noble leaders, had already been given to a township
in which they were expected. Eight vessels with emigrants on board
were ready to sail from the Thames, when the King by an order of
Council forbade their departure, and compelled the intended passengers to come on shore ; fatally for himself, for among those passengers Haslerigge, and Hampden, and Cromwell, with all his family had actually embarked. There are few facts in History which
have so much the appearance of fatality as this." *Quarterly Review*,
Vol. XXV. p. 228.

compelled, and some have not come under it even to this day. The system of doctrine was substantially that of the Savoy Confession ; but churches were allowed to come in either under that, or the Westminster Confession, or the *doctrinal* articles of the Church of England.

In conformity with this Platform was formed the *Consociation ;* which is an assembly of ministers and lay delegates from churches within a particular geographical extent, usually a county or half county ; it is composed of about equal numbers of clergymen and laymen, which last are invariably church members. This body is a judicatory for the trial of all ecclesiastical questions, and its decision is final ; parties are often heard by counsel before it, as in a civil court.

Superior to the Consociation are the *Associations.* These consist of ministers only, and are of two kinds. The general State Association, which meets annually, is the supreme church court; and is composed of delegates from local Associations, for counties and half counties, which meet more frequently. In the local Associations was formerly invested, by law, the power of examining and licensing preachers, and regulating every thing connected therewith ; and this still continues in practice, though no longer enjoined by statute. It must be remarked however that in other respects the legislative power both of the general and local Associations is only that of advising; they have no

H 2

power to compel obedience, but their advice is almost invariably respected.

The General Association of the State sends delegates to the General Assembly of the Presbyterian church of the United States, which meets annually in Philadelphia, and which in its turn sends delegates to the General Association. These delegates are admitted to sit by mutual courtesy, for the Association does not acknowledge the absolute legislative authority of the General Assembly, nor does the Assembly regard the Association as having by right a voice in its councils. The General Assembly is however consulted by the General Association and its advice is generally respected.

Besides the local Associations, *Councils* exist, composed of ministers and lay delegates, which are invited by churches to settle their ministers, and to assist in accommodating any differences that may occur between congregations and their pastors; preachers who have been previously licensed by the local Associations, are re-examined by a Council before ordination over any particular church.

These are the principal features of the ecclesiastical system of the State. The congregations are individually formed on the independent model; having no ruling elders, nor any office-bearers but the Pastor and Deacons. The deacons manage the temporal concerns of the church, and visit and relieve the poor. When a member offends, his conduct must be reported to the whole church be-

8

fore he can be excluded from its communion. The pastors of the congregational churches in New Haven have salaries of from 1000 to 1200 Dollars; £225, to £270 sterling.

There are in the New England States not under 1000 churches upon the congregational model. This includes however those of Unitarian principles, of which there are probably about 50 in all; most of these are to be found in the western part of Massachusetts, a few in Vermont and New Hampshire, and perhaps in Rhode Island, although in this last State the Baptists predominate.

In Connecticut the observance of the Sabbath is not as with us, from midnight to midnight, but according to the ancient Jewish system, from sunset to sunset;—that is they commence its observance at sunset on Saturday, and continue it till sunset on Sunday. In conformity with this principle, the stores are shut on Saturday evening at twilight and business is suspended; the churches are not opened for worship, at least at present, but the inhabitants in general confine themselves to their houses, and spend the evening in family and private devotion. After sunset on Sabbath they consider themselves at liberty to engage in secular matters, but the stores are not opened, and the evening is usually spent with quietness and decorum.

With the exercises of the Saturday evening which this system requires, there could be no difficulty in harmonizing; but my mind could not so easily rid

H 3

itself of former sentiments and feelings with regard to the evening of the Sabbath. In the family with whom I am at present a guest, the Sabbath exercises were concluded immediately after tea, by my host's reading a chapter and engaging in prayer. He then invited me to accompany him to visit a worthy Deacon's family in the neighbourhood; to which I without hesitation agreed, willing to see and know all that I could of their Sabbath occupations. There we found a merry groupe of young people, and it was not without considerable surprise, that I heard the proposal made soon after we entered that one of the young ladies should sing ' *Down the burn Davie.*' In reply to this suggestion I told them that, though I did not wish to prescribe to them the manner in which they should spend the Sabbath evening, yet I could not so suddenly become a convert to their system, and that therefore if they intended to sing songs, I should take the liberty of withdrawing. They argued against what were considered my educational prejudices, but agreed to sing a hymn in place of a song, and spend the rest of the evening in conversation.[13]

We cannot, perhaps, incontrovertibly prove which system of reckoning holy time prevailed in apostolic times; but it is certainly more likely to secure the

---

[13] I have reason to suspect that in proposing the song on the occasion alluded to, the good people only meant to show me the extent of their liberty on the Sabbath evening, and that had I not been present it would not have been thought of. A New Haven gentle-

sanctification of the Christian Sabbath, that after a night of stillness and repose, one entire day from morning to night should be devoted to its duties, than that it should be made up of a fragment of one day, and three quarters of the next. The man of business cannot dismiss worldly concerns from his mind by the mere locking of his warehouse door; and, however conscientious in the discharge of what he may consider his duty, he cannot be so well disposed for meditation, as when he rises to begin a day on which no secular employment is permitted to intrude. Even here, the Episcopalians and the Methodists dissent from the prevailing system, and the consequence is that many avail themselves of this difference of opinion, and neither observe the one evening nor the other. Throughout this State travelling on the Sabbath is strictly prohibited, and the prohibition rigorously enforced; the Mail of the United States is the only privileged conveyance, for the laws of the Federal government, by which it is appointed, are not subject to the control of the local legislature; but neither on foot, on horseback, nor in a private carriage, is it possible for a traveller to escape the Argus eyes of the civil officers.

The Sermons which I have heard in New Haven, the appearance of the congregations, and other cir-

man, who had an opportunity of reading the manuscript of this letter, wrote with a pencil opposite to this portion of it—" *I am persuaded a very uncommon occurrence—I never met with it. Calls are made among intimate friends, but rarely is there jollity or mirth.*"

H 4

cumstances, give me reason to think well of the
state of religion here.

In the College chapel I heard a judicious discourse on the evidence which is sufficient to establish the truth of a miracle.   The Professor successfully combated the doctrine of Hume on this
subject, and proved the validity of the testimony
which we possess, respecting the miracles that are
recorded in Scripture.   In one of the congregational churches, I heard that text again illustrated
which had formed the subject of one of the sermons
that I heard in Boston, Pilate's question " What
is truth ?"   On this occasion, however, the
Preacher treated his subject in the first place as a
question of pure metaphysics, and illustrated it in
a most luminous manner.   I do not recollect having heard on any occasion from the pulpit, a more
masterly exhibition of vigorous thinking and close
reasoning, or language more accurate and appropriate.   It was not however a mere metaphysical
lecture, for the whole train of argument was made
subservient to the illustration of the great gospel
scheme of salvation.   The preacher demonstrated
that every attempt to overthrow the economy of
salvation through Christ Jesus, was in fact beating
the air, and fighting against God.   Immediately
before the sermon, banns of marriage were proclaimed with a loud voice from the desk; I have
not in America been present on any other occasion
when this was done.

At the conclusion of the afternoon's worship, I saw in one of the churches a Sabbath School, consisting of the young persons belonging to the congregation. This was conducted more upon the plan of the Scotish Sabbath Schools than any which I have hitherto seen here, for it was exclusively devoted to religious instruction; it was obviously however a recent attempt, and not matured in the execution. There was a teacher to about every dozen of children, who heard them repeat whatever passage they had voluntarily prepared; there was no system of regular and prescribed exercise, in which they could all join, nor did I hear any attempt made at illustration by parallel passages. A beginning however has been made, and a little experience will soon enable them to improve upon the mode of conducting them.

In one of the congregational churches they have recently introduced the organ, as an auxiliary in Psalmody; but a special stipulation has been made by the more aged and less enthusiastic in harmonics, that no *voluntary* is ever to break in upon the solemnity of worship, or mar its intellectual character; the instrument is allowed to lead and harmonize the voices of the congregation, but to do nothing more.

LETTER V.

LETTER V.

New Haven, August, 1818.

THE buildings of Yale College make a conspicuous appearance when entering the town from the eastward, and the effect is considerably heightened by three churches, which stand at a little distance in front in a parallel line. The ground between the College and the churches is neatly divided and enclosed, and ornamented with trees.

The College buildings are seven in number;[1] five ranging with each other in front, and two behind. Three of those in front are plain but uniform erections of brick, four stories high, containing apartments for the students. A chapel with a spire, and a Lyceum with a belfry, occupy the intervals.

[1] An eighth was erected in 1821. It is exactly uniform to the three larger buildings, and is a continuation of the front line, with space left vacant for a new Lyceum or some corresponding edifice.

Yale College was established at Saybrook in the year 1700,[2] and was incorporated by the colonial legislature in 1701. In 1718 it was removed to New Haven. It was originally intended only for the education of young men for the ministry, but as it gathered strength, from individual liberality and public patronage, the range of its studies was gradually extended, until it now embraces the more essential parts of a complete literary, scientific, and medical education.

The College received its name in commemoration of the bounty of the Hon. Elihu Yale, a son of one of the early settlers; who went to England in early life, thence to India, where he received the appointment of Governor of Madras, and afterwards on returning to England was elected Governor of the East India Company. From him the infant institution received donations at various times to the amount of £500 sterling, and a short time before his death he directed another benefaction to the same amount to be transmitted, but which unfortunately was never received.

Among its early benefactors was the celebrated Dean Berkely, who, having been frustrated in his efforts to establish a College in the island of Bermuda, presented to this institution a farm which

[2] President Dwight's Travels contain, in Letters 16th and 17th, a pretty copious account of Yale College. The reader has here less historical detail but a much more circumstantial view of discipline and study, the whole of which I have derived from official sources.

he had purchased in Rhode Island, and afterwards transmitted to it from England a very valuable collection of books. Sir Isaac Newton, and many other distinguished men presented their works to the library.

Although founded under the sanction of the legislature, and partially endowed by it, the College was for a long time more indebted to individual than to state patronage; for the first ninety years of its existence, the whole amount bestowed by the local legislature, did not much exceed £4500 sterling[3]. When the Federal government however was consolidated, the debts of the individual States were assumed by Congress, and a considerable amount of uncollected arrears of war taxes due to the State, was left at its disposal. In 1792 part of these debts was granted to Yale College, and in 1796 the grant, after a severe struggle to oppose it, was enlarged. By the very judicious management of those who collected the arrears, about 60,000 dollars were realized from them; £13,500 sterling which imparted to the College a degree of vigour which it had not hitherto known, and to this day nearly the whole of its funded income arises from this source.

The affairs of Yale College are under the superintendence of a board of Trustees, consisting of the Governor and Lieutenant Governor of the

[3] Vide North American Review, No. XXXIX. p. 386.

State, six of the Counsellors,[4] and eleven Clergymen. The Faculty consists of a President, nine
Professors, four Medical Examiners, and six
Tutors.[5] The academical studies extend to Literature, experimental and moral philosophy and theology; the medical department embraces a course
of medical and surgical instruction, complete in
all its parts.

[4] A new constitution has been adopted in Connecticut since the
date of this letter, under which the Counsellors have now the title of
Senators.

[5] The following is a list of the Faculty in November 1820.

JEREMIAH DAY, D. D., LL. D., President.

Dr. Æneas Monson, Professor of the Institutes of Medicine.

Dr. Nathan Smith, Professor of the theory and practice of Physic
and Surgery.

Benjamin Silliman, Professor of Chemistry, Pharmacy, Mineralogy
and Geology.

James L. Kingsley, Professor of the Hebrew, Greek and Latin
Languages.

Dr. Eli Ives, Professor of Materia Medica and Botany, and Lecturer on the diseases of Children.

Dr. Jonathan Knight, Professor of Anatomy and Physiology, and
Lecturer on Obstetrics.

Rev. Eleazar T. Fitch, Professor of Divinity.

Rev. Chauncey A. Goodrich, Professor of Rhetoric and Oratory.

Alexander M. Fisher, Professor of Mathematics and Natural Philosophy.

Dr. Mason F. Cogswell, Dr. Thomas Hubbard, Dr. Thomas
Miner, Dr. Warren Fowler, Medical Examiners.

Horace Hooker, Rufus Woodward, William C. Fowler, Edward
Bull, Lyman Coleman, Tutors.

[Since the preceding lines were written, Professor Fisher has
found an untimely grave. He was one of about fifty persons who
perished in the wreck of the Albion of New York, in the bay of

At Yale College the undergraduates during the course of four years are termed, as at Harvard and the other American Colleges, successively Freshmen, Sophomores, Junior, and Senior, Sophisters. It is customary for those graduates who wish to prosecute their studies more fully, to avail themselves of the lectures for several additional years; while they do so they are subject, in common

---

Kinsale, Ireland, on the morning of the 22d April 1822. " The extinction," as a biographer has said, " of genius, of virtue, and of bright hopes !".

Mr. Fisher was born at Franklin, Massachusetts, in 1794. In 1809 at the age of 15 he entered Yale College, where in 1813 he received a Bachelor's degree and finished the course with the highest reputation. After spending some time at the Theological Academy at Andover, he returned to Yale College in 1815, in consequence of being appointed Tutor; in 1817 he was nominated Adjunct Professor of Mathematics and Natural Philosophy, and in 1819 sole Professor of the same branches. The vigour of his mind, the extent of his acquirements, and his unwearied industry, enabled him to discharge his professional duties with a success, which excited the most lively satisfaction in his brother Professors; which bade fair to raise the reputation of the College, as a school for the exact sciences, to a higher rank than any American seminary has yet attained; and which would doubtless have drawn forth the homage of admiration from the older institutions of Europe.

To me as an individual the destruction of the Albion, and the death of Professor Fisher, were both events of most painful interest. The Albion was the vessel in which I returned to my native country; she was then newly launched, and Captain Williams who was lost in her, had been promoted from an older of the packet vessels to her command. We embarked on the tenth of March, and by noon on the thirtieth we were walking the streets of Liverpool. With Mr. Fisher I had become acquainted at New Haven, and had been particularly gratified by his society and conversation. Calling at his

with the others, to the more essential rules of College discipline.

For admission to the Freshman class, it is requisite that the candidate should have completed his fourteenth year, and he must undergo examination upon Adam's Latin Grammar, Clarke's Intro-

apartments in the college, one morning after breakfast, I found him with a duodecimo bible upon the table before him; he had shut it as I entered, and its leaves betokened that it was the subject of frequent study. He enquired particularly about the state of religion in Glasgow, about our benevolent institutions, our Bible, and Missionary Societies; about our clergymen, the support which they gave to such institutions, the style of their preaching, and their theological reputation. He conducted me through several of the apartments of the college; the library, the cabinet of minerals, and the room containing the philosophical apparatus. Long will I cherish the remembrance of that interview and conversation. Early in 1822 I was apprized of his intention of visiting this country, and informed that he would probably be in Glasgow about the month of May. I hoped to have had the pleasure of seeing him for a time the inmate of my own family, and fondly anticipated the intellectual feast which his conversation would afford. But alas! ere May arrived, the Albion was a wreck, and poor Fisher a corpse engulphed in the ocean! "Whatsoever God doeth, it shall be for ever: nothing can be put to it, nor any thing taken from it; and God doeth it that men should fear before him."

Some of the fruits of Mr. Fisher's early talents have been preserved in periodical Journals. He contributed under the signature of 'Nov. Anglus' *Solutions of various questions* in the 5th volume of the 'Mathematical Repository, edited by Thomas Leybourn, of the Royal Military Academy.' He is author under the signature of 'X' of various *Solutions of mathematical questions* in the American Monthly Magazine, begun at New York in 1817; one of these is said to be particularly deserving of notice, *On the most advantageous position of the sail of a wind mill, when the ratio of the velocities of the sail and wind is given.* In the 4th Volume of the 'Memoirs of the Ameri-

duction to the making of Latin, Goodrich's Greek Grammar, and Prosody, Cicero's Select Orations, Virgil, Sallust, Dalzel's Analecta Græca Minora, and the Greek Testament. Applicants for the more advanced classes must have a corresponding increase of age, and undergo examination upon

can Academy of arts and sciences,' are published his *Observations on the Comet of* 1819, *and calculation of its orbit;* this paper was the result of the first actual observations on a heavenly body that he had ever made. To Professor Silliman's ' Journal of Science,' he furnished the following papers:—In Vol. I. *Essay on Musical Temperament,* written when he was about twenty-one years of age, and which called forth from Mr. John Farey, Senior, London, in an essay on *Musical Intervals,* in Vol. 2d of the same journal, the following observation ; "I have before met with nothing like it, in point of utility, in an attentive perusal of nearly every thing which has been printed in the English language on the subject"—In Vol. III. *Remarks on Dr. Enfield's Institutes of Natural Philosophy;* a paper exhibiting his extensive and familiar acquaintance with mathematical and philosophical writers. *On some recent improvements in the construction of the Printing Press,* with a mathematical investigation of its theory and powers. In Vol. V. *On Maxima and Minima of Functions of two variable quantities;* written in part soon after he graduated.

His brother Professor. Mr. Kingsley, in a biographical sketch, which has furnished me with some of the above particulars, says that Mr. Fisher's visit to Europe was undertaken "not so much for the sake of making new acquisitions in science—for the knowledge of European philosophers is found in their books—as to visit the places of public instruction, and examine by actual inspection the mode of communicating knowledge in the foreign universities; to form an acquaintance with men who were distinguished in his own department, and to obtain such information as might enable him more fully to aid, in raising the scientific character of his country, and in promoting the usefulness and prosperity of this college." Professor Silliman in his Obituary adds—"Mr. Fisher was the most extraor-

all the previous customary course of study.   Each individual, on entering, is required to produce certificates of good moral character, and to subscribe a solemn engagement to be obedient in every respect to the laws of the College.   The total number of Academical students and resident graduates is at present 283.[6]

. The three younger classes are each divided

dinary man of his years whom I have ever known.—To his wonderful scientific attainments, he added the finish of classical and polite literature, derived from the best ancient as well as modern sources; his elegant taste embraced the fine arts in their extent and variety, and he was satisfied with nothing, even in the decorum and accommodations of private life, which was not adapted to the same elevated standard."
His Parents still survive at the place of his nativity.   One also lives with whom, had he been spared to return, he was soon to have entered upon the most endearing of earthly relations!

> " There is a tear for all that die,
> A mourner o'er the humblest grave—"

But how wide is the circle of mourners, when they are laid low, who were opening on a career of early and extensive usefulness, who seemed singularly marked out and qualified to enlarge the boundaries of science, and to exalt the intellectual character of a rapidly rising nation!

The Mathematical chair is now filled by the Rev. Matthew R. Dutton.]

[6] At the date of this letter, Yale College was in number of students somewhat under Harvard; since that period however, it has got above the other by about twenty or thirty.   In November 1820 its catalogue exhibited the following summary :—

Resident graduates,	31
Academical students,	319
Medical students,	62
Total,	412

into two parts, to each of which a Tutor is appointed, who assists the Professors in instructing and examining the students; the students of the fourth year, are under the more immediate superintendence of the President and Professors. The three younger classes attend three public recitations or lectures a day, excepting on Wednesday and Saturday, when they have only two. The senior class recites once a day to the President. At every lecture the students are minutely examined on the subject of the preceding one.

The annual ' Commencement' is on the second Wednesday of September, and there are in the year three terms, at the close of each of which is a short vacation.

The following is an abstract of the Academical course :

FRESHMEN. *First Term*—Livy begun, Adam's Roman Antiquities, Webber's Arithmetic, Murray's English Grammar. *Second. Term*—Livy's first five books finished, Analecta Græca Majora, the historical parts, Day's Algebra. *Third Term*—Analecta Græca Majora continued, Morse's Geography, vol. 1st, Irving on Composition, Murray's Grammar reviewed.

In addition to these recitations, the Freshmen attend the lectures of the Professor of Languages, and the private exercises and lectures of the Professor of Rhetoric and Oratory. They present

I 3

in writing, English translations from Latin authors, and specimens of Latin composition.

SOPHOMORES. *First Term*—Morse's Geography, vol. 2d, Playfair's Euclid begun, Horace begun. *Second Term*—Playfair's Euclid finished, Horace finished, Day's Mathematics, parts 2d, and 3d, Cicero de Officiis begun. *Third Term*—Homer's Iliad, Day's Mathematics, part 4th, Conic Sections and Spherical Geometry, Blair's Lectures, vol. 1st, Cicero de Officiis, de Senectute, et de Amicitia finished.

The Sophomores continue to attend the Professor of Languages, and the Professor of Rhetoric and Oratory. They exhibit specimens of English and Latin Composition, and engage in forensic disputations in presence of their instructors. In connexion with the branches of Mathematics, which are specified, they study Mensuration, Surveying, and Navigation.

JUNIOR SOPHISTERS. *First Term*—Spherical Trigonometry, Analecta Græca Majora continued, Enfield's Philosophy begun, Cicero de Oratore begun. *Second Term*—Analecta Græca Majora, vol. 1st finished, Enfield's Philosophy continued, Cicero de Oratore continued, Tacitus, omitting the Annals. *Third Term*—Enfield's Astronomy, Tytler's General History, Vince's Fluxions, Greek, or Hebrew, at the option of the Student.

The Professor of Languages, and the Professor of Rhetoric and Oratory, continue their lectures.

8

The students exhibit specimens of English Composition. Forensic disputations are continued twice a week before the instructors. They attend a course of lectures on Natural Philosophy, Chemistry, and Mathematics.

SENIOR SOPHISTERS. *First Term*—Blair's Lectures, vol. 2d, Hedge's Logic, Locke's Essays, Paley's Natural Theology. *Second Term*—Paley's Natural Theology, Paley's Evidences of Christianity, Stewart's Philosophy of the Mind. *Third Term*—Paley's Moral Philosophy.

The Professor of Languages, and the Professor of Rhetoric and Oratory conclude their lectures. The students continue forensic disputations, and attend the lectures on Chemistry, Mineralogy, Geology, Mathematics, Natural Philosophy, Logic, Metaphysics, Ethics, and Theology.

The Professor of Divinity delivers a lecture on Theology in the College chapel, each Sabbath in term time, completing a course in four years; he also occasionally discourses privately to the senior class.[7]

The English authors which have been mentioned, are studied chiefly as appropriate text books upon

---

[7] A theological school has recently been founded, which is in connexion with the College, and will probably be hereafter incorporated with it. The Rev. Nathaniel W. Taylor has been appointed Professor of Didactic Theology, and the students receive instructions from the academical Professors in the Languages, Rhetoric, and Biblical Criticism. A school of Law is projected, and will probably be soon brought into operation.

which the Professor discourses; and their opinions are of course either enforced or controverted, as they may or may not agree with those of the lecturer. In either case they afford a groundwork for appropriate discussion and illustration; they may also advantageously direct the young enquirer in his private researches, and afford him the means of trying the vigour of his own mind. In the hands of an unskilful lecturer, a good text book is certainly an important advantage; but to one of more shining talents, a faulty manual will occasion comparatively little inconvenience.

. From the preceding sketch it will be apparent that the attention of the student is at no period of the course concentrated upon any particular branch of science or literature, to the comparative exclusion of all the rest. For this reason it is not likely that Yale will produce many 'wranglers' in mathematics, to surpass those of Cambridge, or giants in Greek Literature, to wrest the palm from those of Oxford; but it is very probable that it will send forth a greater proportion of men whose minds are steadily trained to order and activity, and stored with those elements of knowledge which are available in almost every situation, and which may be said to ensure to their possessor, a reasonable degree of success in any train of thinking or research to which, by his inclination, or the exigencies of his future life, he may be led. It is a remark of Cicero's, that

8

no teacher can communicate to his pupil the completely detailed application of his peculiar art, but
after the learner has thoroughly mastered its general principles, he may be safely left to prosecute
by himself the farther investigation. The accuracy of this principle has been no where more
successfully illustrated, than in the history of Scotland. Dr. Johnson, whose habits and predilections
were entirely in favour of the English system of
University education, compared learning in Scotland to " bread in a besieged town, where every
one gets a mouthful, but nobody a bellyful ;" but
every candid observer knows, that this universal
diffusion of moderate education has given a peculiar superiority to the Scotish national character;
—that much more good in the aggregate has resulted from it than from the other system, while
moreover, there is scarcely a department of literature or philosophy, in which Scotland has not produced more than her numerical proportion of eminently great men.

In Yale College the advantages of the English
and the Scotish systems of University education
seem to be in a great measure combined. The
scope for original discussion and elegance of illustration which lecturing affords, is connected with
the more laborious and effective discipline of tutors and examination; the students are not considered as passive recipients of knowledge, but
are stimulated to the active exercise of their own

powers, that they may acquire that command of them which practice alone can give, and which can become habitual only by a continued succession of efforts. Nor are the benefits of public examination unattended to; for the whole of the classes are subjected to a rigorous scrutiny, twice in each year. Each of these examinations occupies from four to six days, and those students who are found particularly deficient in the exercises of the class, are liable at the discretion of the Faculty to admonition or dismission. After the last examination of the fourth year, the faculty decide by a vote upon each student whether he shall receive a degree or not; but the previous probationary course and frequent examinations, together with the rigorous system of discipline which I have yet to detail, send away most of the laggard and defective members, and of those who are allowed to pass, few are of a doubtful kind. Sympathy, however, for poverty or misfortune, and respect for moral worth, are in some cases I believe allowed to operate favourably on behalf of individuals, whose claims in an academical point of view could scarcely be sustained.

The stimulating system of prizes is partially in use. Bishop Berkely established a prize fund, which yields annually 150 dollars; this is given in premiums of 50 dollars each, £11, 5s. sterling, to the students in different classes, who pass the best examination in Latin and Greek. A few others of inferior amount are given for specimens of Latin and English composition, and for public declamation. These premiums are bestowed privately.

The annual ' Commencement', as it is termed, is a kind of festival in New Haven, to which literary men assemble from a considerable distance around. Of the students who have completed their fourth year, a few are selected to deliver public orations on literary, philosophical, or political subjects; after which the customary degrees in Arts, and in Medicine, are conferred upon those who have passed the requisite examinations, and honorary degrees on those whom the College has selected as worthy of them, for eminence in letters, law, medicine, or theology.

I have not had an opportunity of witnessing this ceremonial at Yale College, but I have been present at that of Columbia College,[9] in New York, and I understand that they are very similar in their general features.

On this occasion the Trustees and Professors, preceded by a band of music, and followed by the students, walked in procession from the College buildings to one of the churches. The students wore black silk gowns, which are peculiar to the occasion, and a medal at the breast, the badge of two Literary Societies, with one or other of which

---

[9] In the month following the date of this letter;—the reader will i pardon the anachronism.

all of them are connected. At the upper end of
a temporary platform, near the pulpit, were seated
the President and other members of the Faculty;
and at the lower end, the orators of the day de-
claimed in succession. The band was posted in
the gallery, and played during the intervals.

The opening address, or ' Salutatory' as it is
termed, and the concluding one, or ' Valedictory,'
are generally assigned to the two scholars who
rank highest in the scale of merit; the priority of
the rest is regulated on the same principle. The
addresses which I heard embraced a variety of
topics, a large proportion of which were political;
and frequent allusions were made to Great Britain
and to the recent unhappy hostilities. The composition and delivery were upon the whole respectable, in some instances highly creditable to the
talent of the orators; and if some of them claimed,
on behalf of their native land, a pre-eminence in
arts and arms which we might hardly be disposed
as yet to concede, they would be rigid censors indeed, who would criticise very severely the effu-
sions of youthful ardour on so spirit-stirring a
theme, or frown at their enthusiastic exclamation—

> " 'Tis the star-spangled banner ! O long may it wave,
> O'er the land of the free, and the home of the brave."

Some of the best of the addresses however paid
honourable tribute to the British national character, quoted our poets, eulogized our patriots, our

statesmen, and some of our kings; and manifested, on the part of their authors, a liberality and manliness of sentiment which would have done no discredit to maturer years.

After the ' valedictory' address, the candidates for the Baccalaureate came individually forward. The President, a venerable old man, grasping the student's hands in his, congratulated him in Latin on the termination of his College studies, put into his hand a small red volume with a few words of parting counsel and direction, withdrew the book, and presented him with his parchment diploma bound with a blue riband.

In Yale College, the topics upon which the students declaim at Commencement are selected by themselves, subject to the approbation of the Professor of Rhetoric; and the essays when composed are submitted for his revisal, before being prepared for delivery.

The Medical school which is in connexion with Yale College is of recent institution, but already bears an honourable reputation, as regards the course of study and the ability of the Professors. The lectures commence in the last week of October, and terminate in the last week of March. During the course from eighty to a hundred lectures are delivered by each Professor, on the various subjects of Anatomy and Physiology, Medicine, Surgery, Obstetrics, Chemistry, Pharmacy, Materia Medica, and Botany. The students have also admission to the academical lectures on Natural Philosophy, Mineralogy and Geology. The various branches are investigated in the most scientific manner, and the courses are fully illustrated by demonstration and experiment. The institution possesses an appropriate anatomical museum and library, and the students have also access to the library of the college. A botanic garden has been begun.

Candidates for license and a degree are regularly examined by the Professors, and a board of Physicians appointed by the Medical Society of the State. These have full authority to grant license to practise, and their recommendation secures a degree from the corporation of the College.

By far the most difficult part in the economy of a College is its discipline; particularly in such institutions as Yale, where the most of young men are withdrawn entirely from the superintendence of their friends, and collected together into one large family. The regulations however which are adopted here, seem better adapted to exercise a parental influence over the inmates, than any which have come under my observation.

Each Student on joining the college is placed, at the discretion of his parents or the Faculty, under the particular superintendence of one of the Professors or Tutors, whom he is enjoined to regard as his counsellor, and who considers himself bound to have a watchful eye over the behaviour and improvement of his ward; in a word to make up, so far as that is possible, the want of a father's care. The young men are considered as, in a state of probation till they are matriculated, which never takes place till they have resided in College at least six months. Those whose conduct has been exemplary during this period, are then fully entered as members of the institution; but those who so pass, seldom exceed two-thirds of the class. Those who have not obtained matriculation and who show decided symptoms of insubordination, are dismissed without ceremony, and without any reason being assigned; sometimes a considerable number are thus sent away. The rest remain for farther trial, and are matriculated at various periods as their behaviour entitles them to it; in some instances it is deferred so long as for three years. In this way the disorderly are gradually weeded out, and only the more diligent and exemplary allowed to remain.

When a student after matriculation is guilty of a serious infraction of the College laws, the member of Faculty under whose particular charge he is, sends for him to his apartments, and privately gives him what is technically called his 'first admonition.' Should he again offend, he receives his 'second admonition,' and his friends are informed by letter of his misconduct. This frequently leads to his removal from the College, which is generally so managed as to conceal from his fellow students the real cause of his leaving them. Should his friends not remove him, and should he again deserve censure, instant and disgraceful dismission is the inevitable consequence. For very flagrant immorality, or breach of discipline, the punishment is expulsion; which differs from dismission in this respect, that the sentence is read by the senior Professor before the whole members of the College, and the culprit is rendered incapable of admission to any other in the whole country. These various gradations of punishment have a powerful effect in preserving good order, and all are aware that none but those whose conduct is upon the whole meritorious, will be allowed to complete the course and obtain academic honours.

Till very lately the students of the Senior class exercised, by ancient usage, the discretionary power of summoning before them individuals of the Freshman class, to reprimand them for indiscretions. The intoxication of power, however, has led older and wiser men astray; and as it was found that the exercise of this prerogative caused more mischief than it cured, it has been altogether abolished.

It has sometimes happened in the American Colleges, that a few evil disposed individuals have organized secret and systematic conspiracies; which have resulted in taking possession of the College buildings, and for a time overturning all order and authority. To prevent so far as possible the possibility of such an occurrence, the buildings are so constructed that only a small number of sleeping apartments have communication with each other; to each division, students of various ages and dispositions are allotted, and in most of them one of the Tutors or unmarried Professors has his apartments, so that no disorderly conduct can take place in any of the rooms without the probability of its being discovered. The happy effect of this and the other regulations is demonstrated by the fact, that there has never been any open rebellion in Yale College. There has been but one approach to extensive insubordination, and that was directed not against the Professors, but against the cooks. In this instance the two younger classes absented themselves in a body from commons; and on the reason of such conduct being demanded, they represented that the food had been very carelessly prepared. The Professors replied that their mode of resenting this was disorderly and unconstitutional, and that till they returned to their duty, no enquiry could take place respecting it. The students immediately returned to commons, and presented a petition for redress; examination was instituted, and the complaint proving well founded, some of the cooks were punished and harmony restored.

The hours of study commence in summer at five o'clock, and in winter at six. Morning and evening prayers, with reading of the Scriptures, take place in the chapel, at which every student is required to be present. Regularity of attendance in the class rooms at the hours of recitation, is rigidly enforced, and except during the hours of recreation, which are three or four in the course of the day, no one is allowed to be absent from his apartment. They are forbidden to frequent an inn, or to be absent from commons without special invitation of a friend, and permission of the Professors; they must not attend any ball or theatrical representation during term time, or play at any game of chance. When the number of students exceeds what can be accommodated in the College buildings, the overplus are permitted, at the discretion of the Faculty, to lodge with private families; but they are still subject to the laws which regulate the other students.[9] It has always been observed however, that of those who live out of College, a much larger proportion become obnoxious to censure and dismission, than of those who are within the walls. On Sabbath and public Fast or Thanksgiving days, all the students are required to attend worship in the College Chapel; except those of a different religious denomination, who have obtained liberty to attend some other

[9] ‘ Boarding out,’ as it is called, is now much less necessary, in consequence of the erection of two new buildings, with increased accommodation for lecture rooms and sleeping apartments. (Nov. 1820.)

place of worship. During the remainder of the day they must keep to their apartments, and are expected to be engaged in reading the Scriptures.

The expense of education at Yale College is I believe rather less than at Harvard. The cost of tuition, boarding within the College, fuel and light, washing, use of furniture, books, stationary, &c. is rated by the lowest estimate at from £40 to £50 sterling; to live out of the College costs at least £20 more. The expense of attending the medical school, during the course of five months, amounts to about the same sum. To this must be added, by those who come from a distance, travelling expenses, and boarding during the vacations. Calculating these, and other usual contingencies, I believe that few students can keep their expenditure much under about £100 sterling a year; and some of the more extravagant frequently spend twice as much. The College bills are paid by the academical students three times a year, to the Treasurer and Steward, not as with us to the individual Professors. The President has an annual salary of about £450 sterling, the Professors from £270, to £340. In the medical department the Professors receive no other salary than the fees of the students; with the exception of one who has an annual stipend of £90 sterling. The Professors of Chemistry and Mathematics, besides their salaries as academical Professors, have half of the fees received from medical students and strangers, who attend their classes.

There are three literary societies conducted by the students, called the ' Linonian,' the ' Brothers,' and the ' Calliopean,' with one or other of which all must be connected. Two of these societies have libraries containing upwards of a thousand volumes. Their proceedings are sanctioned by the Professors. A society of a superior kind exists among them which is called the " Phi Beta Kappa," but respecting its nature I can give little information, for its regulations and management are kept profoundly secret. The students are not eligible to it till the latter part of the third year, and not more than about a third of a class are admitted. The President is usually a distinguished citizen of the State, or an officer of the College, and the honour of membership is an object of much ambition. I observe that several of the members wear on their watch Key, the cabalistic letters, Φ Β Κ, with a hand pointing to a star. Among the students there are also a Moral, a Missionary, and a Bible Society.

Yale College is possessed of a valuable library, philosophical apparatus, and cabinet of minerals.

The library contains nearly eight thousand volumes, and is open under certain regulations to the Professors, Tutors, resident Graduates, medical students, and the two senior academical classes.

The greater part of the philosophical instru-

8

ments were purchased in London in 1805, by Professor Silliman, who was despatched on this honourable mission by his brother Professors. This gentleman, after spending the greater part of the summer and autumn in England, attempted to visit Paris by way of Holland, but was unceremoniously stopped on the imperial confines of the ' great nation,' and compelled to make all haste back again; he studied during the winter at Edinburgh College, and returned in the succeeding spring by way of Glasgow and Greenock to New York. He has published a journal of his travels in two octavo volumes; and it is calculated to flatter our national vanity, that two editions have been sold off, so completely, that I found difficulty in procuring in New Haven even a used copy. Mr. Silliman's observations on the national character of the British, are distinguished throughout by the utmost liberality and kindness, and he has evinced a particular partiality to the domestic manners of Scotland. You cannot fail to be gratified by his comments on a Scotish ' good night.'

' The American Journal of Science' has been recently begun here, under Mr. Silliman's editorial care. This publication, like Dr. Thomson's ' Annals of Philosophy,' is devoted to original communications and intelligence on the various subjects of chemistry, experimental philosophy, natural history, the ornamental and useful arts. America furnishes an ample and almost unbroken field for information on such subjects, and I doubt not that this journal will do much to increase the fame of the philosophers of the republic, and to conciliate the respect of scientific men of every country.[10]

Connected with the philosophical department is a most commodious and well furnished chemical laboratory; to which the students are admitted, that they may have an opportunity of gaining a practical acquaintance, with the many delicate and interesting experiments of modern chemistry; an advantage which can never be enjoyed in an ordinary lecture room.

The cabinet of minerals is by far the finest in America; and in Europe I understand there are but few that surpass it.

This superb collection is principally the property of a Colonel Gibbs, an enthusiastic and scientific mineralogist, who with equal liberality and good taste has deposited his minerals within the college walls, as being in every point of view the most suitable place for them. Colonel Gibbs' collection contains about 18,000 well selected specimens, many of which are exceedingly rare and valuable. It was formed by combining two European cabi-

---

[10] A third and enlarged edition of Professor Silliman's British Travels, has followed me across the Atlantic; accompanied by a ' Tour to Quebec' which he has recently published, and which contains much correct information respecting Canada and its inhabitants, characterized by the same manliness and candour which distinguish the former publication. (Dec. 1821.)

nets; the one that of M. Gigot D'Orcy of Paris, one of the Farmers General under Louis XVI. guillotined during the sway of Robespierre, the other formerly belonging to Count Razamuski a Russian, who had taken refuge from political animosities at Lausanne in Switzerland, but on receiving permission to return home sold his minerals to Colonel Gibbs, who was then studying under the celebrated Professor Struve. To these he added · many specimens collected by his own industry. It is believed that a cabinet equally complete could not be purchased in Europe for less than £5000 sterling. Along with these are arranged between five and six thousand specimens, the property of the College and of Professor Silliman, to which additions are frequently made.[u]

The pecuniary resources of Yale College, are unfortunately no way equal to the science and zeal of its Professors. I have already alluded to the unhappy prejudice which prevails, throughout the State, to every thing above the rank of a common English School; and this illiberal sentiment has operated most powerfully to restrain the capabilities of Yale College. The annual income of the institution does not amount at present to £4500 sterling, and of this, only about £800 is from real stock; the whole remaining sum is derived from

[u] In one of the new buildings a spacious hall 84 feet by 42 has been fitted up for the Minerals. (Dec. 1821.)

K 4

the fees of students and other fluctuating sources.
From this income are paid the salaries of the
Professors, Tutors, and other officers, repairs on
the old buildings and the erection of new ones, the
increase of the library and philosophical apparatus,
as well as other contingencies. For all the improvements which have been lately made, the College is entirely indebted to the economizing efforts
of its managers, and the distinguished talents and
industry of its Presidents and Professors. The
reputation which it acquired under the late vene-
rated Dr. Dwight, has been well sustained by the
members of its Faculty who have survived, or succeeded him; and the salutary principles upon
which its concerns are regulated, give the fairest
promise that its superiority will be perpetuated.

Were the Government and people of Connecticut suitably alive to the honour and importance,
in a national point of view, of cherishing this nur-
sery of the liberal arts, they would ' delight to honour' it with their legislative support and bounty.
They would endow new professorships; they would
enable the College to purchase Colonel Gibbs'
minerals, which it is believed he would sell, and
so prevent the possibility of their ever being removed; they would bestow upon the library a permanent fund for its annual augmentation; they
would, in a word, at once raise the institution from
its present almost total dependence on the fluctuating prosperity of agriculture and trade. Thus

would they place upon a secure basis, the prosperity of a seminary which exerts a most powerful and most salutary influence upon the national
character ; which contributes largely to foster that
mental superiority which birth cannot confer, nor
wealth of itself purchase, and which has in all
ages largely contributed to decide the destinies of
nations.[12]

Were we to institute a comparison between
American and Scotish university education, the
result would not, I believe, be in every respect
favourable to ourselves. The systems are essentially different, and each has its peculiar advantages.

In Scotland none of the students live within the
college walls, nor do the Professors exercise any
superintendence over their time, excepting during
the class hours. Throughout the rest of the day
they may be idle or industrious, choose good society

---

[12] A writer in the North American Review, after enlarging on this
subject with a zeal that does honour to a member of a rival institution, adds ;—" To appeal moreover to a feeling which has perhaps
had too great influence over the legislatures, which have successively
withheld the public patronage from Yale, we would add that on the
simple footing of pecuniary account the State is much indebted to
the college. The latter brings annually into circulation in Connecticut many thousands of dollars, and has done so for a long
course of years. It lays no small part of the country under contribution, to increase the wealth of Connecticut; and it were but common justice in the State, to return into the funds of the college, a
small portion of the means which the college gathers for the State."
North American Review, No. XXXIX. p. 396.

or bad, visit the church or the theatre, as they or their friends please. All those who are immediately under the eye of their parents are of course left to their management and superintendence, and this may by many be esteemed incompatible with the American system, but it is not so—the regulations of Yale College do not require that any whose parents reside in New Haven, should either eat or sleep in the college, but they require that by them as well as others, the hours appointed for private study should be so appropriated. With regard to students who come from a distance the advantage is certainly in favour of America, for in place of being left as in Glasgow exposed to the allurements and vice of a populous city, scattered up and down without one to control or to care for them, they are sheltered and watched over with unremitting care; and every effort is made to form their moral character, as well as to instruct them in literature and the sciences.

In Glasgow no restriction exists as to the age at which students enter College, nor as to the amount of reading which is requisite for admission. Boys of eleven and twelve are not unfrequently seen wearing the enviable scarlet gown; and if most of those who enter have a competent knowledge of Latin, and many a trifling acquaintance with Greek, it is owing almost entirely to the excellent system of our Grammar School, for some of the country students bring but very little of the one language, and not a single letter of the other. It would be a manifest improvement to admit none under fourteen or fifteen, and to require an examination on a certain number of classical authors.

The 'curriculum,' as it is termed at Glasgow, includes Latin, Greek, Logic, Moral Philosophy, Mathematics and Natural Philosophy; and excepting the last two, each branch may be said to be studied *individually*, that is without any necessary connexion with the others. Thus, during the first and second year the student's attention is devoted to Latin and Greek, and to them alone; he is quite at liberty to forget, during this period, that there are such things as English grammar, arithmetic, or geography. The third year is devoted to Logic, or rather to the improvement of his powers of knowledge, taste, and communication, with particular reference to the study of general grammar and English composition. Latin and Greek may now be laid almost entirely on the shelf. The fourth year brings the student into the mazes of Ethics and Morals; a little is read of the Latin philosophical writers, and the practice of English composition is continued. During this session it is customary to study Mathematics, but all other subjects are 'beyond the record.' The fifth and last session finds the student in the Natural Philosophy class, and now Ethics, Logic, Greek and Latin, may all be more or less neglected. This finishes the academical course; an examination is

undergone by those who wish a degree in Arts, upon
the various subjects which have been studied, and
excepting those who are preparing for the church,
the legal or medical professions, few think of going
farther.

The system is remarkably different at Yale Col-
legè. No subject occupies the student's attention,
so as to exclude others equally important; all are
studied in their natural succession, but in such a
way as always to keep in view what has been acquired, and thus not allow one thing to jostle out
another. The student takes a larger range also
in Yale College than is obtained at Glasgow;
Arithmetic, Geography, Rhetoric and Forensic
Disputation, Chemistry and Mineralogy, *must* all
be studied during the academical course. It is not
sufficient that in Glasgow most of these branches
may be acquired during the same period, they form
no part of the 'curriculum,' and are very generally
neglected by all but professional students. There
can scarcely then remain a doubt, but that more
general knowledge will be acquired at Yale than
at Glasgow College, by those who study only what
they are forced to do; and of what is thus acquired,
more is likely to be retained.

The *public* examinations are more frequent and
more minute at Yale College, than at Glasgow.
Before entering an advanced class, the students in
Glasgow College are publicly examined on the
studies of the previous year, but in Yale each

class is twice a year minutely scrutinized on the whole range of their previous studies. The private examinations are probably in both pretty nearly equal.

In Glasgow every one who enters is matriculated as a matter of course, and misconduct in the class room is punished by a pecuniary mulct, while dismission from College is so rare, that a case of it may not occur for ten or fifteen years. It is unnecessary to recapitulate the very different regulations at Yale, or to enlarge upon their salutary influence.

The lecture and recitation hours with us are two or three a day, for each class; the remainder of his time is at the student's own disposal. At Yale only a small portion of the day is allowed for recreation; the rest must be devoted to study. The session at Glasgow lasts for six months; the vacation for other six. At Yale the whole three recesses amount only to twelve weeks; probably it would be better that they should occur at one period, but certainly to spend, as we do, six months out of twelve in relaxation, is too much.

There are however in Glasgow College some important features of superiority. The lectures at the private hour to the Latin and Greek classes, upon antiquities, the higher topics of criticism, and their connexion with the philosophy of language and general grammar, are I believe, of a decidedly superior character to any that are usually met with

elsewhere. The exercises also of the Logic class,
as they are at present conducted in Glasgow, have
given the College a celebrity in this department
which no similar institution in the kingdom enjoys.
It is not easy to calculate how much is effected
during this session alone in training the young
mind to habits of industry and accuracy, which
are of the utmost importance in future life, and
are singularly suited to qualify the intellectual
powers for successful exercise, in all circumstances
and on all subjects. The gentleman who has so
long and so ably filled the Logic chair in the University of Glasgow,[13] has had the appropriate,
and certainly most gratifying reward, of seeing
many of his students rise to the highest celebrity
in future life, and of hearing them ascribe their success to the *bent* of mind which they acquired while
under his tuition.

The excitements to exertion which result from
the public distribution of prizes, are in Glasgow
much more numerous than in Yale College; and
this to a certain degree is decidedly advantageous.
The public honours of the ' First of May' have
a powerful effect in exciting the emulation of the
young students; and many an hour during the
long vacation is redeemed from idleness, of which
otherwise no good account could have been render-

[13] Mr. Jardine; author of a volume in which his system of tuition
is fully developed, entitled, " Outlines of Philosophical Education,"
&c.

ed. The allotment of the rewards for prize exercises is conducted with scrupulous precaution, and as the authors remain unknown to the judges till the decision is publicly announced, perfect confidence is reposed in the impartiality of the verdict. It is otherwise however with the distribution of the class prizes; these are determined by the votes of the students, and it sometimes happens that conflicting motives and feelings sway the minds of the voters, and modify the impartiality of their suffrages. The abstract propriety of such excitements has often been questioned; and though many objections are fairly chargeable against them I am inclined to think, that, constituted as the human mind is, more wisdom will be shown by their well-regulated use, than by their total abolition.

Few, if any, bursaries, or exhibitions as they are styled in England, are connected with the American colleges.[14] In Scotland the value of these is exceedingly small, generally about five guineas annually, and very rarely exceeding ten; yet trifling as they may seem, many who afterwards rose high in the literary world, were in a great measure dependent on such aid for their College education.

[14] A bursary is a small annual stipend, resulting from the benevolent endowment of some friend to literature, and appropriated to the assistance of students whose resources are not ample. Bursaries are sometimes in the gift of the Professors, under limitations prescribed by the founders; and at other times appointed as the reward of superior classical attainments.

8

The paramount and peculiar advantage however of. the Scotish Universities, is the low price at which education is afforded, and the facilities which are thus given to those in the humblest ranks of life, of raising themselves to respectability by literary and scientific attainments. Dominie Sampson's College life, is a most appropriate, and by no. means . an overcharged illustration of this. " Abel Sampson," says the ' Great Unknown,' " commonly called from his occupation as a pedagogue, Dominie Sampson, was of low birth, but having evinced even from his cradle an uncommon seriousness of disposition, the poor parents were encouraged to hope that *their bairn*, as they expressed it, *might wag his pow in a poupit yet.* With an ambitious view to such a consummation, they pinched and pared, rose early and lay down late, eat dry bread and drank cold water, to secure to Abel the means of learning." After describing the Dominie's peculiar habits and ungainly appearance, our author proceeds, " He slunk from College by the most secret paths he could discover, and plunged himself into his miserable lodging, where, for eighteen pence a week, he was allowed the benefit of a straw mattress, and, if his landlady was .in good .humour, permission to study his task by her fire. Under these disadvantages he obtained a competent knowlege of Greek and Latin, and some acquaintance with the sciences." After poor Sampson's fruitless efforts at pulpit oratory, it is recorded that " he sought to assist his parents by teaching a school, and soon had plenty of scholars but very few fees. In fact he taught the sons of farmers for what they chose to give him, and the poor for nothing; and to the shame of the former be it spoken, the pedagogue's gains never equalled those of a skilful ploughman."

I doubt not that most readers who are not intimately acquainted with a Scotish College, have regarded this sketch as broad caricature, possessing only so much resemblance to truth as was necessary to identify the portrait; but there are few who have studied in our native country who have not seen living instances of almost equal poverty and perseverance, happily however resulting in very different success. The remarkable, I might almost say instinctive, desire for education which pervades all classes in Scotland, from the castle to the cottage,[15] has in numberless cases

[15] The truth of the following anecdote comes within my personal knowledge. A few years ago a poor woman, in a small village on the west coast of Scotland, was by her husband's death left dependent on her own exertions for the support of herself and four children, the eldest of whom was about eleven years of age. Unable to bear the expense of educating each in the customary way, and yet eager that they should be instructed, she bargained with the village schoolmaster, that for the price of teaching one, he should allow two to attend the school alternately, one the one day and the other the next; by this ingenious device, she procured for both of them the invaluable blessing of education, and furnished a striking instance of the honourable shifts, by which the poor can often acquire for themselves advantages which are seemingly beyond their attainment.

instigated to self-denial on the part of the parents,
and exertions on the part of the children, as great as
are here depicted; and our peculiar system of College education has afforded facilities, which could
no where else have been found, for gratifying this
laudable thirst for knowledge.   The sum of eighteen pence a week, is indeed below the amount of
room rent which I have known to be in any case
paid, but I have known of accommodations being
had for three shillings and sixpence a week, so
much superior to those of poor Sampson, that I
have no doubt many have been accommodated,
even since I went to College, for a sum little exceeding that which the poor Dominie paid; and
many it is well known struggle their way through
the different classes, dependent altogether for their
maintenance on that which was the ' sticket minister's' last resort, the teaching of a small school
during the few hours which they are able to snatch
from their studies and their sleep.   Names of no
small renown may be quoted, who, by their own
experience in this respect, knew

> " ———— how hard it is to climb
> . The steep where Fame's proud temple shines afar!"

The author of these lines himself, the amiable
Beattie, taught his way through the University,
aided only by a small bursary which was won by
his superior merit, and it is said that the early
life of Dr. Adams, the late distinguished rector of

8

the High School at Edinburgh, was a still more striking instance of successful struggling with adverse circumstances. Such instances are sufficient to reconcile us in a great measure to the system of our Scotish Colleges. They could not have happened in England or in America. Whatever advantages may be derived from the students' living within the walls, and from few vacant hours being left to their own disposal, it necessarily follows that little if any difference can be made in the necessary cost of education, lodging and food; and that almost nothing can be done by a poor student to earn his own support.[16]

Setting aside however individual cases, the expense of academical education in Glasgow is extremely moderate. The fee paid to the Professor of each class for one session is three guineas, and was till lately but two. A young man therefore who attends two classes during the same session, as is very customary, pays six guineas in fees; and another guinea will discharge the minor academical charges. The cost of board and lodging in the city varies, of course, according to the inclinations and means of the individual; they may be both obtained for less than

[16] I have subsequently learned that occasionally a few of the students at Yale College receive leave of absence for three or four months to teach some of the district schools; and that others become entitled to exemptions from some part of the College charges, by waiting upon the other students at meals, ringing the College bell, &c. (1823.)

ten shillings, and I believe that the average amount paid by those who live in a respectable way, does not exceed twenty. The allurements to extrava-gance with which a city so large as Glasgow abounds, are certainly numerous; but a powerful barrier is opposed to their influence, when many of the students, so far from having money to ex-pend on frivolities, are dependent for their support in a greater or less degree upon their own exer-tions, even during the time of their attending the classes; and some allowance must be made in other cases for the characteristic habits of the Scotish nation, as to prudence and economy.

I have tried to be impartial in this comparison of the academical system of the two Colleges. To say that both of them are susceptible of improve-ment, is only to say that they are human institu-tions. Both however attain with considerable suc-cess the objects of their institution; they develop the mental faculties of the young, store their minds with literary and scientific knowledge, and train them to active efforts in the discovery and com-munication of truth; the philanthropist will there-fore regard each of them as the source of unmeas-ured benefit to the human race, and he will cordi-ally wish their conductors increased success in their salutary labours.

I was present on one occassion at the splen-did annual ceremonial of the ' Commemoration' at Oxford; beyond all comparison the most im-

8

posing scene of a literary kind that I ever witnessed. The great officers of the University,
heads of houses, and young noblemen, were all
arrayed in their appropriate and gorgeous cos-
tumes, and the highest academic honours were
conferred, with every attention to pomp and circumstance, on men of distinguished reputation in
literature, arms, and hereditary rank; prize essays
were read, and the founders and benefactors of
the several Colleges ' commemorated' with grateful eulogy, in a long Latin oration. To such a
scene as this, Glasgow College and Yale are alike
unable to furnish a parallel, but the relative influence of each institution on the wellbeing of
society, is not thus to be estimated; and both
Scotland and America may reap the most abundant advantage from their academical institutions,
while the utmost simplicity prevails in their or-
ganization and festivals.

LETTER VI.

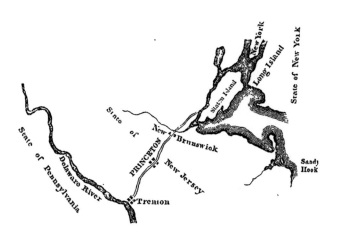

LETTER VI.

Princeton, New Jersey, August, 1818.

A COLLEGE was founded here in the year 1738, which gradually attained to a highly respectable rank as a literary institution. This was more particularly the case during the presidency of the venerable Dr. Witherspoon, who was invited from Scotland to occupy this honourable situation.

Academical institutions, like those of other kinds, are subject to many vicissitudes of fortune; and Princeton College, from the limited number of its Faculty, is more so than some others. In the sister establishments of Yale and Harvard, where the Professors are so much more numerous, a casual mediocrity of talent in one or two, is generally compensated by eminence in the rest; but here where a President, two Professors, and two Tutors, form the whole corporation, much more depends upon their individual abilities.

Upon the President, besides the general super-intendence, devolves the instruction of the Students, in Theology, Moral Philosophy, Belles Lettres, and Logic; one of the Professors teaches the Greek and Latin languages, the other Mathematics, Natural Philosophy, and Chemistry. The co-operation of the Tutors is variously applied, as circumstances may render it necessary. It is obvious, that this system requires no ordinary amount of talent, and extent of acquirement, in the President and Professors. The branches of study which have been enumerated, would afford abundant scope for the skill and industry of at least half a dozen of persons,—it is too much to expect, that men will be readily found capable of presiding, with success, in three or four departments of knowledge, remotely, if at all, connected with each other. On some rare occasion indeed, a happily constituted mind, some man of a thousand, may be found, whose powers and industry are equal to the task which is thus imposed; and when splendid talents are brought into operation on so wide a field, the fame of the college may suddenly rise, and soar in proud pre-eminence over every similar institution; but in arranging the system of a literary establishment, he would be a visionary indeed, who would calculate on a succession of such men, to fill its various departments:—Britain has produced but one Sir William Jones.

There are at present in this college 150 students; .

but were the institution established upon a more liberal scale—and this ought to be the anxious care of the citizens and legislature of New Jersey— it is probable from its local advantages, that its students would soon outnumber those of any other American college. Situate midway between New York and Philadelphia, its proximity to both gives it a decided advantage over both Harvard and Yale. To the immense territory south and west of Philadelphia, it is as yet the nearest academical institution of any considerable reputation; and will certainly, if other things are equal, obtain a preference to those that are two or three hundred miles farther off. The wealthiest families in the Union, and those who scatter money most lavishly, belong to the southern part of it, and if a University can be supported any where, on a liberal scale, they are able to do it. A young man from Georgia, a student at Princeton, informs me that he spent during the first year upwards of £350 sterling, and probably he was not singular in so profuse an expenditure.

A detailed account of the discipline of Princeton would be superfluous, after the information which I have already so fully communicated respecting Yale. You have there a pretty correct sketch of academical education in America, in its most perfect form; and the differences which exist in minor colleges, generally arise from the want of means to carry the system into full operation. Princeton approaches as nearly to perfection as can be expected, and it has had the honour of sending out some of the most distinguished orators and statesmen, that America has produced.

The State of Virginia is about to establish a University of the most aspiring kind, and Jefferson, Madison, and some other of the great names of this western hemisphere, have combined their talents in framing its constitution.[1] What the result in this instance may be, time alone can determine; but from all circumstances it must be apparent, that a great and growing attention is bestowed, throughout the country on Literature and Science.

There are in the extensive territory of the United States, upwards of thirty colleges. A number of these, it is true, particularly in the western and southern States, can only be regarded as academies; there are, however, ten or twelve of decided

---

[1] From first appearances, there seems reason to anticipate that this proposed University will be a total failure; and from the well known sentiments of its founders, on speculative and revealed truth, I cannot much regret that it should be so. When it is established on Christian principles, we shall then rejoice in its success. As a matter of curiosity I subjoin the outline of the academical course, which the Commissioners for the University have projected. They have disposed the subjects of study into 'groupes,' each of which they say, "is within the powers of a single Professor," if so, some individuals of the decade will be no ordinary men.

1 *Languages Ancient;* Latin, Greek, Hebrew.

2 *Languages Modern;* French, Spanish, Italian, German, Anglo-Saxon.

3 *Mathematics Pure;* Algebra, Fluxions, Geometry Elementary,

respectability, and of these five or six are pre-
eminent.

A Theological Seminary has recently been
established at Princeton, by the Presbyterian
Church of the United States. The proximity of
this institution to the College, must be regarded
as a happy circumstance for each ; for the institutions can scarcely fail to be mutually beneficial.
Their combined advantages will probably induce
many young men to select Princeton as their place
of study, who might otherwise have gone elsewhere ;
and the literary intercourse which is likely to take
place between the respective professors, must be
favourable to the development of mental talent,
and the cultivation of acquired knowledge. An
outline of the system of theological education which
here prevails, may be a very suitable sequel to that
which has been given of a classical one.

Geometry Transcendental, Architecture Military, Architecture
Naval.

4 *Physico-Mathematics;* Mechanics, Statics, Dynamics, Pneuma-
tics, Acoustics, Optics, Astronomy, Geography.

5 Physics, or Natural Philosophy, Chemistry, Mineralogy.

6 Botany, Zoology.

7 Anatomy, Medicine.

8 Government, Political Economy, Law of Nature and Nations,
History, (being interwoven with Politics and Law.)

9 Law, Municipal.

10 Ideology, General Grammar, Ethics, Rhetoric, Belles Lettres,
and the Fine Arts.

Additional information on this subject, accompanied with some
judicious observations on the detail of the plan, will be found in an
article in the *North American Review, No. XXVI. p.* 115.

The Presbyterian Theological Academy was founded in 1811, in consequence of an Act of the General Assembly. The funds for its establishment were derived, partly from collections throughout the congregations under the jurisdiction of the Assembly, and partly from private subscriptions. The Seminary has been begun on so extensive a scale, that though the amount which was collected was very considerable, it has not been sufficient to establish it at once in a flourishing condition; and hitherto a part only of the projected plan has been carried into effect. The resources of the Presbyterian Church however are ample, and there is every reason to believe, that farther efforts will not be wanting, till the school is endowed with a revenue adequate to ensure its permanent efficiency.

For lecture rooms and sleeping apartments, a large building has been erected, which is said to have cost nearly seventeen thousand pounds sterling.[2] As yet this house is but partly occupied, and I believe that a number of the students reside in the village.

There are at present only two Professors, but it is intended that there should be other two, and some of the Synods have begun to appropriate funds for this purpose. The Professors have each a salary of four hundred pounds sterling, besides

---

[2] A house for one of the Professors has been subsequently finished at an expense of about £3500 sterling,—this is doing things on a liberal scale.

a house. The students amount to about eighty.
The cost of boarding, lodging and other contingencies, amounts in general to £40 or £50 sterling a year, the tuition is altogether gratuitous.

As yet there are but four exhibitions connected
with the institution, although a large proportion of
those who study have but very limited resources;
measures however have been adopted for their
gradual increase. These exhibitions, or scholarships as they are termed, have each a capital of
about £560 sterling, which must be profitably invested, for their annual value is said to be about
fifty pounds.

The Professors are appointed by the General
Assembly, and every effort is made to provide men
in whose principles, ability, and learning, full reliance may be placed. Before admission, they are
required to declare upon oath, their perfect and
unreserved agreement with the Westminster confession of faith; and the Assembly retains an absolute power to displace at its own pleasure, any
of them who from change of sentiment, or other
causes, may be judged unfit to continue in office.
These precautions are likely to secure the agreement of the theological instructors, with the sentiments of the majority of the General Assembly ;—
if that majority holds sound doctrine, the institution will inculcate the same, but should " the doctrines and commandments of men" hold an ascen-
dency there, it will be impossible to prevent the

source of instruction from being similarly contam-
inated; and this, as was remarked by one of the
present students, is one of the great dangers to be
apprehended from a public school of Divinity, for
an able but unsound Professor may corrupt a
generation. The superintendence of the Seminary
is committed to a board of thirty Directors, whose
authority extends to all but the appointment and
dismissal of the Professors.

Of the Professors who are already appointed,
one lectures on Theology, the other on Ecclesiastical History and Church Government. The next
who is added will probably be devoted to Oriental
Literature.

The course of study is completed in three years,
but young men may enter at any period of the
course. In each year there are two terms; the
first from November 6th to May 12th, the
second from July 1st to September 25th. There
is no penal code of discipline promulgated; it
is presumed that Theological students do not require it.

The duties of the first year commence with the
study of Hebrew, with or without the points;
which is for the present taught by the Professor of
Theology,—after which comes a course of Jewish
Antiquities, in a series of lectures; and the
connexion of Sacred and Profane History, in
which Prideaux and Shuckford are used as text
books.

The second year opens with studies relating to the philosophy of the mind. Questions are proposed, for answer and illustration, which embrace the most important doctrines of that science; and the student is thus led to an acquaintance with the works of Locke, Beattie, Reid, Hume, Stewart, and the other distinguished writers on metaphysics. This is employed as introductory to the evidences and principles of natural religion, as it is called, from which they pass to revealed religion, and thence to didactic theology. Turretin is the text book on this subject; but the interrogatory style of investigation is continued, and the student is required to extend his reading very considerably, that he may become acquainted with the various opinions and systems of different writers. This second division of the course occupies about fifteen months.

During the same period, the other Professor carries the class through ecclesiastical history; on which Mosheim is the text book, but his deficiencies are supplied by lectures. Along with this they have also a very complete course of the historical department of biblical criticism.

During the remaining nine months, the first Professor carries them through polemical theology, in which Stæffer is the text book, and completes the subject of biblical criticism. The other Professor investigates with them the various systems of church government; and the course is completed by lectures, from the one on the pastoral office, and from the other on the composition of a sermon. Apart from the course of public instruction, the students have societies for literary discussion, and for preaching; in the latter the Professors preside, and they may therefore be regarded as a portion of the academical system.

During the course there are repeated examinations before the Directors of the Seminary; a more particular one at the close of each session, and one of yet severer scrutiny at the end of the three years. The student is then remitted to the presbytery, to whose jurisdiction he belongs, by which he is again examined, and should the result be satisfactory he receives from the presbytery license to preach.

As this institution is as yet but in its infancy, much cannot be said as to its success. We may readily suppose, however, that the General Assembly will at all times appoint to its superintendence, the ablest men that the Presbyterian Church can produce, and exercise over it a watchful and fostering care.

I have already alluded[a] to a similar institution at Andover, which is in connexion with the New England Congregational Church. That Seminary differs in some respects from this, and in relation to pecuniary affairs, is for the present in a more flour-

[a] Vide Letter Second.

8

ishing condition. It was founded in 1808; and had its origin in the liberality of three or four wealthy individuals, who not only bestowed funds sufficient for the commencement of the academy, but as it was observed to rise in usefulness and reputation, gradually enlarged the amount of their munificent contributions, till it has become possessed of several commodious buildings, and of four endowed professorships, worth it is said from £300 to £400 sterling a year. The branches for which they are appointed, are biblical literature, sacred rhetoric, ecclesiastical history, and systematic theology; with these they combine the other departments of a theological education, and the establishment is probably as practically useful as if the professorships were more numerous. The chairs are said to be reputably filled;—one of them indeed by a gentleman of high celebrity throughout the whole Union. Besides these advantages Andover possesses about forty Scholarships, which are, however, less in individual amount than the two at Princeton. At present there are in all upwards of one hundred students.[4]

Among theological seminaries the 'Foreign Mission School' at Cornwall in the State of Connecticut is particularly worthy of notice; the more

---

[4] A very valuable correspondent, on whose accuracy I have good reason to place implicit reliance, writes me (1822) that the private benefactions to the Andover Theological Academy since its foundation, have already amounted to very nearly the sum of £100,000 sterling.

so, that there is not in Britain, so far as I know, any similar institution. This academy is devoted to the instruction of young natives of foreign countries, with the view of qualifying them to return home as missionaries or teachers. It was founded in consequence of what, in usual language, would be called the accidental arrival in America, in 1809, of Obookiah, a native of Owhyhee; a young man who showed an ardent thirst for useful knowledge, and who falling under the care of some benevolent and enlightened individuals in New Haven, was, through their instrumentality, made acquainted with the important truths of the gospel. Obookiah made considerable progress in literary studies, and soon evinced an earnest desire to return to his native country as a missionary; and some other individuals of his countrymen having been discovered in America, they were brought together, that they might preserve an acquaintance with their native language, and receive such an education as would be useful to them, should any of them be found qualified and disposed to accompany Obookiah. The providence of God, however, has disappointed

The number of students is rapidly increasing, as the following abstract indicates:—

Summary of the Andover Catalogue for 1821-2.

Resident Licentiates .	5
Senior Class	31
Middle Class . . .	35
Junior Class	61
Total	132

the high expectations which were formed of that young man's future usefulness;—he was carried off by a fever in the early part of this year, shortly before the intended period of his return to his native country. The school continues to flourish, and several boys belonging to the aboriginal tribes of this continent have lately joined it.[5]

Such an institution is in the highest degree praiseworthy; not only on account of the philanthropic and benevolent views of its founders, but because of the wisdom of its leading principle, and because, if prudently conducted, it promises to be a most efficient instrument of good, to nations which are now in the grossest darkness. Native teachers, and preachers, and translators, are no doubt to be the grand means of enlightening and civilizing the heathen world; they are familiar with the language, the customs, the prejudices, the modes of thinking, and the theology of their countrymen, and they are

---

[5] A very interesting narrative of Obookiah's eventful life, has been reprinted here in a cheap form, and is sold by Mr. Lang, Wilson Street, Glasgow, Mr. Johnston, Edinburgh, and Mr. Nisbet, London. It will repay a perusal.

The Foreign Mission School contained in September 1822, eighteen pupils, namely, 6 Sandwich Islanders, 1 Malay, 1 Chinese, 1 New Zealander, 1 Cherokee, 1 Oneida, 1 Tuscarora, 1 Caughnawaga, and 2 Stockbridge Indians; 3 natives of the United States, intending to be foreign missionaries. Seven of these were professors of religion. An Owhyhean was expected soon. In March 1823, two young Greeks reached America from Malta, one 15 years of age, the other 11, who had come over for the sole purpose of enjoying the benefit of the school.

M 3

exempt from the operation of that feeling of dis-
like, which necessarily exists in a large degree
among all men, to the interference of foreigners,
with their religious belief and worship. The extensive commercial intercourse of America with
foreign nations, brings many of their young men to
its shores; and can Christian benevolence more happily take advantage of this circumstance, than by
qualifying such persons, to return as instructors to
'their father's house,' even although this instruction should reach no farther in the first instance
than a knowledge of letters and the useful arts?
The Bible and all its blessings will necessarily
follow. Might not our countrymen take a lesson
in this matter from their western brethren, and
establish such a school in Britain, where there is
a still greater influx of foreigners?

LETTER VII.

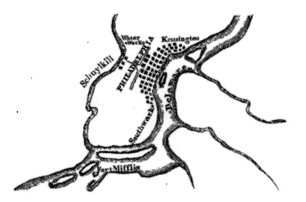

LETTER VII.

Philadelphia, September, 1818.

THE position of Philadelphia, although not equal
to that of New York, is yet well chosen in reference to the character of the surrounding
country. The city stands upon an isthmus about
two miles wide, between the Delaware and the
Schuylkill, five miles above their confluence, and
about an hundred and twenty miles from the sea.
Both rivers are navigable up to the city by the
largest merchantmen. The Delaware is here
about a mile in width; the tide rises and falls
about six feet, and vessels of 1200 tons can come
up to the wharfs. In severe winters, the communication with the sea is still occasionally in-
terrupted; but not so frequently as formerly, nor

for so long at one time, and as the surrounding country becomes cleared of its forests the severity of the winters will be still farther mitigated.

The course of the two rivers at the city is very nearly north and south, but almost immediately above, they diverge; the Delaware to the north-east, and the Schuylkill to the north-west, thus materially facilitating the commercial communication with the interior of the State, and the adjoining one of New Jersey. The Delaware is navigable by large sloops and steam boats to Trenton, about thirty miles above, and the Schuylkill, although above the city comparatively shallow and disturbed with rapids, is navigable by small vessels and rafts to a considerable distance. A little deepening of this river in some places, and the cutting of short canals from one stream to another, would open a communication for some hundreds of miles into the interior. The ground on which the city stands, is covered with a stratum of fine clay; the banks of the Schuylkill furnish a plentiful supply of marble, and the country around is rich in timber, so that materials for building are most abundant.

The appearance of the city from the river is by no means imposing; rather the opposite. The ground is generally level, and the mass of buildings present a dull heavy uniformity; most of those along the bank are by no means elegant, and only a solitary steeple rises above the dense horizon.

The aspect however improves amazingly when you enter the streets, which are wide, straight, and clean, and, with only one exception, cross each other at right angles. The houses are in general of painted brick, but some of the more modern have a flight of marble steps in front, and the lintels of the doors and windows, and even the side walk in front, are of the same beautiful materials.

When Penn laid out the ground for his city, he intended that it should occupy a parallelogram one mile in width, between the two rivers, and that the buildings should be kept within the parallel lines till the intervening space was filled; but the inhabitants found that the bank of the Delaware was a more desirable situation than that of the Schuylkill, and in consequence, buildings have stretched along the former river, above and below the assigned boundary, till the city is here about four miles long, while the streets are not compactly built much farther than half way across to the other river. On both banks of the Schuylkill however a considerable number of buildings have been erected. The populous suburb on the Delaware to the south of the original boundary is called Southwark, that to the north the Northern Liberties, and closer to the river Kensington.[1]

[1] The venerable elm under which according to tradition Penn negociated his celebrated treaty with the Indians, stood at Kensington; and the decayed trunk after being spared by the British army in the Revolutionary war, and weathering many a hard gale, was at

Market street, 100 feet wide, stretches through the centre of the city, from the one river to the other; it is crossed, rather nearer the Schuylkill than midway, by Broad Street, 113 feet wide, and the other streets are at right angles to one or other of these. The cross streets are from 50 to 60 feet wide; those running parallel to the rivers are, with a quaker-like simplicity, which however affords a stranger important facilities in finding his way, named North and South, Front, Second, Third, Fourth, and so on, as they recede from each river; those parallel to Market Street are with more elegance, named after the various kinds of timber with which the ground was formerly covered, Vine, Sassafras, Mulberry, Chesnut, Walnut, Spruce, Pine and Cedar. Water Street, between Front Street and the Delaware, which should have been called *Mud Lane*, and the wharfs which project into the stream, are deviations from the original plan of the city. Dock Street, the only crooked one in the city, was originally the bed of a sluggish stream, which generated

last levelled a few years ago by a hurricane. Portions of it are now eagerly sought after by relic hunters, to be converted, like the Cruick-stone Yew and the rafters of Alloway Kirk, into snuff boxes and other toys. I lately discovered in an old Baltimore newspaper, what is said to be a copy of Penn's treaty; it is in the form of an indenture, and the following are the articles which it specifies as having been given to the Indians, in exchange for the ground between the two rivers, 'as far as a man can ride in two days with a horse.' " 20 guns, 20 fathoms matchcoat, 20 fathoms stroud-

noxious air, and was a few years ago arched over.

Not many wooden houses are now to be seen in the streets; the greater part were extirpated by fires, which on different occasions spread dreadful havoc, and since 1796 their erection has been prohibited. The side walks are wider, and less encumbered than those of New York. Many of them are skirted with Lombardy poplars. In hot weather numerous awnings are stretched along in front of the stores, the footwalks are cooled by frequent ablutions with water, and the atmosphere has a freshness and purity which is very uncommon in so large a city.

Market Street which, to correspond with its situation, should have been the most elegant in the city, is disfigured by a long covered piazza in the centre, of the plainest possible appearance, under which the venders of meat, fish, poultry, vegetables, fruit, earthen and wooden ware, expose their commodities for sale; and on either side are carts and wheelbarrows loaded with additional supplies.

water, 20 blankets, 20 kettles, 20 pounds powder, 100 bars lead, 40 tomahawks, 100 knives, 40 pairs stockings, 1 barrel beer, 20 pounds red lead, 100 fathoms wampum, 30 glass bottles, 30 pewter spoons, 100 awl blades, 300 tobacco pipes, 100 hands tobacco, 20 tobacco tongs, 20 steels, 300 flints, 30 pairs scissars, 30 combs, 60 looking glasses, 200 needles, 1 skipple salt, 30 pounds sugar, 5 gallons molasses, 20 tobacco boxes, 100 Jew's harps, 20 hoes, 30 gimblets, 30 wooden screw boxes, 100 strings of beads." This curious document does not appear in Clarkson's life of Penn.

Upon the whole, however, the streets are much superior to the mass of those in New York, although individually, not one of them can be compared with Broadway, nor is there a walk or a prospect equal to what the Battery affords.

Some of the public buildings do honour alike to the liberality of the citizens, and to the classical taste of the architects by whom they were designed. The banking house of Mr. Girard, presents an elegant front almost entirely of white marble. A lofty Corinthian portico, of fluted columns, rises from a flight of steps to the full height of the building, and corresponding pilasters are extended on both sides. The Bank of Pennsylvania is a still more perfect structure, and makes a nearer approach to classical models than any that I have ever seen. The whole building, including even the roof, is of white marble. Its form is a parallelogram one hundred and twenty-five feet long, and fifty-one feet broad; at each end is a flight of ten steps supporting a chaste Ionic portico of six columns, with an entablature, and pediment. The entablature is carried round the building, but the sides are otherwise plain. Under the porticoes, the Grecian character has been carefully preserved, and in neither is there any opening but a single door in the centre.

This magnificent edifice is said to have been designed from a temple at Athens, and the very remarkable correctness of its principal features, combined with the appropriate and beautiful material of which it is composed, produce a most pleasing effect on the spectator's mind, and forcibly impress him with the sad inferiority of modern decoration, to the simple elegance of Grecian models. The situation which this noble edifice occupies is low and confined, and materially injures its effect.

The foundation has just been dug for a building for the Bank of the United States, the front of which is also to be in the purest Grecian style and of white marble.[2]

None of the other buildings are particularly deserving of notice. Two imitations of the Gothic have been attempted; the one a Bank, the other a Masonic Hall. The buildings are necessarily on a small scale, and the fatal incongruity of red brick walls, with white marble buttresses and pinnacles, must strike every one who has seen an ancient Gothic building.

Philadelphia is furnished with a copious supply of pure water, which is conveyed in pipes throughout the whole city. This has been found here, as every where else, to be eminently conducive to the health and comfort of the inhabitants, and has materially aided in lessening the danger of fire,

[2] This structure has been completed, and is highly spoken of. The front is a portico of the full height of the building, consisting of eight columns of the chastest Doric, rising from a flight of steps and supporting a corresponding entablature and pediment. (1822.)

and the prevalence of infectious diseases. In all that respects the virtue of cleanliness, New York would do well to take a lesson from the rival city. The water is raised by the steam engine from the Schuylkill, about two miles above the city, where the river is nearly a quarter of a mile wide, and about thirty feet deep at low water; it is then thrown into a capacious reservoir, close by the bank of the river, and 100 feet above its level, where all the grosser particles gravitate, before its distribution by the pipes. No filtration takes place. About 700,000 gallons are raised every twenty-four hours.[3] In former times the water after being raised from the Schuylkill, was thrown into a small cistern house at the intersection of Market Street and Broad Street, from which it was distributed into the various street pipes. This cistern house is not now in use, but the building remains, and is ornamental to the street; it is of a circular form surmounted with a dome, and surrounded with gravel walks and trees.

Among the public institutions in Philadelphia which a stranger should visit, are the Penitentiary

[3] Very considerable improvements have been recently made on the Water Works. The steam engine has been superseded by a water wheel, 15 feet in diameter and 15 feet wide, which makes 11 revolutions a minute, and works a pump of 4½ feet stroke, discharging its contents 22 times a minute. The quantity of water raised in 24 hours exceeds one million of gallons. Other two wheels of the same size and power will soon be ready for operation. (1822.)

8

and the Pennsylvania Hospital. The first I did
not see in consequence of having postponed my
application till I had but one forenoon at command, and then the hour of admission did not
suit me. I was assured, however, that it was in
almost every respect similar to that at Boston,
which has been already described. One of the
managers stated to me that the defects of the present system are so numerous and apparent, that
they intend to erect a new prison, on a scale large
enough to admit of almost every inmate being kept
in solitary confinement.[*] The criminal code of
Pennsylvania is merciful to a proverb. Murder
'of the first degree,' that is, when proved to have
resulted from cool and deliberate design, is the only

[*] This design has been carried into effect since my return home,
and an attentive correspondent has favoured me with the following
particulars of the construction of the prison. The new Philadelphia
Penitentiary is surrounded by a strong wall 30 feet high, enclosing a space of ground 650 feet square; the entrance gate is
fortified with a portcullis, and on each side are flanking towers containing the keeper's apartments; at the corners are bastions for
sentinels. The cells 250 in number and one story high, are disposed
in a circle, 75 feet from the nearest part of the outer wall; the open
ground at the corners is planted with vegetables. The cells look
inward with an iron railing in front, and a round observatory for
the superintendent, 60 feet in diameter, occupies the centre of the
ground. Each cell measures 10 feet by 12, and they are separated
from each other by walls rising 4 to 6 feet above the roof, and
projecting 20 feet in front, capped with stone and armed with iron
pikes. A common sewer passes under the cells. There is no possibility of intercourse between the prisoners, so that the efficacy of
solitary confinement will now undergo a fair trial. (1822.)

capital crime. The Quakers however, have a rooted
aversion to return such a verdict, in any circumstances, and a jury is so seldom altogether
free from this feeling that capital convictions are
exceedingly rare—it is a common saying here, that
it requires more interest to get hanged, than to be
made Governor of the State.

Pennsylvania Hospital serves at once the
several purposes of a Lunatic Asylum, Infirmary,
Lying-in and Foundling hospital. The building is
large, and although of brick not inelegant; it stands
in the centre of one of the square divisions formed
by the crossing of four streets, and the whole of
the surrounding space is the property of the institution. In front is a circular grass plot, in the
centre of which is a statue of William Penn, with
the ' charter of privileges' in his hand—it strikingly
resembles his portrait in West's well known painting of his treaty with the Indians.

This institution although partially charitable is
not altogether so. No patients are admitted gratuitously, except those of the poorest classes; all
others pay a regulated board, which varies from
about 15s. to 45s. sterling a week. There are
however a number of out-door patients, who are
attended and supplied with medicines gratuitously,
at their own houses. Clinical lectures are
regularly delivered to students of anatomy, and
the fees are devoted to the support of an Anatomical Museum and Library, to which the students

have access. The museum contains many valuable preparations, models, casts, and drawings; the library consists of about three thousand volumes, and both it and the museum are rapidly increasing. The institution is now possessed of another permanent source of revenue, in West's splendid painting of "Christ healing the sick in the temple," presented by the venerable President of the Royal Academy, who is a native of Pennsylvania, as a pledge of his regard for the benevolent institutions of his native country. A small building has been erected for exhibiting this picture, and a quarter of a dollar is required for admission.[5]

Peale's Museum is another object of popular interest. This is a private collection, and like many similar establishments, contains a good deal that is worth seeing, mingled with many miscellaneous monstrosities which are not worth house-room. My attention was chiefly attracted by the gigantic skeleton of the mammoth or mastodon.

A human being shrinks into insignificance beside the bony fabric of this enormous antediluvian; for such we may safely call it, notwithstanding of the fashionable scepticism of those who are in all things too philosophical to accept of ex-

---

[5] A more recent traveller states that the exhibition of this painting " yielded 8000 dollars, £1800 sterling, the first year, and 5000 dollars, £1125 sterling, the second; and it is supposed that it will hereafter afford to the hospital an annual revenue of £500 sterling." *Howison's Upper Canada*, p. 338.

planations of natural phenomena from the sacred volume. It is not a partial inundation, nor any supposable succession of them, which could have covered the whole earth, to the tops of the loftiest mountains, with the spoils of the sea, and with the remains of animals, some of them altogether unknown even to historical tradition, and others incapable now of existing in the regions where their bones are found. The deluge is an explanation of all these wonders, to which the Christian will devoutly and satisfactorily recur, leaving comfortless infidelity to its own pathless wanderings.

The skeleton of the mammoth resembles very much that of the elephant, carrying like it two great tusks in front. The principal difference is found in the grinders; which in the elephant are flat on the top, with the enamel penetrating the whole material,—but in the mammoth rise into ridges, or processes as anatomists term them, somewhat as in those of the sheep, with the enamel in the form of an outer crust or case, enveloping but not penetrating the bone. Some naturalists have supposed from this peculiarity that the mammoth was a carnivorous animal; but a scientific gentleman remarks to me that this was impossible, as it has like the elephant no front teeth, and its neck is too short and its tusks too long, to have admitted of its holding and devouring its prey as carnivorous animals do. He thinks it probable that it lived upon shrubs, and the smaller branches of trees, for crushing which, the grinders seem to be well adapted. It only occurs to me in reply to this remark, that the enormous trunk of the mammoth may have served to catch and crush the smaller animals, and convey them into the mouth. Conjecture however in such cases is both unavailing and unimportant; it is sufficient that we have in the existence of these bones unanswerable demonstration, that in earlier times an animal has existed, much more enormous in bulk than the largest that is now known to tread the surface of the globe. This skeleton which is, I believe, not so large as some others that have been found, is 11 feet high over the shoulders, and measures 31 feet from the extremity of the tusks to the end of the tail, following the curve.[6] It was found in 1801, in

[6] An attentive correspondent has been so kind as to procure and forward me the following additional particulars respecting the skeleton of the mammoth:

	Feet.	Inch.
Height over the shoulders,	11	0
———— over the hips,	9	0
Length from the chin to the rump,	15	0
From the point of the tusks to the tail, following the curve,	31	0
The same in a straight line,	17	6
Width of the body,	5	8
Length of the under jaw,	2	10
Width of the head,	3	2
Length of the thigh bone,	3	7
Smallest circumference of the same,	1	6
Length of the tibia,	2	0
Length of the humerus, or large bone of the fore leg,	2	10
Largest circumference of the same,	3	$2\frac{1}{2}$

Smallest

a marl pit in the State of New York; others have been found near the *licks*, or salt springs, in the State of Ohio. The skeleton is nearly entire, except in the cartilaginous parts which are supplied by cork.

In contemplating the power of so colossal a limb, and the tension of the muscles which must have strung it, an impressive commentary is suggested to that singularly beautiful passage in the book of Job, " Behold now Behemoth which I have made with thee; he eateth grass as an ox! He moveth his tail like a cedar; his sinews are wrapped together. His bones are as strong pieces of brass; his bones are like bars of iron. Behold he drinketh up a river and hasteth not; he trusteth that he can draw up Jordan into his mouth!"

An Academy of the Fine Arts was founded

	Feet.	Inch.
Smallest circumference of the same, ...	1	5
Length of the radius, ...	2	5½
Circumference round the elbow, . . .	3	8
Length of the scapula or shoulder-blade, . . .	3	1
Length of the longest vertebra, . . .	2	3
Length of the first rib, ...	2	0
Length of the longest rib, without cartilage, . .	4	7
Length of the breast bone, ...	4	0
Length of the great tusks, ...	10	7
Circumference of a molaris tooth, ...	1	6½

	Pounds.	Oz.
Weight of the under jaw, ...	63½	0
—— of a tooth, ...	4	10
—— of the whole skeleton, ...	1000	0

here in 1805. It was shortly after incorporated
by the legislature, and a building was erected with
suitable apartments for study and exhibition rooms.
One of the apartments contains a few specimens of
antique sculpture, and casts of most of the celebrated
statues. Among the modern specimens is a bust
of Washington by Canova, and one of West by
Chantrey. The painting room is more richly
stored, and can boast, if the catalogue is correct, of
several paintings by the old masters; among these
are three by Titian, one by Raphael, one by Cor-
reggio, which is said to have been executed for
Charles III. of Spain, and was purchased for £340,
three by Rubens, one by Dominichino, one by Te-
niers, one by Vandyke, one by Paul Veronese, one by
Rembrandt, four by Murillo, and three by Salvator
Rosa. These are but a few of the old paintings, and,
amongst a crowd of moderns, are some of great
merit by native artists, the chief of whom appear
to be Allston and Lesslie. From Allston's[7] pencil,
is a beautiful picture of the dead man raised to
life by touching the bones of the prophet Elisha;

[7] A writer in the North American Review claims on behalf of
his country the honour of having produced the first historical painter
of the present day, and this rank he assigns to Mr. Allston. ' The
modern school of painting,' says he, ' bids fair to flourish among
us, and that not merely from flattering pretty faces and appealing to
personal vanity, but in the historic department of the art. We
hope we do not go out of our way to pay a compliment to our
fellow citizen, who has now founded upon a series of works, that
have stood the test of English and of American criticism, the reputa-

and·by Lesslie is a painting which I thought excellent, exhibiting William of Deloraine unhorsed
and wounded by Lord Cranstoun.   His goblin
attendant has seated himself on the warrior's hel-
met, and opened the mysterious book to devour
its contents, while an airy phantom, like the spirit
of the storm, stretching downwards behind him,
extends his arm to prostrate the over-curious imp
by the side of the bleeding mosstrooper.

Philadelphia possesses a valuable public library
containing upwards of twenty thousand volumes,
and another containing about four thousand.
There is also an Athenæum, although on a much
smaller scale than that of Boston; it is well supplied with British periodical publications, and I
have spent several hours in it very agreeably, skimming the more interesting portions of the recent
journals.

·. In a literary point of view Philadelphia enjoys a
respectable rank among American cities, but as yet
Boston is far before any other.   I was not a little
surprised to learn by the ' Picture of Philadelphia,'

tion of being the first historical painter living. We should be glad
to have the work of Cammucini at Rome, or Girard at Paris, or
David at Brussels, indicated, that deserves to be preferred to Mr.
Allston's Uriel, Jacob's vision, or Jeremiah.   In England certainly,
he has left behind him no rival in this branch of his art.'   *North
American Review*, No. *XXX. p.* 181.   This is a matter respecting
which there will be no doubt a difference of opinion, but if Mr.
Allston's pencil so far surpasses in power those of rival artists, by
all means let his country and himself enjoy the honour of it.

that in 1811 it contained fifty-one printing offices, employing one hundred and fifty-three presses, and I believe that since that period the number has increased. A considerable proportion of these must be supported by newspapers, of which there are no fewer than eight published daily, besides many once, twice, and three times a week; but after deducting what are necessary for these, there must remain a very respectable number devoted to literature of a more permanent and aspiring kind.

Philadelphia has produced the finest and most accurate specimens of typography that have yet appeared in America, and there is a decided superiority in most of the works printed here, to those executed either in Boston or New York. There are two letter foundries, and several printing press makers. The Columbian press, invented by a person of the name of Clymer a native of Philadelphia, appears to be in many respects very superior to any other that I have yet seen.[8]

Many periodical works have at various times been published here, some of which are still continued; and though their success has been in no instance equal to that which is at present enjoyed by

[8] Mr. Clymer has subsequently come over to London, and obtained a British patent for his press, which has been extensively adopted and is universally approved of. The first of them that came to Scotland has now been at work for four years in our office, where we have presses on six different constructions, but though two or three of the kinds are excellent, our workmen consider the Columbian as decidedly the best they have ever pulled. (1823.)

the North American Review, yet some of them
exhibit a large proportion of respectable talent.[9] For
reprints of the heavier British books, Philadelphia
is quite famous.   The Encyclopædia Britannica
was begun in 1790, by Mr. Dobson, an enterpris-
ing countryman of ours.   When the first half
volume was published, of which 1000 were printed,
he had but 246 subscribers; they increased however so rapidly that of volume second 2000 were
thrown off; the first was soon after reprinted, and
in a short time he found it extremely difficult to
procure a sufficient number of printers and engravers, to carry forward the work with sufficient
rapidity.   Dr. Rees' larger work, and that of
Dr. Brewster are at present in progress.   The
Edinburgh and Quarterly Reviews are regularly
reprinted at New York; and several of our other
popular periodical works in different parts of the
Union.

It is a mistake to suppose that books are cheaper
in America than in Britain.   The works of our
modern authors, indeed, which at home are exclusive property, loaded with an enormous copy
right, and which we can purchase only in the shape
of handsome octavos or more elegant quartos, suffer here instantaneous transmutation into an humble

---

[9] The Analectic Magazine, published in Philadelphia, was for a
considerable time edited by the elegant author of the Sketch Book,
and Bracebridge Hall. Some of the papers of the former work were
first published in the Analectic.

duodecimo, occasionally of most plebeian aspect, and for two dollars or less you may obtain the verbal contents of most of the Albemarle Street two guinea volumes; but in all books of which the copy right has expired, our British editions are superior in execution and accuracy and quite as low in price, as those which are published in America.

In historical engraving I have seen no specimens of American art which are very superior. Westall's illustrations of our modern poets have nearly all been copied, but there is a harshness in the engraving which contrasts very disadvantageously with the productions of Heath. In the execution of bank notes, however, Philadelphia may challenge the world. Messrs. Murray, Draper, Fairman, & Co. have distinguished themselves by some remarkably ingenious discoveries, which have been applied with singular success to this branch of the art; and their notes, which you meet with in every quarter of the Union, are distinguished by an originality of style and delicacy of execution which much surpass those of our native country, and if they do not afford a perfect protection from forgery, must at least render it exceedingly difficult. [10]

[10] A more minute account of this inimitable style of engraving might have been given, but that its appearance is now familiar to all who take any interest in such subjects; and specimens from the London establishment of Messrs. Perkins and Heath, are to be met

Philadelphia is the seat of a celebrated College. This institution was begun under the auspices of Franklin, and was originally only an academy and charity school. Material alterations were made at different periods in its management and regula-tions, and it was incorporated by the legislature of the State, first as the College of Philadelphia, and afterwards on a more extended scale as the University of Pennsylvania. Although respectable in other departments, this seminary is most highly celebrated as a medical school, in which respect Philadelphia is regarded as the Edinburgh of the United States.

In a religious point of view, Philadelphia though strongly characterised by the peculiarities of its quaker origin, is not so much so as I had previously imagined. The Friends are now prodigiously outnumbered by those of other persuasions, and I believe that of themselves many who retain the name of the sect, have laid aside some of the peculiarities by which the more rigid are distinguished. This is particularly the case with those of younger years ;—in dress there seems to be a kind of hesitating approximation to conformity with modern taste ;

with every day. Its value may be appreciated by the fact, that none have spoken so highly of it as the best engravers of our native country. The most curious and most useful part of the discovery, is that process by which metal plates of the same design may be multiplied by pressure, to any extent, and with as much facility as impressions are obtained on paper (1823).

and there are some individuals to be found, who, though careful in writing to retain the well known formula in date, address, and signature, have no objections in conversation to concede the usual courtesies of polite intercourse. Passive obedience and nonresistance have been generally esteemed essential to Quaker principles; but a considerable party in this city separated from the main body, during the Revolutionary war, in consequence of maintaining the propriety of fighting for the national independence. They still continue to be a distinct class, justifying an appeal to the sword in defence of national rights.

I was conducted one afternoon lately, by a Friend of the old school, to see their principal place of worship and burying ground. The meeting house is large and very plain, and is divided into two compartments, one for males, the other for females. My conductor remarked that in this house met the largest deliberative society in the world, in which every individual has a vote. This is on occasion of the annual meeting of the Quakers in the United States, when there are generally 1500 persons present, all of whom have an equal right of speech and suffrage.

The burying ground, behind the meeting house, is the only one of the kind that I ever saw. The surface was as level as a bowling green, excepting a small portion at one side where a few grassy hillocks indicated the mansions of the dead.

8

My conductor remarked that the Friends had buried in that ground since the days of Penn. The resurrection of the body, he said, formed no part of their religious belief, and they considered it improper to erect any memorial over the departed, as if any part of *the man* were buried, or to preserve a distinction between the graves of one family and those of another. In accordance with these sentiments, they begin to inter at one corner of the enclosure; and go regularly on, digging one grave by the side of the preceding one, till the whole ground has been gone over. The surface is then completely levelled, and a new series of sepulchres begun.

All this was new to me, and somewhat revolting. That the society of Friends denied the resurrection of the body, I did not previously know. Neither was I aware that they set themselves to eradicate that principle in our hearts, which leads us to cling in fondness to the remains of the departed object of our affections, and to hallow the spot where the beloved dust reposes. This is far too philosophical for me, and I cannot help thinking offers violence to one of the purest, kindliest sympathies of the human heart. It is well to discountenance the laboured, and very frequently fabulous eulogies, with which tomb-stones are so profusely bedaubed; but to plough down the field, and leave it like the sand on the sea-shore devoid of trace or memorial—to put it out of my power to say 'my friend lies there,' is to lacerate feelings which have been cherished and honoured in all ages, by all, even the best of men. " Where thou diest, I will die, and there will I be buried !" " Why trouble ye the woman ?" said the blessed Jesus, " she hath wrought a good work upon me ; for in that she hath poured this ointment on my body, she did it for my burial." What can suggest a more exquisitely touching picture of a bleeding heart, than these affecting words, " She is gone to the grave to weep there !" All this must be un- intelligible to a Quaker, if he is really consistent in his professed belief.

I attended at the meeting house one sabbath af- ternoon, to see their mode of worship; the only occasion on which I ever did so. The meeting did not continue longer than an hour, and the worship was certainly in the highest sense of the word intellectual, for not an individual opened his mouth. Some wore their hats, others put them off, and the aspect of many by no means betoken- ed any great degree of mental abstraction.

Of the principles of the majority of the sect, I have been able to learn very little ; indeed it would not be easy to ascertain exactly their confession of faith. I have met with individuals who maintained very decidedly the essential doctrines of evangeli- cal religion, but I also found others whose senti- ments seemed to approach very nearly to infidelity. Their almost total neglect of public instruction must necessarily occasion, among those who think at all, a great diversity of sentiment upon speculative subjects. Their benevolence and philanthropy, however, are as conspicuous here as every where else; the early and most successful managers of the Penitentiary were principally Quakers, and a gentleman of the same body was pointed out to me, who is one of the most efficient managers of the Pennsylvania Hospital. The whole civilized world owe a debt of gratitude to the Quakers, for their long and unwearied labours in the cause of general philanthropy;—and if slavery is to be abolished in this country, it will probably be effected through their instrumentality.

There are altogether nearly sixty places of worship [11] in Philadelphia; including most of the usual denominations, with some of German origin unknown in Scotland. During the few sabbaths

[11] An attentive correspondent, whose kindness I have already had occasion to acknowledge, has transmitted the following enumeration of the churches and chapels in Philadelphia, as they stood in June 1822. 12 Presbyterian, under the General Assembly, including one for Africans, and one building;—11 Methodist, including four for Africans;—9 Episcopalian, including one for Africans, and two building;—6 Baptist, including one for Africans;—5 Quakers, including one of Free Quakers, and one building;—4 Romish;—2 Reformed Dutch;—2 German Calvinists, in one of which service is conducted in the German language;—2 German Lutherans, one also adhering to the vernacular tongue;—1 Associate Reformed;—1 Reformed Presbyterian, or Covenanters;—1 Swedish Lutheran;—1 Moravian;—2 Universalist, including one building;—1 Socinian;—1 New Jerusalem;—and 2 Jewish Synagogues. Total 63, including five building.

which I have spent here, I can of course have heard but a small number of their preachers and shall be brief in my account of them.

In one of the Presbyterian churches I have been four times present. The clergyman who officiates here is rather advanced in life, of a sedate and intelligent countenance, and a spare habit of body. He possesses a considerable command of language, and in prayer much felicity of expression; he has scarcely any action, his voice is rather weak and his enunciation slow, yet earnest and impressive. He exhibits an intimate acquaintance with the Bible, a strong conviction of the importance of its truths, and a lively desire to impart instruction. On one of the occasions referred to, he lectured on the concluding verses of the ninth chapter of the Gospel by John, in connexion with the commencement of the tenth, and stated with much simplicity the grand doctrine of the atonement. At another time he delivered a very judicious discourse on the work of the Holy Spirit, and continued the illustration of the same subject, in the form of a lecture on the parable of the sower, as recorded by Mark. From the parable of the mustard seed, he discoursed on the progress of the gospel in heathen countries, and the approach of that time, when 'incense and a pure offering,' should be offered to the Lord Jesus, from the rising to the setting of the sun.

In the Associate Reformed, or Antiburgher

church, I heard an old fashioned but very good sermón, from one of our own countrymen. The service on this occasion, carried me in mind completely across the Atlantic. We had a Scotish minister, a Scotish precentor,[12] and a Scotish congregation; the discourse was delivered with a strong national accent, the psalms were of the version which is in common use at home, and were sung to some of our well known old fashioned tunes. Such a combination of circumstances, brings the recollections of ' auld lang syne' into powerful excitement; and the wandering Caledonian who could be present without a glow of kindly feeling to the whole assembly, must be fashioned of most unusual materials.

At a Baptist congregation I heard a discourse from a young divine, who there was much reason to fear had made a very unsuitable choice of a profession. He was however only a temporary occupant of the pulpit. The regular pastor, whom I afterwards heard, is a man of good talents and so far as I could judge correct doctrinal sentiments, but there was a degree of mannerism in his reading and speaking, which strongly recalled certain lines of Cowper's which I shall forbear to quote. I heard him lecture on the first and second chapters of Ezra, when he illustrated the historical narrative in a very instructive manner; he afterwards

[12] *Anglice*, Clerk.

expounded with great success those most important words, ' If ye believe not that I am he, ye shall die in your sins.' I wished very much to have heard one of the African preachers who is highly spoken of,· but for want of a proper guide I failed in my attempt to find his church.

I have visited two Sabbath schools in Philadelphia. One of these meets between sermons, and is devoted to instruction in reading. The other assembles in the evening, and is devoted entirely to religious instruction. In the course of my wanderings in the United States, I met with no Sabbath school excepting this and the one at New Haven which at all resembled the Scotish ones. The scholars in this are chiefly of females; they are divided into several classes, two of which are taught by ladies, and the others by young men. The principal deficiency that I observed in the management was the allowing each scholar to please herself, both as to the passage which she prepared, and as to the length of it. Experience proves that this system is essentially prejudicial to the improvement of the scholars, who should all have a prescribed exercise, and so far as possible the same one. A considerable degree of attention and diligence was apparent among the scholars; though as in all American schools, rather more latitude of speech and behaviour prevailed among them than is altogether beneficial.

Philadelphia I should be inclined to think, is

O 2

scarcely so cheerful a place of residence as New York. Whether I may have been led to this opinion from having spent a shorter time in it, or from the greater prevalence of Quaker manners, or from some other accidental cause, I shall not pretend to determine. The surrounding country is very beautiful, and there are many pleasant villas and flourishing little towns upon the banks of both rivers.

At Bordentown, twenty-six miles above the city on the west bank of the Delaware, is the seat of the ex-King of Spain, Joseph Bonaparte, who has assumed the title of Count de Survilliers. I saw his house,[13] as the steam boat passed down the river, rising on the brow of a hill surrounded on all sides with a dense forest of pines. The view

---

[19] This house has since I left America fallen a prey to fire, and some valuable pictures and statues perished in the flames. The inhabitants of the neighbouring village having been very active in attempting to save the costly furniture, the Count shortly after addressed a letter of thanks to them through the newspapers. The ex-King however was in novel circumstances in addressing his republican neighbours, and his letter as might have been expected, partook more of the gracious style of the sovereign than the grateful tone of the citizen. He assured them with some degree of pomposity that he regarded the scupulous honesty and undaunted courage which had characterized their exertions, as proofs that the inhabitants of Bordentown ' properly appreciated the interest which he had always felt for them.' A somewhat saucy reply speedily appeared in which the Count was informed that they held his benignant smiles very cheap, and that in giving him their assistance during the fire, they were actuated by the common impulses of humanity and nothing more.

from the windows must be very commanding, and as he surveys it, what a contrast of ideas must crowd upon his mind! Paris — Madrid — the banks of the Delaware;—the brother of Napoleon—the King of Spain—the obscure American recluse! How singularly happy may be the evening of his eventful life, if in the stillness of this retirement, he should be led rightly to meditate on that futurity where an existence awaits him more glorious or more dreadful than all that he has yet known. At Trenton, four miles above Bordentown, was the seat of General Moreau, while in this country. His stables are seen close by the road. On the banks of the Schuylkill General Vandamme, another conspicuous name in the annals of recent events, has a very fine villa. He has had the good sense to withdraw from European broils, but if one half of what has been told of him be true, he merited a very different termination to his history.

There are several very large wooden bridges across the Schuylkill, in the neighbourhood of Philadelphia. Most of them have three arches, but near the water works there is one of a single arch, 340 feet 9 inches in span. The river is here forty feet deep, and the sinking of piers would have been a hopeless undertaking. This bridge, like most others in this country, is roofed over and closed in at the sides, with small openings like windows for the admission of light. The roof is use-

O 3

ful not only in preserving the bridge from the
influence of the weather, but also in compact-
ing the fabric, but it gives the bridge a heavy
look without and a gloomy appearance within.
These roofed bridges exhibit a style of architecture
which is unknown in our native country.   Over-
head a massy frame work binds the whole edifice
together; sometimes immense hoops bending from
beam to beam suspend the various arches, each hoop
composed of six or eight enormous planks laid surface to surface and bound together by iron bolts;
in others the floor is suspended by massy chains or
iron rods, descending from upright beams.   Strong
however as these bridges appear to be, the autumnal floods and the breaking up of the ice in
spring are frequently fatal to them; in the month
of May last I was ferried across two rivers, close
by the ruins of extensive bridges which had been
recently swept away.

Two unsuccessful attempts have been made by
the citizens of Philadelphia to cut a canal between
the Schuylkill and the Susquehanna; with the intention of gradually completing a water communication between the Delaware and the great western
lakes.   In these abortive efforts upwards of fifty
thousand pounds sterling have been fruitlessly
expended.   The failure however seems to have
arisen rather from mismanagement, than from any
impracticability in the scheme.   The example of
New York has given a new stimulus to canal enter-

prize, and probably future travellers may have to commemorate that the State of Pennsylvania has been equally successful. Baltimore has good reason to deprecate such a result, as it would most probably divert to the Delaware much of the inland and foreign trade which at present flows into the Chesapeake.

LETTER VIII.

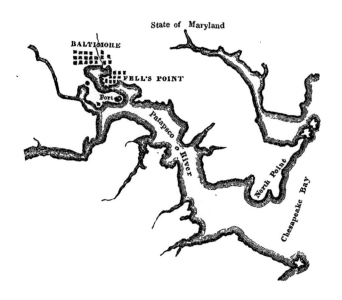

LETTER VIII.

Baltimore, September, 1818.

BALTIMORE is built at the top of a small bay in
the river Patapsco, near its entrance into the
Chesapeake, and consists of two portions, nearly
a mile asunder; the upper of which is properly
speaking the town, and the lower called Fell's
Point is the harbour. The water comes up to
the town but it is shallow and in general none
but coasters go past the Point. The bay is formed
and protected by a peninsular tongue of land
which stretches downwards into the river; the
entrance is narrow and is completely commanded
by a fort, which sustained a heavy bombardment
during last war.

The town is built with considerable regularity,
upon portions of three hills and their intervening

valleys; many of the streets cross each other at right
angles, and they are in general spacious and well
paved.   A large proportion of the buildings are of
brick; the more ancient, in consequence of inattention to painting, have rather a gloomy aspect, but
the modern ones resemble in every respect those
of New York and Philadelphia.

In public buildings Baltimore aspires to distinction, but some of the most considerable are as
yet only in progress.   A massy brick edifice
which is intended for an Exchange has been
roofed in; externally it is remarkable for dimensions rather than elegance, and of its internal
appearance I can say nothing.   Two new churches
are going forward, the one destined to be a Romish
Cathedral the other a Socinian Chapel.   They
stand very near each other, rather above the city,
and as yet a considerable space is open around
them.   The style of the respective buildings strikes
me as somewhat appropriate to the system which
it has been erected to support.

The Cathedral is built of dark coloured stone
in the form of a cross, with a dome over the centre,
but the length is not nearly so great as in our
ancient churches; the walls and roof are finished
and a shoal of Irish labourers are busied on the
interior.   It is rather singular that they have not
attempted the Gothic in this building; probably
the great expense of that style may have been the
cause of the Roman Doric being preferred.   The

principal entrances are arched, and a few pilasters
carried round the walls are its principal ornament ;
the size and disposition of the windows, with the
crossing of the transept, have been so managed as
to throw into the body of the church a strong
depth of shadow, the holy gloom of which will
doubtless be esteemed highly conducive to genuine
religious emotion, and which at least we must
grant to be no way inappropriate in that ritual, of
which the burning of candles forms so important
a portion.

The Socinian Chapel, a more lightsome and
tasteful fabric, is nearly finished, and although
not a large building is said to have cost upwards
of twenty thousand pounds sterling. In front is
an arched portico, and in the tympanum of the
pediment is a *stucco* angel descending from a cloud;
the walls are covered externally with composition,
lined and painted to resemble stone. The interior
is profusely decorated. The pulpit is of polished
marble of various colours, with a baptismal font before it of the same material; upon the wall behind
are two white marble slabs, resembling the tables of
the Law in the ancient pictures of Moses, upon
which are inscribed a few texts of Scripture.[1] The

---

[1] I noted these passages in my memorandum book and subjoin
them for the gratification of enquirers. The one table bore in full
length 1 Tim. i. 17. Phil. iv. 6. Mark xii. 29. Matth. v. 16.
2 Tim. ii. 19 :—the other John xvii. 3. Matth. vii. 12. Heb. xii. 1, 2.
and xi. 14.

ends of the pews are beautifully carved and bronzed in imitation of the antique. The ceiling is covered with rich stuccoed work, and in the gallery is a large organ the front of which is very tastefully finished in the form of the ancient lyre. The effect of the whole is certainly very splendid; but the more splendid it is, the more must we regret the purpose for which so costly an edifice has been erected.

Two public monuments have been recently begun; the one to Washington, the other to commemorate the attack on the city during last war, and to record the names of those who fell in its defence. Washington's monument occupies the front of a rising ground a little above the city; the other the centre of a square within it.

The name and the deeds of Washington stand so conspicuously pre-eminent in the history of this nation, that to rear a suitable monument to his fame must be a matter of no trifling difficulty. The structure must be magnificent and durable, above all ordinary edifices, which aspires to outshine or outlast the splendour of his name. Probably this is one reason why no national monument has hitherto been erected to the Father of American liberty. The Baltimore one is the first of an architectural kind that has been attempted. Two statues however are in progress; one by Canova to be placed in the State House of Raleigh, the capital of North Carolina, the other by Chantrey for the town of Boston.[2]

The Baltimore monument is a plain column rising from a square base, to be surmounted by a colossal statue by some artist whose name I have not heard. The work has advanced as yet but a short way, so that it is impossible to form a correct idea of the ultimate effect; the situation however is commanding and it must eventually form a conspicuous object in the distant prospect. The fabric is brick within, and white marble without, with a spiral staircase in the centre. No loop holes have been left for the admission of light; the stair is consequently very dark, and when the column attains to its full height will be somewhat disagreeable to ascend.

[2] A writer in the North American Review thus writes with regard to these rival statues and their sculptors. " With respect to this statue, the only work of Canova, as far as we are aware, which our country can boast, if indeed it has already reached Raleigh, we can speak only of the model in clay. The likeness is certainly not strong, and the artist complained of the want of materials to deduce it from; a circumstance the more to be regretted, as no countenance is better ascertained than Washington's, and if materials were not put into his hands, it could not be because they do not exist. We apprehend, moreover, that the costume of the statue will not suit the American taste. Gen. Washington is represented sitting, with a tablet supported by his left hand, on which he is about to write the constitution of America, with a style which he holds in his right. Though thus occupied as a civil legislator, he is clad in the Roman military dress with the brazen cuirass, half of the thigh, the knees and legs bare, and military sandals. It seems to us that this dress is in itself unbecoming, besides being inconsistent with the legislative or

The Battle Monument is also of white marble,
but much smaller.   It consists of a reeded column
with a crossed fillet at the top and bottom, erected
upon a square base tapering in the Egyptian style
and rusticated.   The shaft is not unlike the Roman
fasces, without the axe ; one side of the base exhibits a door, which in a very hot day suggests
the luxurious idea of an ice house ; the other
sides contain slabs on which are to be inscribed
the names of all those who fell in defence of
their 'altars and hearths,' as the helmets of our
yeomanry express it.   The operations on this
erection are for the present suspended ; the base
has been built, and the materials for the column lie
scattered around it, but the carved blocks are still
in the packing frames in which they were brought

civil occupation represented.   The only costume that we can imagine
less becoming than the ancient military dress, is the modern military
dress, the hussar boots, faced coat, and hair clubbed up with pomatum, in which we understand Mr. Chantrey will dress Gen. Washington in the statue designed for Boston, according to the theory of
the English School, which enjoins the closest possible imitation of
nature, and adherence to historical truth.   Neither of these principles
is just in the art.   Nature is to be imitated, only in her noble, select,
and pleasing parts, and historical truth adhered to no further than it
adds to the beauty, grandeur, and charm of the work ; provided that
the deviation be not such as to shock our judgments.   Look at the
statue of the Queen before St. Paul's in her hoop and toupet.   We
would have had Gen. Washington's statue in the true classical dress,
the ancient civil senatorial robe, call it Roman or Greek, alike removed from the indelicate bareness of the Roman armour, and the
fantastical cuts and folds of our modern tailoring." *North American
Review, No. XXVII. p.* 385

from Italy.   In architectural design this monument is so perfectly anomalous that we cannot but regret its premature erection; in a few years, probably, the citizens will learn to regard it with the same feelings which are now excited by the Edinburgh monument to Nelson.   Its situation however is well chosen, the material is beautiful, and so far as these go even strangers will regard it as an ornament to the city.   The event which it commemorates will always secure it the affections of the natives.

Fort M'Hendry at the end of the peninsula saved the town from capture during last war, although it was then but ill prepared for an attack; the batteries were in a poor condition, it had no covered ways, and the magazine was not bomb-proof. A shell struck the corner of the magazine in a slanting direction, and shattered the wall; had it penetrated, the capture of the fort would have been inevitable.   Since that period the works have been greatly strengthened, and bomb-proof barracks, covered ways, and magazines, have all been erected. The fortification is of a pentagonal form, and consists of an inner and outer line of batteries.   The inner line is of brick and is mounted with the lighter guns; the outer breastwork is of turf and the guns are of a large size.   Between the lines are furnaces for heating shot.   The old walls still exhibit the scars of the attack, and several deep hollows in the ground show where shells had buried themselves.

Behind the principal fort are two small batteries at a short distance from each other. The British squadron sent out a detachment of boats during the night, hoping to effect a landing behind Fort M'Hendry, which they succeeded in passing unobserved; not aware that there were other batteries beyond it, the sailors set up a premature shout of triumph, which immediately brought down upon them an unexpected cannonade; several of the boats were sunk and the rest compelled to return.

Fell's Point is like other sea ports somewhat dirty; and the yellow fever when it was prevalent, committed great ravages here, while Baltimore was comparatively healthy. In the harbour at present is a beautiful sharp built schooner, evidently intended for warlike purposes, and pretty well known to be fitted out for the coast of South America; she will carry about a dozen of guns. The Baltimore ship builders particularly excel in the construction of such vessels, and it was their astonishing fleetness of sailing which enabled the privateers to pick up so many of our merchantmen during last war. They are very low in the water, and broad in the beam; the masts are sloped very much backwards, and they sail exceedingly close to the wind. Very few of them were captured by our cruisers, and those generally in consequence of some accident. Two instances of this kind I

7

have heard of. A very fine privateer brig of this description left New York on her first cruize, the weather was very foggy, and at no great distance from Sandy Hook she descried a pretty large vessel which she supposed was a merchantman; she of course ran down upon it with all speed, but discovered when it was too late that the anticipated prize was a British seventy-four gun ship:—the crew were constrained to surrender without firing a gun. Another privateer of a similar description, happened to fall in at sea with one of our large frigates; trusting to her superiority of sailing she made no haste to get out of the way, but tacked about till the frigate had got nearly within gun shot, when she stretched upon the wind and bore off. Out of the frigate's reach she again lay to, awaiting her pursuit; at that critical moment the wind which had hitherto blown pretty fresh died suddenly away, and her sails flapped against the masts, the frigate's boats were instantly manned, the privateer lay in helpless inactivity on the water, resistance was in vain, and the fable of the hare and the tortoise was again realized.

The harbour of Baltimore presents I understand but a very dull scene now to what it once did. During the European continental war, when America engrossed the carrying trade of nearly the whole world, a flourishing commerce crowded the harbour with vessels, and the custom-house with business; but Mr. Madison's proclamation of war was

the signal for its ruin, and the termination of
hostilities in Europe having left other nations at
liberty to claim their share in the interchange of
commodities, the quays are now half deserted, and
the store-houses comparatively empty.   As the
United States however recover from their present
mercantile difficulties, and as the back country
becomes more thickly settled, the increasing demand for foreign produce and manufactures must
by degrees bring back the good old times, when
Fell's Point was crowded with merchantmen, and
the storekeepers of Baltimore exulted in the dimensions of their ledgers.

Eastward from the town is yet to be seen the
breastwork of turf which was hastily thrown up
when General Ross landed to attack it.   The rifle
of some expert marksman was the means of saving
Baltimore on this occasion.   It might seem that
an individual bullet could be of but little avail as
to the result of a battle—it can kill but a man;
but when that man is a commanding officer, and
such an officer as Ross, the bullet that kills him is
decisive of the day.   In the defence of a difficult
pass, a wood, or an entrenched post, the American
backwoodsmen are unequalled; they can with difficulty be got to stand in open ground, and have no
confidence in battalion movements, but give them
the stump of a tree, a fence, or a hillock of earth,
over which they can level their piece, and the
youngest boy among them will ply the work of

destruction with a deliberate certainty of aim, which is disastrous in the last degree to the battalions of the enemy.   It is not known who killed General Ross; common report attributes the effective shot to some one of a few lads who were posted behind a bush, but one of the most opulent citizens, a Scotsman by birth, who with the rest shouldered his musket on the occasion, tells me on the authority of the general who commanded, that no reliance can be placed on that report.

This important event took place on the twelfth of September, and I was the other day present at a review, which annually commemorates the successful defence of the town.   As I am no way skilled in military tactics, I cannot pretend to criticise the evolutions which I saw.   The young men belonging to the town wear in general a blue uniform, and make a creditable appearance; the country militia wear no uniform at all, and have a very *tag-rag-and-bobtail* kind of aspect.   The day was excessively hot, and some of them marched to the field in their shirt sleeves, where blackened with dust, perspiration and powder, they presented a somewhat ferocious appearance.   A small body of sharpshooters were on the field in a dark grey uniform, which had a remarkably neat appearance; we are accustomed to green for this description of troops, but I doubt whether the grey will not in general answer the purpose of obscurity and concealment fully as well.   On the flanks were sta-

tioned some companies of artillery, at right angles
to the main line; and the contrast which different
battalions exhibited was no where more conspicuous
than among them.   I was highly amused with a
corps of old fellows who strongly reminded me of
the Edinburgh city guard, while it was yet in
being; they wore long tailed coats and cocked
hats, and their hair was larded with pomatum and
powder.   The working of their guns was a serious
business; there was a sad chasing of each other
for a cartridge, much prompting and directing
about thrusting it in, and to fire and sponge were
works of undisguised danger and difficulty.   An
unfortunate position made their awkwardness still
more conspicuous, for close beside them were
posted the ' Independent Blues,' a body of trimly
dressed, active young fellows, who handled the
rammer and the linstock with exemplary dexterity,
and if the rules of good breeding and military
discipline had not prevented them, would have
fired at least two shots for one of the venerables'
beside them.   The troops paraded at ten o'clock
in the morning, and did not leave the ground till
four in the afternoon; they had an hour's interval
however at noon, and there were on the ground
numerous itinerant venders of peaches, pastry, and
soda water.

I witnessed since my arrival here, a spectacle of
a different kind, and one that is more rarely seen
in the United States, the execution of two men for

mail-robbery.   Flagrant as this offence is esteemed
among us it is not a capital crime here, unless
when accomplished by the aid of deadly weapons,
or with such a show of violence as may put those
who travel with the mail in fear of their lives.   In
the present instance the lives of the driver and
passengers had been threatened, and as the perpetrators were old and notorious offenders, the law
was allowed to take its course.[5]

Baltimore prison is built on a sloping ground
rather out of town, and has a large open court
yard, every part of which is well seen from different
parts of the rising ground which environ the city.
The gallows was erected within the yard and the
hills around were covered with spectators.   I am
no frequenter of such scenes, yet I was desirous of
witnessing the effect of so unusual and tragic an
occurrence on an American assembly.   On reaching

[5] Robbery of the mail is very frequent in the United States; yet
all things considered, not so much so as might be expected.   Re-
mittances from one part of the Union to another, even of large
sums, are generally made by transmitting bank notes in letters
by the Post Office; scarcely a mail bag is made up for any of
the larger cities, which does not contain in this way large sums
of money.   The mail is totally unprotected; there is no guard,
and the driver carries no arms.   In the more frequented roads
the bag is now carried in a kind of boot under the driver's seat,
but in the country it is tossed carelessly into the bottom of the
stage waggon, to annoy with trunks and portmanteaus the feet
of the passengers.   On one occasion while travelling in one of
these vehicles, I observed a cut in the bag beside me, large enough
to admit a man's hand.

the brow of one of the hills, soon after the unhappy
men had been turned off, I found every commanding position covered with spectators. The multitude
seemed to differ from what a similar catastrophe
calls forth at home, chiefly in the superior respectability of their appearance. There were plenty of
all classes, but a decidedly large proportion were
well dressed, and females of various ages, and ap-
parently all conditions, were not wanting. It was
manifest that curiosity is quite as active a principle
here as at home; and that an American crowd as
well as a British one is powerfully influenced by
that singular characteristic of our nature, a fondness for tragic spectacles. The distance at which
I and those around me stood, prevented us from
seeing very plainly the more minute circumstances
of the work of death, but the general aspect of
the ' gallows tree' did not, it was obvious, excite
very keen feelings of commiseration for the suffer-
ers; the spectators gazed towards the fatal spot,
pretty much as they would have done had it been
an eclipse of the moon or a house on fire.[4] I had
in my pocket a small perspective glass, which I
offered to two young ladies who happened to
stand near me; they seemed quite pleased with
the accommodation, and continued to use it alternately till the whole of the melancholy scene

[4] A fair ' Englishwoman' sketches a remarkably different picture
of an American execution ; perhaps the variation in our stories may
have arisen from her never having seen one.

was over. The bodies on being cut down were immediately buried in the corner of the prison yard.

A visit to the Penitentiary of Baltimore, has suggested no remark upon the system which I have not already made. The condition of the prisoners is perfectly comfortable, and to judge from their appearance you would suppose them quite contented with it; they show to visitors the various articles of manufacture in which they are employed, and explain the steps in the process with as much willingness as ordinary workmen, and without any symptoms of shame that they should be found in such a place. There are at present about 360 prisoners, two of whom are Scotsmen; a third died a few days ago. The keeper informed me that one of them evinced a strong desire to save his country the disgrace connected with his delinquency, for when first examined he called himself a native of North Carolina.

The Hospital is a large building a short way out of town, and is said to be under excellent management. A splendid collection of anatomical models in wax is exhibited in it, at the charge of a dollar for each visitor; the admission price is high, but it is in fact a contribution to the funds of the institution, and is therefore cheerfully paid. The nature of the figures is not such as to invite a minute description of them, but they appear to be very beautifully executed.

The State of Maryland has all along been distinguished by a sedulous attention to the advancement of learning; and for several years considerable sums of money have been annually voted by the legislature for the support of schools and colleges. In all these appropriations it is an express and honourable stipulation that no distinction shall be made in favour of any religious sect, but that both the management and the benefit of the institutions shall be free to persons of every denomination. In 1807 a Medical College was founded here, and in 1812 its charter was extended so as to embrace the other departments of science and literature; it then received the appellation of the University of Maryland. As yet the medical department is the only one which has been brought into operation. There is also an older College, called St. Mary's, which though a Romish establishment, is said to have educated some of the first literary men in the United States; it was not empowered to confer literary Degrees till 1805. It is mentioned as a proof of the liberality of the conductors, that no religious test is required at this institution, either for admission or for a degree; but probably not the less danger is to be apprehended from this circumstance. *Timeo Danaos et dona ferentes.* Voluntarily to prevent Protestants from coming under their influence, was never the system of Papists; it is much more characteristic of their policy to receive with professions of liberality all who offer, and then to put in operation their proselyting skill.[5]

A school is conducted here on the Lancasterian plan, which contains about three hundred children. I thought on visiting it, that the teacher's manner to his pupils, was most unnecessarily harsh and repulsive; and, although their proficiency appeared to be creditable, that more might be effected by one who knew how to conciliate the affections of those over whom he ruled. I understand that a change is not improbable, for the pedagogue is discontented with the amount of his salary, although it is equal to that of a Professor in most of the colleges. [6]

Baltimore is celebrated for the fineness of its flour; the superiority of which arises from the perfection at which they have arrived in the machinery by which it is manufactured. I have recently visited a mill driven by steam, in which manual labour is so completely excluded, that the sailor who delivers the grain at the wharf is the last person who applies his hand to it, till it descends into the barrel in the shape of superfine flour. It is difficult to convey a proper idea of machinery without the aid of drawings, but I trust you will be able to

[5] For farther information respecting the state of education in Maryland, and other parts of the United States, the Reader is referred to an article in the North American Review, No. XXXIII.

[6] The individual alluded to left Baltimore soon after my last visit to it.

comprehend the following rude outline of the process. A covered trough which projects from the
mill to the edge of the wharf, receives the grain as
it is emptied from the vessel; within this trough is
an axle revolving longitudinally, around which are
thin pieces of wood projecting into the trough, and
continued along in a spiral line. As the revolution
of the screw of Archimedes raises water, so this
axle by revolving among the grain forces it backward in a regular current from the wharf to the mill.
The grain on reaching the inner end of this trough
is received into a succession of little tin buckets,
which are strung upon an endless belt revolving
upon two wheels, the higher of which is in the
garret floor. As these buckets turn over the
upper wheel they empty their contents into a box,
from which the grain is conveyed to the fanners,
where it is thoroughly cleaned. From the fanners
it is conducted into the hoppers, in the floor below;
here eight pairs of stones are kept constantly at
work. From the stones the flour descends into a
long wooden trough, similar to that into which the
grain was first thrown; and another spiral screw,
revolving here, urges it gradually forward to another series of buckets, which carry it to an upper
story, and discharge it under a machine for cool-
ing it. This consists of a spindle revolving perpen-
dicularly, with a horizontal shaft crossing it near
the floor, in the under part of which are teeth
formed of thin slips of wood, which nearly touch

the floor, and which are so disposed in relation to each other, that while they stir the flour round, they at the same time convey it inwards to the centre. The flour is thus spread thinly over the floor, and as the teeth revolve among it, it describes circles successively smaller and smaller, until it falls through an opening into the bolting machines in the story below. Here are three bolting cylinders, producing the various degrees of common, fine, and superfine flour; and from them it is finally received into barrels, ready for inspection and shipping. This mill manufactures with ease a thousand bushels a day; and the flour which it produces, always commands an advance on the average market price.

The essentially republican constitution of this country, is daily forced upon a stranger's observation in various ways. At present a vigorous competition is going forward in this city, for the office of Sheriff;—I copy the following advertisements from the newspapers :—

" SHERIFFALTY.

" Samuel Merryman offers himself to his fellow citizens as a candidate for the office of Sheriff, for Baltimore city and county, at the ensuing election. Having been employed as deputy Sheriff, by William Merryman and John Chalmers, Esquires, during their respective terms of service, his experience justifies the hope that he will be found capable of performing the duties of that important station; and he pledges himself to do so with impartiality and diligence, if elected." .

Immediately under this address appears the following :—

" SHERIFFALTY.

" The subscriber, at the instance of a number of his friends, offers himself as a candidate for the Sheriffalty of Baltimore county, and respectfully solicits the suffrages of his fellow citizens.   He has for some time past been employed, and still remains in the employ of the present Sheriff, and flatters himself he will be capable of giving general satisfaction, in the discharge of the several duties of the office.

JOHN STITCHER."

The claims of these rival candidates seem so equally balanced, that the independent electors might chance to find themselves in the same condition as the animal between the two bundles of straw ; but here comes a third, with more formidable qualifications, and I should not be at all surprised to learn that he carries his point, against both Messrs. Merryman and Stitcher :—

" SHERIFFALTY.

" INDEPENDENT CANDIDATE.

" The subscriber begs leave respectfully to offer himself to the consideration of the voters of the city and county of Baltimore, at the ensuing election, as a candidate for the office of Sheriff.   For the information of his fellow citizens, (friends he has none, nor ever had any,) he would state, that he is in political principles independent of either party ; in religion a Christian ; in moral character an honest man ; and by profession, an artist whose business it is to shorten the fire-wood of his neighbours, without the use of axe—vulgarly called a wood sawer.

" Although he is aware, that there are men who will refuse their support on account of his occupation, yet he believes that a majority of his enlightened fellow citizens will rather look at the man, than the sawer—at the abilities, than the coat that covers them.   And although he cannot boast of having been in the employment of the Sheriff, yet he flatters himself that his qualifications for the office would not suffer by a comparison with either of his competitors. Should he succeed in obtaining a majority of the suffrages of his fellow citizens, he pledges himself to fulfil the duties incumbent on the Sheriff of Baltimore County, with impartiality and fidelity.

JAMES MOONEY."

A wood sawer in America, is scarcely a step higher in the scale of society than a coal porter is with us; the occupation is a cleaner one, but otherwise they appear to be pretty much upon a level. His occupation is to cut fire wood into the proper length for burning, and to carry it from the street into the yards or dwelling houses of his employers. The joke however does not end here. An advertisement appeared a few days after those which I have quoted, intimating that the rival candidates would, on a particular evening, publicly address their fellow citizens in support of their respective claims to their suffrages. This, it is said, must have been inserted by some wag, who wished to amuse himself and his fellow citizens at the expense of the aspirants for popular favour; yet the requisition operated imperatively on the appearance of the candidates, for had any one of them declined the wordy contest, it would probably have so displeased the independent electors, as to nullify completely his chance of success. I attended under the piazza of the market place, to hear the speeches; day light was gone, but a few candle ends were stuck against the wall, and by the faint light which they afforded I saw an orator elevated somewhat above the crowd of auditors, and haranguing away very much to their satisfaction, as their frequent shouts and cheers testified. I could not get near enough to understand the topics of discourse, or his mode of illustrating them; nor could I learn whether or not the wood sawer was the declaimer, but the word *wotes* once or twice reached my ear, from which it was evident, that he kept well in view the main object of his thus essaying the art of Demosthenes. [7]

The aspect of Baltimore in religious matters, is upon the whole a gratifying one. The Popish cathedral and college, and the Socinian chapel, must have suggested to you that error is not wanting; but it is gratifying to be assured that its influence is not paramount. Many are to be found here who have not bowed the knee to Baal; and faithful pastors who are not ashamed of the gospel of Christ, nor indolent in proclaiming and defending it.

Notwithstanding the magnificence of the Socinian chapel, the sect I understand is not numerous. A few individuals are wealthy, and sanguine in their expectation, that the splendour of the building, and the philosophical character of the worship, will induce persons of cultivated taste to flock to their standard. Those with whom religion

---

[7] Such a scene as this, is peculiar to the southern part of the country; in most of the northern and eastern States advertising for office is unknown.

is a matter of taste, may perhaps so choose to manifest their claim to it; but so long as they thus legislate between God and their own consciences, it is a matter of comparative indifference in what place they profess to worship him.

Of the disciples of the church of Rome, the number is much greater; for Maryland is, as regards the United States, the head quarters of popery. It was indeed originally a popish colony, established by the efforts of George Calvert, Lord Baltimore, a nobleman who having become a convert to the Romish faith, after filling offices of high political trust under James the First of England, relinquished his situation at court, and turned his attention to the establishment of this colony. He showed however by the laws which he promulgated, that he continued free from one of the most odious characteristics of popery; religious liberty was established and maintained in its fullest extent, so much so, that when the Quakers were persecuted in New England, and the Puritans in Virginia, both found an asylum in Maryland, in which they enjoyed unfettered liberty of conscience and of worship.

During my residence here I have attended worship with congregations of various denominations. In two Episcopalian churches, the contrast as to doctrine and ceremonial was as great as can be well supposed. In the first I heard a discourse from a passage in the apocryphal book of

Ecclesiasticus :—" Fear not the sentence of death."
The sermon to which this was a prelude, was, I
am sorry to say as apocryphal in its doctrine as in its text. God speaking by an inspir-
ed prophet has said, " their fear toward me is
taught by the precept of men,"—a passage too
appropriately applicable in the present instance.
The interior of the church in which this clergy-
man† officiates is very splendid; rows of Corinthian columns support the roof and galleries, and a
great deal of gilding and decoration is lavished
around. Some rags of popery are unfortunately
interspersed—*Laus Deo,* for instance, upon the
organ, and I. H. S. encircled by rays upon the
back of the pulpit.

The other Episcopal church was as remarkable
for plainness as this for decoration; not that it was
of the ' barn order' of architecture, as an English
traveller is said to have wittily remarked of some
of our Scotish churches, but it was free from much
of the tinsel finery which is so often seen. The
clergyman and the service were both equally distinguished by their adherence to simplicity. The
minister in a black gown went at once into the
pulpit, where he read prayers and delivered his
sermon, without conforming to the usual but unmeaning ceremonial of changing his robes. When
the sermon was finished, he offered up an extem-
poraneous prayer, of considerable length and
great devotional fervour. To complete the exter-

8

* St. Paul's
† All Souls Kirk

nal characteristics of this congregation, they have no organ,[7] or instrumental music of any kind; a choir is placed in front of the gallery which leads the singing, and the congregation pretty generally unite in it.✻ These variations from customary form in Episcopalian worship, are favourable symptoms of the spirituality of the congregation, and its pastor; and I am most happy to add, that the discourses which I heard delivered from the pulpit, were in the strictest sense of the word evangelical; the grand truth of the gospel that "Jesus died for sinners and rose again for their justification," was perspicuously stated and powerfully enforced. I have heard this minister on various occasions, and the opinion which I first formed respecting him has been strengthened by every subsequent discourse. He expounds the scriptures in an instructive and convincing manner, and the doctrine of the cross is the leading topic of his illustration. " Seek ye first the kingdom of God and his righteousness," was his text on one occasion; and on another he addressed us from that passage in the prophet Isaiah, " Behold ye that kindle a fire and compass yourselves about with sparks; walk in the light of your fire, and in the sparks that ye have kindled. This shall ye have of mine hand, ye shall lie down in sorrow !"

[7] It is not without some degree of regret that I have learned that an organ has been subsequently introduced. (1822.)

Q 2

from which he proclaimed a loud alarm to unbe-
lievers, grounded on the certainty and awfulness
of future punishment.

The ministrations of this worthy and zealous
pastor are not confined to the Sabbath.   On
Wednesday evening he has a meeting for prayer,
in a large room near his church, at which a very
considerable number attend.   I did not hear of
this till I had but one Wednesday to spend here,
and have of course been but once present.   At
this meeting nearly all the formalities of Episcopa-
lianism were excluded; the prayer book was not
introduced, and excepting that the assembly kneel-
ed during prayer, there was nothing from which
any one could have guessed at the denomination
to which it belonged.   After a fervent prayer, the
minister addressed us from the words of Hosea,
" O Israel, thou hast destroyed thyself; but in me
is thine help !"—the address was a faithful and
affectionate exhortation to Christians to recollect
what by nature and practice they were, and in
whom their hope was found.   On concluding the
address he called by name on one of the members
of his congregation to pray; after prayer the
females present sang a hymn, the minister then
named another person, who also prayed; a second
hymn was sung, and the blessing was pronounced.

The spirit of the discourse which I heard in
the Presbyterian church, was, I regret to say,
very inconsistent with the scriptural statement that

7

" there is none other name under heaven given among men, whereby we must be saved," but the name of Jesus Christ of Nazareth. The preacher virtually set aside the doctrines of original depravity, regeneration and atonement; not indeed by in so many words denying them, but by inculcating sentiments which were utterly subversive of their belief.

The pastor of the church in connexion with the Associate Synod, I have heard several times with much pleasure. " If I wash thee not, thou hast no part with me," was selected as a text, from which he successfully refuted the reasonings of those who make mere morality, and personal reformation, the ground of a sinner's hope. On a communion Sabbath he illustrated, from the words in the Song, " I am my beloved's and my beloved is mine," the intimate and endearing connexion which exists between Christ and his church, and the consequent obligation under which every member of it is placed, to exhibit in all his conduct the influence of that spiritual union, without which he is altogether dead. The number of church members is not very great; a row of tables was placed down the centre passage, and they were only twice filled. Those who first sat down were addressed by the pastor, who then seated himself as a communicant at the second distribution, at which another minister presided.

At the Baptist church I have been once present. The pastor is a native of France, who speaks the

Q 3

English language with tolerable correctness, but not without a considerable tinge of his vernacular idiom and pronunciation.   He selected as his text, " This child is set for the fall and rising again of many in Israel ;" and if his discourse was not characterized by any great degree of talent, it was as I thought scriptural in doctrine.

The Cameronian or Reformed Presbyterian congregation is a small one, but a young and zealous minister of very considerable talent has been recently appointed over it, under whom it is not improbable that the number will increase.

Sabbath schools have been in operation in Baltimore for some time, but the inhabitants have not yet fully learned to appreciate their value.   The teachers tell me that they find considerable difficulty in persuading the children to attend regularly, and too frequently the parents, when spoken to on the subject, show by their answers that they almost consider it a favour to the teachers to allow their children to be taught by them !   I was sorry to observe however in a school which I visited, that even some of the teachers were frequently either late or absent; so long as this lukewarmness exists among them, it is in vain to expect punctuality in the scholars.

The Sabbath is upon the whole decorously observed in Baltimore, yet I have seen black girls sitting in the evening at Washington's monument selling peaches, and it was but too obvious that they were not without customers.

If I may judge from my own experience, the natives of Baltimore are exceedingly kind and hospitable to strangers.   I met almost every where with an open-hearted warmth of reception which is exceedingly gratifying.

LETTER IX.

Washington, September, 1818.

I HAVE now the honour of addressing you from
the metropolis of the United States. It is common
here to call Washington ' the city in the woods,' I
was therefore somewhat surprised to find that there
is little or no wood near it. The aspect of the city
indeed would have been much improved by a few
trees, to fill up the vacancies, and thus afford
something for the eye to rest upon between one
group of buildings and another. The soil however
is poor, and the probability is that there has never
been much timber on this spot; I have noticed
none of the stumps which are usually left when the
forests are felled.

The position which was selected for the Federal
city, is a point of land embraced by the forking
of the river Potowmak, about one hundred and

twenty miles from its junction with the Chesapeake, and about two hundred and fifty miles from the sea. The principal branch of the river flows down upon the west, and unites with the smaller one from the eastward in front of the city. Ships of war of the largest size can float in safety three or four miles above the junction of the streams. It was expected that this situation would have been found particularly favourable to commercial enterprize, and consequently that the population would rapidly increase; hitherto however these hopes have not been realized. Georgetown, about a mile above upon the principal branch of the river, monopolizes the inland trade, and Alexandria seven miles below intercepts the foreign; while the barrenness of the surrounding country is discouraging to settlers. The prosperity of Washington therefore seems to be in a great measure dependent on its advantages as the seat of government, and these in a new government, economical even to penuriousness in the salaries of its public officers, cannot as yet be very important.

Great however or trifling as they may be, the city did not till very lately enter upon the full enjoyment of them. Great doubts were entertained whether it was to continue to enjoy the presence of the chief magistrate, and supreme legislature; and capitalists felt no inclination to invest their money in property which was not otherwise valuable, and which might therefore be suddenly and irretrievably depreciated. But what the natives were at a loss to decide, the British may be said to have decided for them. The burning of the Capitol and the President's house during last war, has settled the question, and it seems to be now ascertained to the satisfaction of speculators, that Washington is to continue, at least for a considerable time to come, in the undisturbed enjoyment of her metropolitan privileges. How an event so disastrous should lead to consequences so propitious, may seem to be in some measure a paradox, but it is one of easy explanation. When the rebuilding of these edifices came to be the subject of deliberation in Congress, the question as to the removal of the seat of the legislature was necessarily discussed; national feeling however co-operated powerfully with other considerations to influence the decision, the proposal was at once scouted, and the requisite amount was enthusiastically voted to efface the memorials of British triumph. Preparations were instantly made to rebuild the Capitol and President's house with more than their original splendour, the value of building ground and of houses took an immediate start, and Washington now exhibits abundant proof of the enterprize and elasticity of the national character.

The original plan of the city was on a most extensive scale. A parallelogram more than four miles and a half long, and two miles broad, was regularly divided into streets, avenues, and squares, and should the anticipations of its founders be realized, this will after all be but the nucleus of the future metropolis. The streets are laid out towards the cardinal points, crossing each other at right angles; the avenues intersect these diagonally, so as to avoid the tiresome sameness which is observable in Philadelphia, and extensive squares are to be placed at the crossings of these transverse lines. The avenues are from 130 to 160 feet wide, the streets from 80 to 110.

To lay out the plan of a city however is one thing, and to build it is another; of all the regularity and system which the engraved plan exhibits, scarcely a trace is discernible upon the ground. Instead of beginning this gigantic undertaking in a central spot, and gradually extending the buildings from a common focus, they appear to have commenced at once in twenty or thirty different places, without the slightest regard to concentration or the comforts of good neighbourhood; and a stranger looking round him for Washington, sees two houses here, and six there, and a dozen yonder, scattered in straggling groups over the greater part of three or four square miles. Hitherto the city does not contain above fourteen thousand inhabitants, but these have taken root in so many different places, that the public crier, a black man whom I have just seen performing the duties of his calling, is obliged to make the circuit on horseback. Pennsylvania Avenue is almost

the only place where the line of communication
can be traced. This stretches from the Capitol to
the President's house, a distance of rather more
than a mile, with double rows of gravel walks and
poplar trees, and a good many buildings have been
erected on both sides of it, with considerable attention to neatness and continuity. This however
is but a small portion of the intended avenue,
which according to the plan is to stretch out in
both directions, till it is eventually about four miles
in length.

A short way from the Capitol, Pennsylvania
Avenue is crossed by the Tiber, a little muddy
stream, or creek according to American phrase-
ology, which filters through flags and rushes into
the Potowmak. A wooden bridge is thrown over
it, but the stage driver who brought me from Baltimore preferred fording the stream, to cool the feet
of his horses. Moore in one of his poetical epis-
tles dated from the ' Modern Rome,' makes a sar-
castic allusion to this classic stream, but, if Weld
is correct, the name was given it by some early
settler, before the site was chosen for the Federal
city, and therefore its founders are not answerable
for what at first seems a piece of ridiculous affec-
tation.

As the Capitol and the President's house are
both of freestone, we are rather disappointed to
find them covered with white paint. The grain
of the stone is indeed rather coarse, and a good

many hard white pebbles are imbedded in it, yet the walls would certainly have looked better in their natural colour. The truth is, the buildings were both originally unpainted; but the unceremonious usage which they received from our troops at the capture of the city, so effectually begrimmed their visages that it was found impossible to eradicate the defilement. To have demolished and rebuilt the walls, would have been a very costly expedient, and as the least of two evils, the painter's brush was resorted to; here and there however, above some of the windows, the black wreathings of the smoke are still discernible through the white covering.

Of all the errors committed on our part during that unhappy war, this was undoubtedly one of the greatest. Setting aside the question as to its abstract defensibility, on the ground of retaliation or otherwise; it is obvious that it was in the highest degree impolitic; because its immediate effect, as might have been anticipated, was to break down party spirit among the Americans, and to unite them as one man in support of the measures of their government. The firebrand was no sooner applied to their Chief Magistrate's Palace, and the National Senate House, than thousands who had from the beginning maintained a systematic opposition to the contest, at once came forward and took up arms to maintain it; their national feelings were roused into powerful excitement, and

they joined in one loud voice of execration at the destruction of their national edifices.   Our ministers,
had such been their object, could not have devised
a more effectual way of strengthening Mr. Madison's hands.   Had our troops recorded their triumph upon the front of the buildings, and left
them uninjured, the indignant feeling of humilia-
tion would have wreaked itself on those by whose
imbecility the capture of the city had been occa-
sioned, and who escaped so nimbly when it fell
into the enemy's hands.   But the burning of the
buildings saved Mr. Madison; a thirst for revenge
of the insult overcame every other feeling, and the
war became thenceforward, what it had not been
before, decidedly popular and national.

No more than the wings of the Capitol had been
completed when the city was captured.   They
have risen from their ashes, and are again roofed
in; the centre also is beginning to appear above
the ground.   Each wing is pretty nearly square,
and consists of a basement and principal story,
surmounted with a low circular dome bearing a
small lantern.   The basement is rusticated, and al-
ternating with the windows of the principal story
is a row of Corinthian pilasters.   The centre is to
resemble the wings in its general features, but will
project considerably beyond them.   The building
wants simplicity.

The House of Representatives will occupy a

magnificent hall in the right wing of the building.
The Speaker's chair is to be placed near the wall,
and the seats and desks of the members will be
disposed in semicircular lines round it, rising as
they recede. Beyond the members' seats will be
an extensive gallery for spectators. Twenty-two
splendid Corinthian columns with corresponding
pilasters are to surround the outline of the semi-
circle, and the wall behind the Speaker's chair.
Part of these are already erected. The shaft of
the columns is of a kind of puddingstone from
the banks of the Potowmak, composed of numerous pebbles of various sizes and colours, and ad-
mitting of a good polish. The capitals, which
were executed in Italy, are of white marble, and it
is said cost upwards of a hundred pounds sterling
each. The appropriate foliage of this splendid order is most exquisitely elaborated. I am disposed
to think, however, that had the columns been altogether of white marble, the effect would have been
much more pleasing. As the workmen are still
busy with this hall, I am unable to be more minute
in my description.

. Among a multitude of workmen who are now
employed on the building, I chanced to enter into
conversation with an Irish marble cutter, who has
been here for some months. He said that a large
proportion of the workmen were from Scotland
and Ireland; their wages are from one to two
dollars a day, it costs them about three dollars

a week for board and lodging, and he is able to save about one half of his wages.

The President's House is a handsome building of considerable dimensions, occupying the brow of a rising ground near the bank of the river and commanding a most extensive and beautiful prospect. In the centre of the side towards the river is a semicircular projection, and Corinthian pilasters,[1] rising between the windows to the full height of the building, support a balustrade which goes completely round. The principal front however is on the other side, rather a singular arrangement I think, where a plain but lofty portico of four columns rises above the entrance door. Among heaps of rubbish around the building I saw several fragments of the old capitals of the pilasters, which had been cracked by the conflagration and thoroughly blackened with smoke.

The walls of the President's House are now restored to their former condition, and carpenters and upholsterers are busied in giving to the interior more than its original splendour. The walls of some of the rooms which have been finished are covered with very rich French paper studded with gilt flowers. I saw in one of them a full length copy in oil of Stuart's portrait of Washington; the original is, or at least was, in the possession of the

---

[1] I speak from recollection in calling these pilasters *Corinthian*. My memorandums are silent on the subject, and it is therefore not impossible that I may be wrong.

Marquis of Lansdown, and is the same from which the beautiful engraving by Heath was executed.

Along with the Capitol and the President's House the public offices were also destroyed. There were at that time only two, which have been rebuilt, and other two have been added; they are appropriated to the departments of the treasury, state, navy, and war, and stand near the President's House, two on each side.

No less than five libraries perished in that ill-fated conflagration, two of which were of considerable value. Many public documents and some curious papers connected with the history of the revolution were also destroyed. As a recommencement of a national library, Congress has purchased from Mr. Jefferson the whole of his private collection, containing about ten thousand volumes. In turning over a few of Mr. Jefferson's books I found a copy of Professor Dalzel's Collectanea Græca Majora which bore the following inscription in the autograph of the editor :—

Ad virum honoratissimum

et doctissimum

THOMAM JEFFERSON S. R. S. Edin.

a fœderatis Americæ civitatibus

ad Regiam Majestatem Christianissimam

cum plenâ potestate legatum

hunc librum observationis causâ

misit

ANDREAS DALZEL.

A similar one appeared on the Minora.

8

The models in the Patent Office would have
shared the fate of the Capitol, but for the intercession of the person who had charge of them.
He strenuously pled with our officers that they
might be spared, representing that they had no
relation to warlike affairs, that many of them were
ingenious and useful, and that to destroy them
would be to wage war against the arts, and against
general improvement.   This appeal was effectual,
and the models were left uninjured. Its success
makes one regret that no such intercession took
place on behalf of the libraries and national archives,
to which the same argument applied with tenfold
force. A gentleman who witnessed the whole process of destruction, stated to me his opinion that
General Ross would probably have been induced
to abstain from the destruction of the Capitol and
the President's House, had suitable exertions been
made by the civil authorities.   The whole of these
however, officers of state and local magistrates, re-
gardless of all but their personal safety, took to
their heels by common consent, and left the public
buildings to their fate.   Old Anchises should have
shamed them all :—

> " Vos agitate fugam !
> Me si cœlicolæ voluissent ducere vitam,
> Has mihi servassent sedes.   Satis una, superque,
> Vidimus excidia, et captæ superavimus urbi."

The Patent Office exhibits a singular assemblage

R 3

of nicknacks, for the greater part of the models
seemed to me to deserve no better appellation,
though I dare say they are quite as important as
many of those useful inventions which are every
month recorded in the corresponding office in
London. A boat was pointed out to us which was
to be propelled by machinery, but it unfortunately
turned out that the machinery was a sufficient load
for the boat without any other cargo. The frame
of a tent bed made of iron graced another shelf;
but the originality of the invention was more than
questioned by some wag, who had written on the
label affixed to it ' Og King of Bashan had an
iron bedstead.'   Patent churns were numerous ;
and if you search minutely, patent cradle-rockers
and patent brooms may also be discovered. Our
conductor particularized as an invention of real
utility, a machine for cutting iron nails; the introduction of which has completely superseded,
throughout the United States, the use of hammered
ones.

The expense of obtaining a patent here is only
thirty dollars; £6, 15s. sterling. The securing
of copy right is a still cheaper process. One copy
of the book is deposited in the Secretary of State's
office, and a fee of sixty cents, about half a crown,
is paid to the clerk of the District where the author
resides, for an entry of the claim ; another half
crown is paid for a certified copy of this entry,
which must be advertised for four weeks in the

newspapers, and copied at full length on the back
of the title page of the book. ∴The term of copy-
right is fourteen years, but in the event of the
author's surviving, a repetition of the same process
secures it for other fourteen. There is a good deal
of cumbrous and unnecessary machinery in all this,
but it is much more favourable to authors and en-
terprizing publishers than the exaction, as with us,
of eleven copies of the work, however voluminous
and expensive. There is one impolitic regulation
on this subject; an alien cannot hold copy-right
until he has resided in the country at least two
years at one time. Poor encouragement this for
an emigration of authors, to give a stimulus to the
national literature ! Not only is an alien deprived
of the power of personally holding copy-right, he
cannot even convey a title to another person. Were
the ' Great Unknown' to cross the Atlantic, and to
continue the manufacture of his literary ware at
the usual rate of three publications per year, by
which he would at home, according to report, net
at least three or four times as many thousands of
pounds sterling, for two whole years he could not
gain a dollar by his writings; he might publish
them, but before three days flew past,² two or three

---

² Rapidity of publication is as well understood in America as any
where. I copy the following from a New York newspaper which
has recently reached me (May, 1823):—

 " *Despatch in printing.*—The new novel, Peveril of the Peak,
was received from England in New York on Monday at Ten A. M.

pirated editions would make their appearance, without his having it in his power to suppress them. There is at least a semblance of good policy in most of the American statutes respecting foreigners, and by some of them considerable advantages are offered to emigrants, but the framers of this law seem to have regarded *quilldrivers*, as a race by no means likely to increase the energies or resources of the nation; and therefore as an effectual barrier to the importation of such learned lumber, they have condemned them to a state of pauperism for two whole years after their arrival, proclaiming all that they may produce during this period to be lawful prey to depredators of every kind. The same impolitic, and so far as I can see, unjust law, applies also to patents.

The navy-yard, about a mile south east of the Capitol, occupies nearly forty acres of ground, on the margin of a small inlet of the eastern branch of the river. Before visiting it I had neglected to

and was printed, published, and sold on Tuesday, within 28 hours after the same was received. Another English copy of the same work was received per the Custom House, New York, at Twelve o'clock on Wednesday—at One o'clock forwarded to Philadelphia by the mail. In Philadelphia it was printed on Thursday, and on Friday 2000 copies were put in boards by Six o'clock in the morning. The English copy of Moore's Loves of the Angels was taken out of the Custom House in New York on a Monday in February last, —at Eleven o'clock A. M.; was immediately sent to Philadelphia, and 250 copies of the work printed were received at New York on Thursday following by Eight o'clock A. M. and the same copies were sold and circulated that afternoon."

provide myself with an introduction to the commanding officer, and reached the gate before I recollected that this would be necessary. As the
only remaining chance, I walked boldly past the
sentinel, hoping to get in unchallenged; ere I had
gone many paces, however, the serjeant of the
guard hailed me, and having ascertained that I
was an interloper ordered me to turn. I made no
remonstrance, but observing at a short distance
from the gate a marble monument, I asked and
obtained permission to inspect it. I found it to
be a monument to the memory of some American naval officers, who fell several years ago in an
attack on Tripoli. It consists of a column upon a
square base, surmounted with an eagle, and surrounded by allegorical figures as large as life. The
shaft of the column bears the beak and stern of
three vessels of the antique form, projecting from
it at equal distances from each other. The figures
are allegorical of History, Fame, Commerce, and
America. History is in the act of recording on
her tablet the heroic achievements of the departed
warriors; Fame has mounted upon the base to
crown them with laurel; Mercury carrying the
cornucopiæ, as the representative of Commerce,
bewails their untimely fate; and Columbia, a beautiful female decorated with feathers, is pointing
two little chubby boys, one of whom carries the
Roman fasces, to the commemorative device. On
the front of the base is a sculptured basso relievo

representation of the bombardment. The other three sides are occupied with inscriptions; one contains the names of those who fell, another intimates that the monument was erected by their brother officers, and on the third is inscribed—

FAME HAS CROWNED THEIR DEEDS,

HISTORY RECORDS THE EVENT,

THE CHILDREN OF COLUMBIA ADMIRE,

AND COMMERCE LAMENTS THEIR FALL.

This last inscription is, to say the least of it, superfluous, for the art of the sculptor is worth nothing if it requires such an expositor under it. The monument was executed in Italy and is very beautiful, but the spectator regrets to observe that the fingers of some of the figures have been broken off. We are not left in doubt as to the perpetrators of this outrage, for a small square tablet bears the mortifying information—

MUTILATED

BY BRITONS,

25TH AUGUST, 1814.

This inscription might also have been spared. It is not at all improbable that some of our soldiers, in the wantonness of victory, may have been the guilty individuals, for the monuments in Westminster Abbey abundantly manifest the propensity which prevails in the inferior classes of our country-

men to similar acts of vandalism; many of the
smaller figures there, have been deprived not only
of their fingers, but of their heads, and the
real cause of wonder with respect to this one is,
not that so much but that so little mischief was
done. The person who ordered the inscription,
however, should have reflected that it immediately
suggests the question " How came ' Britons' to be
here ?" and it is possible, if the answer to this question is followed up by others which naturally occur, that the disgrace of allowing the fingers to be
taken off, might eventually appear to be at least as
great as that of having done it. A few years hence,
nothing could have been seen in Washington to
remind a visitor of its having been once in an enemy's hands, but so long as this monument remains
in its present state, the humiliating fact is conspicuously recorded.

Postscript, February, 1819.

A second visit to this city has given me an opportunity of visiting Congress, which was not in
session when I was here formerly.

The Senate and House of Representatives meet
at present in plain brick buildings close by the
Capitol, where temporary halls have been fitted
up for them. The galleries of both houses are
open to every person; I found in them auditors of
every description, workmen without their coats in
one place, and elegantly dressed females in an-

other. The utmost quietness and decorum however prevailed.

The President of the Senate wears no costume; he appeared in a blue coat with gilt buttons, and occupied a plain elbow chair with a small canopy over it. Each senator has a writing desk before him, and many of them were either writing letters or reading newspapers. They were all in plain dresses, and many wore jockey boots.

I found the Senate discussing the propriety of making compensation to a British subject in Upper Canada, for a small vessel which had been captured by an American cruiser on Lake Ontario, before the declaration of war. The vessel had been sold, and the proceeds paid to the clerk of one of the Districts of the State of New York, to await the decision of a court; the court decided that the capture was illegal and ordered restitution, but in the mean time the clerk had become a defaulter and eloped. A bill had in consequence been brought into the Senate, containing a provision for making good to the owner of the vessel the sum which he had thus lost Various individuals spoke shortly on both sides of the question. Some opposed the bill, on the footing that the individual aggrieved ought to have recourse upon the legal securities of the District Clerk, and said that it would be giving to a British subject an advantage which would not have been conceded to a citizen of the United States. I had however the pleasure

of hearing the Hon. Rufus King, one of the senators for the State of New York, speak warmly in
favour of the bill. He said that the nation was
bound in honour to make good to a foreigner the
decision of the court; that in similar circumstances
an American citizen would have most certainly
obtained redress in Great Britain, and that he
had never known an instance of such a decision
there, in which prompt and ample compensation
had not been made. The question was ultimately
carried in the affirmative.[3]

The house of Representatives was in committee,
and I found Mr. Sargeant of Philadelphia concluding a long speech, which had been begun the preceding day, on the subject of the United States'
Bank. A committee, which had been appointed to
investigate some alleged misconduct on the part of
the Bank Directors, had reported an opinion to
the House that the charter of the Bank had been
violated, and consequently forfeited entirely. Mr.
Sargeant combated this opinion, and was arguing
while I was present, that although the facts were
proved to be exactly as the committee had reported,
the charter was still good, for such delinquencies
had all been provided for in that charter, and

---

[3] The bill alluded to was afterwards thrown out in the House of
Representatives, in consequence, as a member of the house told me,
of it being somehow or other informal. I cannot help suspecting
however, that disinclination to the object of the bill was the true
cause.

specific penalties attached to them; the penalties he
said were incurred, but the charter was still perfectly valid.   I left this gentleman speaking, and
his opinion in the end prevailed.

The aspect of the House of Representatives is
still less dignified than that of the Senate.   The
house was pretty full, but many of the members
were lounging beside the fire reading newspapers,
others were clustering round the windows, and few
eyen of those who remained at their desks were
attending to the orator, most of the others being
busily engaged in writing letters, and some carefully
weighing them to ascertain that the enclosures did
not exceed the weight which their franks covered.
In the House of Commons, it struck me that the
members showed a good deal of indifference to the
discussions which were going forward; the triple
bows of the wigged messengers between the door
and the bar, seemed sufficiently childish; the
peremptory order of the Speaker, ' strangers withdraw,' somewhat uncivil to strangers; the confusion which took place in clearing the gallery, and
the elbowing and pushing at filling it again, not
a little annoying and vexatious; but after all there
is more senatorial decorum in the House of Commons than in the House of Representatives.   It
appeared singular that so many members should
attend the debates while so few seemed to be in-
terested in them, and I thought that those whose
legislative exertions were confined to gazing out at

the window, or toasting their toes at the fire,
might with more propriety enjoy themselves so at
home. I have since learned from a member of
the House, as some explanation of this, that in
place of forty members constituting a quorum as
in our House of Commons, it requires in the
House of Representatives a majority of the whole
number. The total number of members, which
is increasing every year, is at present 118, consequently at least 59 must be assembled at every
deliberation, and as a great many subjects are
necessarily of a local nature, and interesting to
very few, it is no wonder that many should avail
themselves of the newspapers, or of pen and ink,
to 'give time a shove.' The question which I
heard discussed was one that regarded the existence
of the United States' Bank, which had been established but two or three years before, chiefly with
a view to facilitate the financial operations of government; and in which a great deal of money had
been made and lost, by sudden and unprecedented
fluctuations in the value of its stock, which after
rising from 100 to upwards of 150, had recently
fallen to 93. It was however no way surprising that
they should be tired of a speech which had lasted
two days, and that on a subject which had engrossed a great part of the session, to very little
purpose; the orator is esteemed one of the ablest
men in the house, but an animated debate is one
thing, and a lecture another. Instances are not

wanting of members occupying the floor for three successive days; the house adjourning when they get tired, to resume the thread of discourse the following day. The writing desks are bad things, were it for no other reason than that they encourage indolence and inattention; the benches of the House of Commons scarcely admit of lounging; besides it is to speak and not to write that the members are sent to Congress.

It would not however be fair to try the American Congress by a comparison with the British Parliament. There is little similarity either in the materials or in the manner of their construction. In America, a young, thinly peopled, and republican country, almost every person is engaged in the active business of life; and the equality of succession to property, and the necessarily frequent division of it, prevents almost entirely the accumulation of large fortunes. A great proportion of those who compose her representative assemblies are men of no wealth and sometimes of little education, many of them second rate lawyers, others merchants, well stored with commercial information, and a few who find a seat in Congress a convenient thing were it only for the salary which is connected with it.[4] Great

---

[4] Eight dollars, thirty six shillings sterling, for every day that Congress sits, with an allowance of the same sum for every twenty miles that the member has to travel to and from Washington. A seat in Congress is worth rather more than two hundred pounds sterling a year.

Britain on the other hand is an old country, over-flowing with population, where a monarchy, heredi-tary nobility, and feudal tenures, are necessarily connected with large fortunes, and with the entire leisure of their possessors for legislative or other pursuits ; a country where many receive an educa-tion expressly intended to qualify them for the service of the state, and where many members of the representative assembly, so far from requiring a stipendiary compensation for their attendance, are able to expend immense sums in procuring their election. Yet with all these disadvantages the wisdom and integrity of the American Congress have ere now put to shame the more practised politi-cians of Europe, and her diplomatic agents have often evinced themselves more than a match for the starred and titled plenipotentiaries of our own and other countries.[5]

[5] In a review in the North American of Tomline's Life of Pitt, some remarks occur on the usages of Parliament and Congress which I doubt not will interest the reader. The article alluded to is written with much candour and good sense, and the reviewer expresses him-self respecting George III. and his favourite minister, in terms of kindliness and approbation which we should hardly have expected from a republican critic. In alluding to the King's letters he says, " we think the character of a monarch who could manifest such undeviating firmness, such remarkable good sense, and such devotedness to the con-stitution of the country, deserves to be recorded and published." On Parliament he makes the following observations :—

" We cannot but observe that the habit of offering exaggerated and unmeaning commendation to talents and learning, has been long practised in the House of Commons, and abounds especially with those who are politically opposed, and whose measures are at the same

The building of the Capitol has advanced so considerably since the period of my former visit, that several apartments in the right wing have been finished, and one of them is now occupied by the Supreme Court of the United States.

This Court is almost the only one which has adopted an official costume; in all the inferior courts throughout the country, except I believe those of South Carolina, the judges are to be distinguished from the counsel or the jury, only by their position

time the subject of violent and, to our feelings, unbecoming crimination and condemnation.   Neither of these habits is to be observed in the same degree in the debates of the American Congress.   Part of this difference may be accounted for, from the circumstance that as the government has no representative, no minister in either branch of Congress, the principal cause and stimulant of personal censure or compliment do not exist; for one naturally leads to the other.

" There are several peculiarities in the British House of Commons, that procure vast facilities and advantages to individuals endowed with great talents.   The first peculiarity is, that the discussion is confined exclusively to half a score of members, for during the great debates to which we have referred in this article, seldom more than that number took a part.   It is true that occasionally there starts up in these debates a new member, who makes what the reporters call a maiden speech, which is heard with great attention, reported with great care, and then, in all probability, the name and the voice are for ever lost, amidst the din and shouts of the chiefs of the epic. In those maiden speeches we have observed that the most fatal symptoms are well set and well prepared sentences and periods, certain moral truisms, and frequent references to the Greeks and Romans.   Such symptoms are commonly mortal.   But unless these members speak with promise, they are heard a second time with great indifference, and finally scraped and groaned down, if the less positive expression of the feeling of the house, by one half the members going into the coffee rooms, and the other half going to sleep, is not accom-

on the bench. This is probably a point on which the Americans have mistaken the reverse of wrong for right. It was all very well to lay aside the antiquated and grotesque wig, which buries the intellectual organ under curls and pomatum, but to strip the administrator of justice of every distinctive garb, was depriving the judicial office of an accessory which has a very powerful influence on the human mind.

The Supreme Court is composed of five judges, and I found them like the House of Representatives

panied by a prompt obedience. Whatever advantages may attend the practice of allowing the Commons to select their own orator, it has an air of great rudeness; and we are able to account for it in no other way, than by supposing that it was first exercised under some of the arbitrary sovereigns to stifle those who were obnoxious to their censure. No such custom existed during the Commonwealth, and as many members spoke then as now in our Congress.

" A good deal also may be learned from the constitution of the house. Many members are sent there merely to vote, who would probably greatly displease their patrons if they should attempt to speak. Many who spend great sums to obtain seats have no constituents, and an M. P. is only serviceable to such persons for the purpose of franking letters, of adding a little to their distinction and dignity in drawing rooms and at dinner parties, and as being one proof, besides the right to carry a gun, that a man is a gentleman. And after all, this is one of the least expensive modes which an Englishman adopts to prove his claims to that condition. Men seldom go to Parliament for the mere purpose of speaking for their constituents, inasmuch as the members of the House of Commons have constituents in a more enlarged sense than the members of the American Congress, because from the circumstances of our country, there is a much greater variety of interests in it requiring more specific representation. It often happens, however, that instructions are sent in relation to certain privileges and customs, by virtue of which members of the House of Commons are forced to speak; as was most particularly the case in

engaged upon the subject of the United States'
Bank. This national establishment is by no means
popular throughout the Union, and some of the
State legislatures imposed a very heavy tax upon
the branches which were established by it within
their jurisdiction. The payment of this tax was
resisted by the Directors, and the question as to the
right of the local governments to impose it, came
before this court in the form of an appeal. During

relation to the Slave trade. There is, notwithstanding, as we observed
above, a class of members whose sole object is the honour and dignity
of a seat in Parliament. They care little in what way they get there;
and being there, have no particular constituents, whose interests they
are called to defend. They have not as with us each thirty five
thousand constituents who can reward them with their approbation
and often with State offices, whereby such weight is acquired at home,
that the national government is forced to extend its patronage to
them:—by which circuitous process many a member of Congress,
who would be immediately defeated on the floor of the house in any
attempt to gain influence by taking an active part in the debates, is
still enabled by means of long speeches painfully composed and
delivered, and diligently printed and distributed through the post
office, to acquire or sustain that popularity among his constituents,
which shall send him up to the executive government, clothed in all the
importance of a powerful local interest.

" Another peculiarity of the English House of Commons is, that a
division takes place every night; and though such a subject as the
Missouri question might be renewed for twenty nights successively in Committee on the State of the nation, yet there is always a
certain degree of variety, freshness and animation, produced by a
knowledge that a decision is about to take place. This peculiarity
is a consequence of that which we have mentioned. The third peculiarity is, and it is one which will always make greater orators than we
are likely to have in this country, because they will always have more
experience, that men of great promise and ambition can enter the

the few minutes that I spent here I heard some arguments, by the counsel for the State which had imposed the tax, in support of its right to do so. He argued that by the Federal compact the various States had relinquished in favour of the general government only the rights of levying importation and exportation duties, of making war and peace, and of coining money; but that they still retained and daily exercised the power of imposing internal taxes, and that there was nothing in the constitution

House of Commons at the age of twenty one, an age at which an individual seldom can enter even a State legislature in this country. Fox was chosen to the house before he was twenty, Pitt before he was twenty two.

" Again, Parliament is a profession, and a man becomes as skilful and as much attached to it as to that vocation by which he earns his bread. The distinguished men in the House of Commons, remain there twenty and thirty years, and many of them as long as they live. The consequence of this is, that they not only become greater men themselves, but learn to do the business of the nation with greater despatch. We believe that the members from Virginia and South Carolina remain in Congress longer than those from the New England States, where an opposite policy, either arising from the caprice of the people, or the circumstances of the candidate, prevails to a fatal degree." *North American Review No XXXIV. pp.* 157, 189, 190.

By the constitution of the United States, every thirty thousand free citizens are entitled to send one member to the House of Representatives, who must be at least twenty five years of age, and holds his seat for two years. Qualifications for voting vary in the different States; in that of New York, every one possessed of a freehold of the value of 50 Dollars, £11, 5s. sterling, or occupying a tenement of the annual rent of forty shillings currency, that is 22s. 6d. sterling, is entitled to vote. This is to all intents and purposes universal suffrage.

S 3

of the United States' Bank which freed it from the operation of this right. I did not remain to hear the speakers on the opposite side, but the decision was ultimately given in favour of the bank.[6]

In an adjoining room is at present exhibited Colonel Trumbull's[7] painting of the Declaration of Independence. This is one of a series of historical paintings commemorative of the Revolution, which Congress has commissioned this artist to execute for the purpose of adorning the new Capitol. In commemorating the event which gave birth to this great republic, the painter has placed before us most of the individuals who composed the general Congress, by which the Declaration of Independence was decreed and published; and the

[6] An article in the North American Review makes reference to to this decision in the following terms:—" The first question was whether Congress had the power to incorporate a bank, and in the discussion of it, the incidental and derivative powers of Congress, the choice of means and their adaptation to the ends proposed, were fully examined, and the court determined that the creation of a banking corporation, was a proper and fit instrument for carrying on the fiscal operations of the government.—The court having determined that Congress had the power to erect a bank, and this power being necessarily supreme, it followed that a power to create implied a power to preserve; the unlimited power of a State to tax was a power to destroy; and the exercise of such a power being inconsistent with the preserving power, it could not coexist with it, but must yield to that power which was in its nature sovereign and supreme." *North American Review No XXVI. pp.* 110, 111.

[7] This gentleman carried arms in the early part of the Revolutionary war, and his father, who was then Governor of the State of Connecticut, was distinguished by his efficient exertions in the same cause. Before the conclusion of the struggle the son quitted the

committee which was appointed to frame the document, in the act of presenting the draught at the table. I am no judge of such compositions, and may therefore be guilty of presumption in expressing any opinion, but I cannot help thinking that the painter might have selected a more interesting period of time in this great transaction. The picture indeed cannot be said to represent the *declaration* of independence, for though the instrument had been drawn up, it had not yet been adopted, much less made public. The great object has been to get together into one group the portraits of those self-devoted men, who were the principal actors in this event; but in effecting this the result is really calculated by its total want of epic grandeur to

army and went to London, to study painting under his distinguished countryman the late President West. Here he was arrested under suspicion of being a spy and committed to the Tower. The following anecdote respecting his confinement, which I transcribe from Professor Silliman's Travels in England, deserves to be universally known. It is given in Colonel Trumbull's own words.

" I was arrested at 12 o'clock at night of the 19th November, 1780, in London, on suspicion of treason—I was then principally occupied in studying the art of painting under Mr. West. Mr. West well knew that his attachment to his native country gave offence to some individuals who were about the king's person. He therefore went the next morning early, to Buckingham house, and requested an audience of the king; it was granted, and he proceeded to state the origin and nature of his acquaintance with me, concluding that whatever might have been my conduct in America, he could conscientiously state to his Majesty, that since my arrival in London the principal part of almost every day had been passed under his roof, and indeed under his eye, in the assiduous study of his profession, leaving little or no time for any pursuit hostile to the

remind us somewhat of the Vicar of Wakefield's family picture. To the left of the canvass in the foreground is seated the President, John Hancock, immediately before him is the committee, consisting of Jefferson, Franklin, Adams, Livingstone, and Sherman, the last of whom is in the quaker garb, and Jefferson is in the act of laying the scroll upon the table; to the right and in the back ground are the other members of Congress, most of them seated, and all as demure as if they had been assembled to attend a funeral. No opportunity was afforded in such a scene for the delineation of character, or the representation of animated action and intense emotion. The painter was not

interests of Great Britain. The King after a moment's hesitation, made this answer : ' Mr. West—I have known you long ; I have confided in you ; I have never known you to mislead me ; I therefore repose implicit confidence in this representation. This young gentleman must in the mean time suffer great anxiety ; he is in the power of the law, and I cannot at present interfere. But go to him, and assure him from me, that in the worst possible legal result, he has my royal word that his life is safe.' Mr. West came to me with this message immediately, and you may well believe that it softened essentially the rigours of an imprisonment of eight months." Professor Silliman adds,—" If you consider who was the King's prisoner, that he was in his view a rebel, and had just come from fighting in an elevated station against him ; that his father was a most active and efficient head of. one of the most actively and inveterately rebellious States, I think you will allow that the King's answer, which amounted to this—" should the courts of law condemn him to death, I will save his life by a pardon," constitutes one of the finest passages of kingly history, and could never have proceeded from a little mind."—*Silliman's Travels in England*, 3d Edit. Vol. I. p. 241.

allowed to give scope to his imagination; for the
event was too recent, the room in which it took
place too plain, and too well known, and the meeting of a deliberative assembly altogether too com-
mon-place a subject, for any considerable deviation from historical truth. The real value of the
picture consists in the portraits, all of which are
believed to be authentic; most of them Mr. Trumbull executed from life, for he began to collect the
requisite materials many years ago, and the rest
he copied from pictures believed to be accurate.
Of the portraits of a small number of those who
composed the Congress no trace could be discovered, and these are therefore not introduced.[8]
The size of the picture is eighteen feet by twelve.

As to the state of religion in Washington I can
give you but little information; I have not happened to spend a Sabbath in it. There are two
Episcopalian churches, one Presbyterian, one Associate Synod, two Baptist, two Methodist, one
Quaker, and one Romish. The Popish chapel is
dedicated to St. Patrick; it is a small building and
somewhat paltry, but I saw in it a beautiful white

---

[8] Of the fifty six individuals, whose signatures are affixed to the
Declaration of Independence, only the following five were living
while I was in America; so far as I know the number has not been
subsequently reduced:

> Thomas Jefferson, of Virginia.
> John Adams, of Massachusetts.
> Charles Carroll, of Maryland.
> William Floyd, of New York.
> William Ellery, of Rhode Island.

marble font for *holy water* which has lately arrived from Italy. Standing within the basin is a figure of St. Patrick about twelve inches in height, wearing the mitre and sacerdotal vestments, and in the attitude of pronouncing a benediction on the water. The execution is beautiful, and we cannot but regret that one of the noblest of the fine arts should be so frequently pressed into the degrading service of this system of delusion.

Of society and manners here I know almost nothing, for both my visits have been very short. Respecting public characters I must be equally silent, for none have been pointed out to me except Commodores Decatur [9] and Rodgers. They are both plain looking men, and were not in uniform when I met them. Commodore Rodgers' affair with the Little Belt, before the commencement of last war, has given us an idea that he is a man of more bluster than bravery; Americans however say that we are mistaken, and that during the war while commanding a fifty gun frigate, he actually hove to, and offered battle to a British seventy four gun ship, which she declined ;—I cannot help however doubting the accuracy of this story.

[9] This brave officer has fallen in a duel since my return. That detestable practice is lamentably prevalent in America, and is sometimes accompanied with circumstances of peculiar barbarity. In going the second time to Washington, I passed the ground where a duel was fought but a week or two before, with muskets, at ten paces distance ; the one party was shot dead on the spot, the other dreadfully mangled, and I believe afterwards died.

LETTER X.

LETTER X.

Alexandria, September, 1818.

THE secluded spots where men of historical celebrity have spent their hours of rural or of literary
retirement, have ever been objects of interest to
the traveller. A powerful principle in our nature
impels us to seek a kind of personal familiarity,
with those scenes which occupied the attention of
the more distinguished individuals of our race; to
which they hastened for relaxation from the fatigues
of public life, and where they sought and found a
solace amid all its disquietudes. The Sabine farm
and the Tusculan villa have awakened the enthusiasm of many a classical wanderer, and could the
field be identified in which Cincinnatus was dragged away from the unfinished furrow, to drive
back destruction from his country's gate, how
would the heart of the patriot bound within him
as he paced its surface, and recalled the circumstances in which the unambitious Dictator returned

to the plough! The classic soil of Italy it may
never be my favoured lot to tread; but America
can boast of a hero second to none of Greek or
Roman fame, and who could land upon its shores
without the eager desire to visit Mount Vernon?

This beautiful spot is about ten miles below
Alexandria, on the banks of the Potowmak. In
leaving the Federal city the traveller crosses the
main branch of the river by a wooden bridge, very
nearly a mile in length. This is a simpler erection
than the bridges over the Schuylkill; it has no roof,
and consists of a floor of planks, supported upon
piles, and level from end to end. A portion of it
suspended in the form of a drawbridge at the deepest part of the channel, admits of the passage of
vessels up or down the river. There is a similar
bridge of very nearly the same dimensions, across
the Cayuga lake, in the upper part of the State of
New York. These prodigious structures may be
mentioned as proofs, among many others, of the
enterprize and perseverance which are essential
ingredients in the national character.

The country between Washington and Alexandria is similar to that around the capital. The
surface of the ground in the neighbourhood of the
river is agreeably diversified with woods, mea-
dows, and sloping inequalities; but the soil, wherever it has been broken up, seems to consist principally of light sand and gravel.

Alexandria, seven miles from Washington, is

a commercial town of considerable activity, containing about nine thousand inhabitants. The harbour is capacious, and vessels of the largest size can float alongside the wharfs. The town is compactly built, on the plan of Philadelphia; the streets are wide, well paved, and better lighted at night than those of most American towns. The principal articles of export are flour, biscuits, and tobacco. It is said that 200,000 barrels of flour have been inspected here in the course of a single year. The biscuits, or *crackers* as they are universally called, are quite celebrated, and are shipped in large quantities to all parts of the United States, and even to the West India islands. The principal manufacturers are two worthy countrymen of ours; one of whom served his apprenticeship in a well known baker's shop at the ' foot of the burn close,' in our native city. It is quite gratifying to meet with a townsman when one is so far from home, and this pleasure I have unexpectedly enjoyed more than once. In Baltimore I became acquainted with an old gentleman, now a marble cutter, who wrought as a mason at the erection of ' Spreull's land,'[1] and who could talk to me of several individuals whom I intimately knew.

One of the cracker bakers was rather unceremoniously used, by some of the British ships of war which went up the Potowmak to Alexandria, to

---

[1] A *land* is the Scotish appellation for a tenement which accommodates several families under one roof.

9

co-operate, had that been necessary, in the attack upon Washington. They took the liberty, it seems, of emptying his cellars of a good many barrels of flour, without favouring him with any thing in the shape of payment. He acknowledges, however, that they performed the exploit in as civil a manner as could well be supposed; for when he went on board to represent that something by way of a fair exchange, would sweeten his recollections of the transaction very materially, the officers insisted on his sitting down and drinking wine with them to promote their better acquaintance, and after thus oiling the hinges of friendship, they dismissed him with many smooth words, and good natured recommendations to think no more about the flour. The old gentleman jocularly offered to sell me a bill on the British Treasury, for ' goods delivered.' We cannot help regretting that any one should have it in his power to relate such anecdotes of our naval commanders; they are not at all in accordance with the usages of modern warfare, nor with that honourable system which characterized the march of our armies through France. I cannot believe that it has been customary with our naval officers so to plunder private property in defenceless towns; and in such circumstances as the present, I should be inclined to hope that were an application made to our government, with proper evidence of the fact, reparation would yet be made. Our countryman, however, a good old gentleman, has set it down in his Ledger as a very ' bad debt.'

At Alexandria I was favoured with an introductory note to the Honourable Bushrod Washington, the General's nephew, and one of the judges of the Supreme Court, to whom Mount Vernon now belongs. I believe that strangers are politely received at the mansion house without any introduction, but it was of course more agreeable to be possessed of it, and I accidentally obtained the company of two young gentlemen who were going a pilgrimage to the same shrine. The road to Mount Vernon after running along for a short way within view of the Potowmak, strikes off into the woods on the right; the day was hot, and we found the shelter of the trees very grateful, but coming to a place where the road divided we chanced to take the wrong one, and after proceeding about a mile were indebted to a black girl for being set right again.

At the bottom of the avenue to Mount Vernon, the gate was opened to us by an old negro who had survived the master of his youth, and who now receives from many a visitor substantial tokens of the universal respect which is entertained for his memory. The avenue is narrow and in bad order, it has indeed more the air of a neglected country road, than the approach to a gentleman's residence. The mansion house, an old fashioned building of two stories surmounted by a small turret and

weathercock, stands on an elevated situation on the
western bank of the Potowmak; it is built of wood,
but the walls are cut and plastered in imitation of
rusticated freestone.   The back part of the house
is to the river; at the other side are two small
wings at right angles to the principal building,
and connected by piazzas which bend towards
them so as to form a kind of irregular crescent.
Opposite the hall door is a circular grass plot
surrounded by a gravel walk and shaded on both
sides by lofty trees; two beautiful chesnuts were
pointed out to me, which sprung from nuts planted
by the General's own hand.   On the two sides
are the vegetable and flower gardens, in the latter
of which is a greenhouse.[2]

The mansion house was originally built by
Washington's uncle,[3] who had served in the British navy under Admiral Vernon, and commemorated his regard for his commanding officer by the
name which he gave to his estate.   Some partial
alterations were made on the house by the General, but report says that he subsequently regretted

[2] In the British edition of Marshall's Life of Washington is a
very accurate front view of Mount Vernon; in Weld's Travels a
view is given of the back part of the house and the bank of the
river, but it is exceedingly incorrect.

[3] In Marshall's life of Washington, it is said that the house was
built by his elder Brother; my journal states his Uncle, and my
memory strongly corroborates its testimony as to the information
which was given me at Mount Vernon; it is possible however that
I may have misunderstood what was told me.

9

that he did not entirely rebuild it. It is an old fashioned, perhaps not a very comfortable residence, according to modern ideas of comfort, but it ought now to be considered sacred, and have the most unremitting care bestowed on its preservation. He will be worse than a Vandal who presumes to pull it down. In the hall hangs a picture of the Bastile, and in a small glass case above it is an ancient key, which formerly turned the bolt of one of the dreary locks in that house of sighs. It was sent out to Washington by the Marquis la Fayette, after the destruction of the Bastile, as an inscription affixed in his hand writing records. Over the mantel piece of one of the parlours is a small framed miniature of the General which was cut out of a piece of common earthen-ware. It is a singular fact that this is regarded by the family as the most accurate likeness that exists. The general contour of his face is well ascertained, and there is a strong similarity in most of the portraits: yet those who knew him best agree that there was a certain expression in his countenance, which is quite wanting even in Stuart's painting, and in the engraving which was executed from it. This very ordinary kind of daub, which was broken out of a common pitcher, and probably executed by some potter's apprentice, is said to possess more of this intellectual characteristic than any of the other portraits.

At the back of the house a lofty piazza stretches

T 2

along the whole length of the building, and before it the ground slopes rapidly towards the river
and soon becomes quite precipitous. On the bank
is a small tea-house, which affords a most commanding view of the surrounding scenery. The
Potowmak widens into a bay before you, and bending round the base of Mount Vernon, seems almost
to insulate the promontory on which it stands;
then sweeping in the opposite direction round the
projecting shore of Maryland, and lost for a time
behind its vast forests, it re-appears in noble expanse about ten miles below, with the sunbeams
flashing from its surface, and rolling its mighty
current into the yet more ample bosom of the
Chesapeake.

A little to the right of the tea-house, and nearer
to the edge of the bank, is the tomb of Washington. Here under the peaceful shade of oaks and
cedars, lie all that earth contains of him by whose
energy and patriotism the United States became a
nation! No venerable cathedral rears its arches
over his remains; no sumptuous mausoleum em-
balms his memory.

"Si monumentum quæris, circumspice!"

His country is his monument; his country's liberty
his only panegyric!

Washington in his will designated the spot in
which he wished to be interred, and particularly
directed that the body should not afterwards be

removed. The cemetery is nothing more than a plain brick vault, almost level with the ground; it is encircled by venerable oaks, and some beautiful red cedars are growing in the mould which covers the roof. Visitors were formerly allowed to see the interior, but some person having had the rudeness to strip part of the cloth from the coffin, all access to it is now forbidden. Subsequently to this prohibition, the servant who had been intrusted with the key conceived the horrible idea of robbing the vault, with the purpose of carrying off the body to Britain to exhibit it for money! His intention was happily discovered and the nefarious outrage prevented; it is difficult indeed to imagine how it could have been carried into effect without immediate detection, but the projector must have been a fool to imagine that such atrocity would have been countenanced in Britain, or that he would have been permitted for a single day to carry on so abominable a trade.

The State of Virginia applied to the relatives of the General for permission to remove the body to Richmond, to erect a monument over it; and it is said that notwithstanding the specific injunctions of the will, the family were persuaded to consent to this proposal. Several years however have since elapsed, and as no provision has yet been made for carrying the proposed plan into effect, it is generally believed that no claim will now be founded upon that permission. Congress it is reported wish to transfer the body to the seat of government, and to entomb it under the centre dome of the Capitol. If it is ever removed from its present situation certainly the Capitol is its only suitable resting place; no individual State should be allowed to possess a deposite which, if the family relinquishes it, is undoubtedly the property of the nation, and should pass into no other guardianship. Beyond all question however, the proper place for Washington's ashes is where they are. The secluded spot harmonizes with every idea which we have formed of his character, while the powerful influence of local associations, gives vividness to our conceptions, and intensity to our emotions. In the Capitol every thing would have an opposite tendency. It is a building which Washington never saw, and which is no way connected with his personal history; it has once been reduced to ashes, and what would in all probability have been the fate of the body, had the removal taken place before that event? In visiting the tomb of Nelson in the vaults of St. Paul's, it is not the wondrous achievements of the hero which chiefly occupy our thoughts—there is nothing in those damp and dismal caverns which is at all in harmony with such recollections. An attendant pilots you, by the yellow glimmering of a tallow candle, through tartarean darkness to the quarry of granite under which he is buried, and while wandering round it, your thoughts are engrossed by the opening which was made in the floor of the church to lower the coffin through, and of the prodigious labour it must have cost to pile up over it such ponderous masses of stone—Nelson you scarcely think of, your ideas are all engaged about those who buried him. At Mount Vernon no such distraction takes place. You look round upon scenery which Washington often contemplated; you tread the turf over which he walked; you see the gardens in which he amused himself; the trees which he planted; the house, the rooms, the chair, which he occupied; and the humble vault which he himself chose for the repose of his dust. Every thing is consistent—the effect harmonious and powerful—Mount Vernon alone should be Washington's grave.

On the opposite bank of the Potowmak, and a very little way farther up, is a small intrenchment, named Fort Washington, which commands the channel of the river. Had it been vigorously fought when our vessels went up the river to Alexandria, it is believed that it might have arrested their progress. When our troops however were on their march to Washington, the officer who commanded it blew it up and made off. There was no sufficient cause for such a proceeding, yet it is said that he obeyed to the letter the orders of his superior officer. I was quite gratified to hear from a gentleman of Judge Washington's family, that

T 4

when the British ships of war passed Mount Vernon, they honoured the memory of the departed hero by lowering their fore-top-sails; and their bands, as another gentleman informed me, played Washington's March. That was indeed a manifestation of most correct and honourable feeling, on the part of the commanding officer.

I have mentioned that the avenue to Mount Vernon had a neglected appearance, I am sorry to add that similar neglect pervades other parts of the establishment. The flower garden and greenhouse have nearly gone to decay; the tea-house on the bank of the river is almost in ruins, indeed its upper story, from which a more extensive view may be obtained, is at present totally inaccessible, for the ladder to it retains but one foot at top and another at bottom. Even the door of the vault is to all appearance so crazy, that I think a kick would go far to knock it to pieces. It is painful to observe such an air of desolation, in so interesting a spot, and I would cherish the hope that it will speedily be removed.

After having spent an hour or two at Mount Vernon, Judge Washington politely invited us to accompany him to a Barbecue, which was to take place in the afternoon close by the road to Alexandria. The very term was new to me; but when explained to mean a kind of rural fête which is common in Virginia it was not difficult to persuade us to accept the invitation.

The spot selected for this rural festivity was a very suitable one. In a fine wood of oaks by the road side we found a whole colony of black servants, who had made a lodgement since we passed it in the morning, and the blue smoke which was issuing here and there from among the branches, readily suggested that there was cooking going forward.

Alighting from my horse and tying it under the shadow of a branching tree I proceeded to explore the recesses of the wood. At the bottom of a pretty steep slope a copious spring of pure water bubbled up through the ground, and in the little glen through which it was stealing, black men, women and children, were busied with various processes of sylvan cookery. One was preparing a fowl for the spit, another feeding a crackling fire which curled up round a large pot, others were broiling pigs, lamb, and venison, over little square pits filled with the red embers of hickory wood. From this last process the entertainment takes its name. The meat to be *barbecued* is split open and pierced with two long slender rods, upon which it is suspended across the mouth of the pits, and turned from side to side till it is thoroughly broiled. The hickory tree gives, it is said, a much stronger heat than coals, and when completely kindled is almost without smoke.

Leaving the busy negroes at their tasks—a scene by the way which suggested a tolerable idea of an encampment of Indians preparing for a feast after

the toils of the chase—I made my way to the out-
skirts of the wood, where I found a rural banqueting-
hall and ball room.   This was an extensive platform
raised a few feet above the ground, and shaded by
a closely interwoven canopy of branches.   At one
side was a rude table and benches of most hospitable dimensions, at the other a spacious dancing
floor; flanking the long dining table, a smaller one
groaned under numerous earthen vessels filled with
various kinds of liquors, to be speedily converted,
by a reasonable addition of the limpid current from
the glen judiciously qualified by other ingredients,
into tubfulls of generous toddy.

A few of the party had reached the barbecue
ground before us, and it was not long ere we mustered altogether about thirty ladies and somewhere
about an hundred gentlemen.   A preliminary cotillon or two occupied the young and amused the
older, while the smoking viands were placed upon
the board, and presently Washington's March
was the animating signal for conducting the ladies
to the table.   Seating their fair charge at one side,
their partners lost no time in occupying the other,
and as there was still some vacant space, those who
happened to be nearest were pressed in to occupy
it.   Among others the invitation was extended to
me, and though I observed that several declined
it, I was too little acquainted with the tactics of a
barbecue, and somewhat too well inclined to eat,
to be very unrelenting in my refusal.   I soon how-

ever discovered my false move. Few except those
who wish to dance choose the first course; watch-
fulness to anticipate the wants of the ladies, prevent
those who sit down with them from accomplishing
much themselves, the dance is speedily resumed,
and even those who like myself do not intend to
mingle in it regard the rising of the ladies as
a signal to vacate their seats. A new levy
succeeds, of those who see more charms in a
dinner than a quadrille, and many who excused
themselves from the first requisition needed no
particular solicitation to obey the second. The
signal for rising did not seem on this occasion to
excite much notice; and some prolonged their
sitting till they had an opportunity of bestowing
on the third levy, the pleasure of their company.
Some experiments began now to be made upon the
virtues of the toddy, and it was not long ere the
capacious lakes began to be effectually drained off.
Let me not be misunderstood however; I saw not
the slightest approach to intemperance. Jollity
and good humour were not wanting, but there
was nothing which trenched upon sobriety either
in speech or behaviour. There might be others
present besides Judge Washington who had seats
on the bench, but the judicial dignity was no way
compromised by any part of the proceedings.

While local politics and other matters engrossed
the conversation at table, others less inclined to the
sedentary position stationed themselves round the

dancers.   The cotillon was the favourite figure,
and the platform was just large enough to admit
of two at a time.   There ' music rose with its
voluptuous swell,' and exercise flushed the cheek,
and enjoyment brightened the eye of the fair Vir-
ginians.

But the sun drove on in its diurnal career; and
as my poor steed had fasted since early in the
morning, I thought it time to take leave of the
entertainment and make the best of my way to
Alexandria.   I left them about five o'clock, and
learned that very shortly after, the assembly broke
up.

LETTER XI.

LETTER XI.

Albany, October, 1818.

I HAVE now made two passages in a steam boat on
the Hudson; the river in which this system of
navigation was first successfully attempted. Of
this honour we cannot deprive America, and it
were unmanly and ungenerous to attempt it. A-
mericans are very far from pretending that Fulton
was the first projector of steam vessels, but they
are entitled to maintain that he was the first who
succeeded in bringing them into operation; and
there can be little doubt that in doing so, he very
materially improved on the plans which others had
proposed.[1]

---

[1] " The merit of a great original conception cannot be denied,
but the talent of its possessor is frequently eclipsed by the improvements it afterwards undergoes, and the splendid combinations in
which it is involved. The Marquis of Worcester seems to have
had the first crude notion of a steam engine—Newcomen constructed one, but the name of Watt is immortalized in the history

We can state with truth that experiments were made on the Forth and Clyde Canal many years ago to ascertain the practicability of what has now succeeded; and although it is said that the attempt was abandoned solely in consequence of the injury which was done to the banks, by the violent agitation of the water, yet it is not probable that the result was in other respects very encouraging, for had it been so, there was sagacity enough in our countrymen to have transferred the system to river navigation.

Fulton was indebted for his ultimate success to the efficient aid of the late Mr. Livingstone, Chancellor of the State of New York, who supplied the funds for his experiments. Mr. Livingstone's friends were at first inclined to censure what they esteemed his temerity in embarking in so *vapouring* a scheme, but a few months wrought a wonderful change in their opinions, and his family is now reaping the rich fruits of his enterprize. The only legislative encouragement which the projectors received, was an exclusive right for a term of years, of navigating steam vessels in the

---

of the arts as the efficient author of the invention.   The application of steam to the propelling of boats is not a new idea; nay, experiments were long since instituted to prove its efficiency. The bright and ample honour of our Fulton, is, that he succeeded where others failed, and that he carried into execution what others had abandoned as impracticable and senseless," *North American Review, No. XXXIV. p.* 242.

waters of the State of New York.[2]   This was however a prodigious monopoly, for it includes the navigation of the Hudson, Lake George, Lake Champlain, the lower part of Lake Erie, the American side of Lake Ontario and the St. Lawrence, Long Island Sound, and the bay of New York. Large sums have been paid to the Company by various individuals for liberty to navigate different portions of these waters.

The steam boats on the Hudson are much larger than any which we have seen at home, and in many respects very different in their construction. I have sailed in one which contains upwards of 120 permanent sleeping births, and these are frequently inadequate to the accommodation of the passengers.[3]

[2] This monopoly was for a time silently acquiesced in by the neighbouring States, but of late they have begun to manifest great discontent that New York should send shoals of steam boats into their harbours, while their steam vessels are not allowed to enter those of New York; and as a retaliatory measure the States of New Jersey and Connecticut have interdicted New York steam boats from approaching their shores. Lawyers of great eminence have given it as their opinion that the power which has been assumed in granting this monopoly, is completely inconsistent with the Federal Constitution, and the question is now awaiting the decision of the Supreme Court at Washington.   (1822.)

[3] The vessel here alluded to is the Chancellor Livingstone, which was the largest and finest steam vessel in the United States, while I was there. . Through the kindness of a friend in New York, and another in Greenock, I am enabled to subjoin an accurate statement of the Chancellor Livingstone's dimensions, power of engine, rate of sailing, and cost, as contrasted with those of the

The distance from New York to Albany is reckoned at 160 miles, and the fare including

Majestic, the largest of the steam packets which ply between Greenock and Liverpool. The American Vessel was built in New York, and her engine made at Fulton's works at Powle's Hook; the British one was built by Mr. Scott of Greenock, and Mr. Napier of Glasgow furnished the engines.

	CHANCELLOR LIVINGSTONE.	MAJESTIC.
Length of Keel	154 feet	125½ feet.
Length of Deck	165 feet	144 feet.
Breadth of Beam	32 feet	23½ feet.
Breadth over the Paddle Boxes	—	39½ feet.
Draught of Water	7¼ feet	9¼ feet, with 80 tons fuel.
Register Tonnage, exclusive of the Engine Room	—	239 tons,
Register Tonnage, including the Engine Room	520 tons	345 tons.
Nominal power of the Engine	75 horses	2 of 50 horses each.
Diameter of the Cylinder	40 inches	40 inches each.
Stroke of the Piston	5 feet	3½ feet.
Diameter of the Paddle Wheels	17 feet	16 feet.
Breadth of the Paddle Wheels	5 feet 10 inches	6½ feet.
Diameter of the Fly Wheels	14 feet	None.
Average velocity in smooth water by Steam alone	8¼ knots an hour	10½ knots an hour.

three meals is seven dollars, or thirty-one shillings and sixpence sterling. An additional dollar how-

	CHANCELLOR LIVINGSTONE.	MAJESTIC.
Greatest velocity with favourable wind and tide	12 knots . . .	15 knots.
Cost of Vessel, rigging and furniture	£11,700 sterling .	£10,000 sterling.
Cost of Engine . .	£13,500 sterling .	£5,000 sterling.
Total cost	£25,200 sterling .	£15,000 sterling.

It will be observed from the above statement, that the cylinder of the Chancellor Livingstone's engine is exactly of the same diameter with that of each of the two in the Majestic, yet the power of the American engine is rated at 75 horses, and the others at 50; this is accounted for by the longer stroke of the piston in the American engine. The machinery of the Chancellor Livingstone rises 4½ feet, and the top of the piston 15 feet, above the deck. In the Majestic the machinery and piston are all under the deck. This arrangement, which is universal in the American steam boats, gives a longer stroke to the piston, and the increased power enables them to enlarge the diameter of the paddle wheels; it however raises the centre of gravity so much, that it seems at first sight scarcely capable of application to vessels which go to sea, and carry sails, which none of the American boats did when I was there. Since my return however, a steam ship has been established between New York and New Orleans, and a steam brig between New York and Norfolk, which are rigged with schooner sails, and in both, as the cuts in the newspapers indicate, the machinery and piston rise considerably above the deck. The Majestic has three masts, with schooner sails, and spreads when in full sail 3000 yards of canvass. Her shortest passage from Liverpool, a distance of 245 miles, was performed in 19½ hours, exclusive of stoppages, which is at the rate of rather more than 12 knots an hour, and she once ran from the Craig of Ailsa to Greenock, a distance of 60 miles, in 3 hours and 40 minutes, which exceeds 15 knots an hour. The Chancellor

ever is levied by the State from each passenger, and appropriated to the fund for cutting the great canal, between Lake Erie and the Hudson.[4]

Livingstone burns pine wood, and carries her fuel on wings projecting in front of the paddle boxes. She has two chimnies, several feet asunder, and the pilot occupies a position a little behind them upon a stage raised above the machinery, steering by a wheel, from which tackling is carried round to the rudder.

The American steam vessels have nothing corresponding to our second cabin or steerage. The principal cabin of the Chancellor Livingstone is 54 feet long, and 7 feet from the floor to the beams; the width in feet I have not, but it accommodates with ease two parallel ranges of dining tables, of the full length of the apartment. The Ladies' cabin is upon deck, immediately over the other, and is 36 feet long. The forward cabin is entirely a sleeping apartment, 40 feet long, with a longitudinal partition in the centre. The sleeping births are along the sides of the vessel, in two tiers; the principal cabin contains 38, the forward cabin 56, and the Ladies' 24, in all 118; but these are often inadequate to the accommodation of the passengers, and mattresses are laid out upon settees on the floor. There are other 17 sleeping births, for the captain, pilot, and crew, making a total of 135. She carries 24 hands, including engineers, sailors, stewards, cooks, &c. She was built when materials and workmanship were very high; it is said that she could now be constructed for little more than one-half.

[4] This tax like every other was exceedingly unpopular, and it is obvious that although levied from the public its inconvenience was principally felt by the steam boat company, for passengers by the sloops, which are numerous and excellent, were not subject to it. So much was this felt, that the steam boat proprietors have subsequently found it their interest to relieve the public of it altogether, by compounding with the State for an annual payment of five thousand dollars. As this is a voluntary offset from their yearly profits, of more than eleven hundred pounds sterling, it is evident that they must have been very considerable. They have at the same time lowered the passage money to six dollars. (1822.)

7

We sailed from New York at nine o'clock in the morning. The weather was unfavourable to the enjoyment of the excursion, for the wind blew strong a-head and the air was piercingly cold; mere pleasure however was not my object, and I had no resource but to submit.

For a considerable distance the Hudson is the boundary between the States of New York and New Jersey. Jersey city as it is called is nearly opposite the lower extremity of New York, and about three miles farther up on the same side is a noted duelling ground, called Hoboken. Hither 'men of honour' resort from New York, to vindicate their claim to this envied appellation, and by eluding the laws of men and defying those of God, unanswerably demonstrate the extremity of their courage. A small white obelisk was erected here to mark the spot where General Hamilton fell, by the hand of Colonel Burr, but it is said to be going rapidly to decay. To Hamilton's genius the United States are indebted for some of the most invigorating principles in their national constitution, and had the political system which he advocated been more extensively adopted in the Federal compact, the republic would probably have made a nearer approach to a perfect constitution. It is much to be lamented that a life so valuable to his family, his country, and mankind, should have been staked on the decision of so unhallowed a tribunal. Burr was pointed out to me

U 3

in the streets of New York. He has never been tried for the offence, for as the duel was fought in New Jersey, the State of New York can take no cognizance of its result, and so long as the survivor keeps out of the territory of New Jersey, he is safe from the operation of its laws. Although the crossing of a stream, however, thus protects the person of the murderer, he cannot be said to have gone without punishment even of a temporal kind. The Republican party to which he at first belonged shun him as an apostate; and after having failed to ingratiate himself with the Federalists, he earned their thorough detestation, by sacrificing to his resentment the man who was their most illustrious ornament.[5]

[5] Close by Hoboken is Weehawken, a romantic spot about 200 feet above the level of the river, from which a most commanding prospect is enjoyed of the bay and surrounding scenery. In 1821 a lively little satirical poem was published by a Mr. Hallack of New York, from which the following descriptive stanzas are extracted :—

> " Weehawken, in thy mountain scenery yet,
>   All we adore of nature in her wild
> And frolic hour of infancy, is met;
>   And never has a summer's morning smil'd
> Upon a lovelier scene, than the full eye
> Of the enthusiast revels on—when high
>
> Amid thy forest solitudes, he climbs
>   O'er crags that proudly tower above the deep,
> And knows that sense of danger, which sublimes
>   The breathless moment—when his daring step
> Is on the verge of the cliff, and he can hear
> The low dash of the wave with startled ear.

7

About a mile above New York and nearly opposite Hoboken, is the village of Greenwich, now almost an integral part of the city. Around it are many neat buildings, the greater part of which, as well as the village itself, were erected in former times as a retreat from the yellow fever. [6] Above,

> Like the death music of his coming doom,
> And clings to the green turf with desperate force,
> As the heart clings to life; and when resume
> The currents in his veins their wonted course,
> There lingers a deep feeling—like the moan
> Of wearied ocean when the storm is gone.
>
> In such an hour he turns, and on his view,
> Ocean, and earth, and heaven burst before him.
> Clouds slumbering at his feet, and the clear blue
> Of summer's sky in beauty bending o'er him—
> The city bright below; and far away,
> Sparkling in golden light, his own romantic bay.
>
> Tall spire and glittering roof, and battlement,
> And banners floating in the sunny air:
> And white sails o'er the calm blue waters bent.
> Green isle, and circling shore, are blended there
> In wild reality. When life is old,
> And many a scene forgot, the heart will hold
>
> Its memory of this; nor lives there one
> Whose infant breath was drawn, or boyhood's days
> Of happiness were pass'd, beneath that sun,
> That in his manhood's prime can calmly gaze
> Upon that bay, or on that mountain stand,
> Nor feel the prouder of his native land."
>
> _Fanny, a Poem, Stanzas XCI—XCVI._

[6] The subsequent and repeated return of this malady, after an absence of many years, has again driven the citizens to Greenwich for shelter. (1822.)

Greenwich, the banks on the right slope with a gentle declivity to the water, and are in general thickly wooded; on the left they are frequently broken and precipitous. About fifteen miles up the river, Kingsbridge heights appear on the right, and below them Haerlem creek, [7] as it is called, which stretches with an irregular curve from the Hudson into Long Island Sound, giving to the Manhattan territory its insular character, and limiting the jurisdiction of the city corporation of New York.

The New Jersey shore becomes now bold and precipitous, and for several miles an abrupt wall of granite raises its bare forehead on the left, to a height of nearly two hundred feet. The Palisades, as this range has been most appropriately denominated, form a striking feature in the landscape; they are in general from two to three hundred feet from the water's edge, in some places the front has been broken, and irregular masses of rock tumbled downwards to the water, but for the most part it is smooth and perpendicular like the wall of an ancient fortress, while here and there a solitary pine tree, ' moor'd on the rifted rock,' seems, like the banner of a citadel, to wave a proud defiance from the edge of the cliff.

---

[7] The reader of Knickerbocker's History of New York will recollect that here the renowned sounder of brass, Antony Van Corlaer, met with his untimely fate, presumptuously essaying while half tipsy to swim across the creek ' in a dark and stormy night.'

With the Palisades terminates the State of New
Jersey, and we approach a wider part of the stream
which the early Dutch settlers dignified with the
appellation of the Tappaan Sea, but which was in
after times modified into that of Tappaan Bay.
This lake as we may call it is about ten miles long,
and the banks are from four to seven miles apart,
presenting a very considerable variety of landscape;
' here the bold promontory crowned with embow-
ering trees advancing into the bay—there the long
woodland slope sweeping up from the shore in rich
luxuriance—whilst at a distance a long waving line
of rocky heights throw their gigantic shades across
the water.' [8] In many places the ground has been
cleared of wood, and country seats and snug farm
houses, flanked by capacious barns, give variety
to the scene; in other situations however the for-

[8] Knickerbocker, Vol. II. Chap. 2.—Mr. Irving's fascinating
pen has now invested the beautiful scenery of the Hudson with all
the charm of classic ground. The reader need scarcely be reminded
of Rip Van Winkle and the Legend of the Sleepy Hollow. The
Sleepy Hollow we are told lies ' in the bosom of one of those spacious coves which indent the eastern shore of the Hudson, at that
broad expansion of the river denominated by the ancient Dutch
navigators the Tappaan Zee, and where they always prudently
shortened sail and implored the protection of St. Nicholas.' Let
not future voyagers up the river, fail to explore the sequestered glen
on their right, where Ichabod Crane sighed for the smiles of Katrina
Van Tassel, and where the ill-omened apparition of the gallop-
ing Hessian wrought such wo to the enamoured pedagogue. The
mountain side where Rip encountered the dolorous party at nine
pins, and partook of their soporific flagon, is yet at a distance.

ests are yet untamed, and afford the traveller a
glimpse of what America formerly was, when none
but the Indian traversed its shores, and only the
bark canoe glided over its waters.

On the traveller's left is Rockland county, a favourite resort of the early Dutch settlers; the race
is hitherto so unmixed, that very little English is
spoken in any part of the county. Some of the
land on the right contains good freestone, and has
been valued so high as 1500 Dollars an acre;
about £340 sterling.

I was particularly struck, in my progress up this
lordly stream, by the multitude of thriving little
towns which at short intervals stud its banks.
They are generally of wood, and some are obviously of recent origin, but in others a sprinkling
of brick buildings gives an aspect of comparative
antiquity and a promise of permanence to the
settlement. All of them have wharfs projecting
into the river, which are never without sloops
loading or discharging; in many of them banks
are to be found and courts of justice.

Schooners are a favourite kind of vessel in
America for the coasting trade, but in the rivers,
and particularly on the Hudson, none but sloops
are employed; in going up the stream we met a
great number going down before the wind to New
York. The Hudson river sloops are proverbial
for their neatness. They are not deep in the water, but very broad in the beam and sharp in the

bows; carrying a large cargo and giving space for
a comfortable cabin, but drawing little water and
sailing fast. The rigging is abundant and in excellent order, the vessel clean, showily painted,
and occasionally decorated with a handsome figure
head; altogether very superior in appearance to
any of our river craft. The number that are employed upon this river have been estimated at two
thousand, of 40 tons and upward.

Somewhat above the Tappaan Bay there is a
contraction and sudden bend of the channel, and
the stream, after washing in its descent the bases
of the mountainous range denominated the Highlands, makes a circuit round a bold head-land
called Verplank's Point which projects from the
eastern shore. The turn is so sudden, that in
going up the river the banks at a little distance
seem to close completely in, and it is not till you
have approached very near it that the narrow channel appears upon the left, through which the river
issues from the mountainous region. Before we
reached this part of our course a most agreeable
change took place in the weather. The clouds
broke, and the rays of the sun burst through;
the wind subsided into a gentle breeze, the temperature of the air became perceptibly milder, and
we entered the alpine region under the cheering
and beautifying influence of a lovely autumnal afternoon, rendered doubly enlivening by the previous contrast.

Verplank's Point commands a fine prospect of
the river. The bank swells up with a gradual but
rapid slope, the brow of it is crowned by a neat
family mansion, and a little below, the roof of the
tea-house appears from among the trees. Behind
rise the lofty hills among which we were about
to pass, and you could almost imagine yourself on
the margin of Lochlomond or some other of our
Scotish lakes. Our floating leviathan now entered
the narrow channel, and we were soon surrounded
by the Highlands of the Hudson. These are said
- to form a part of the eastern or Blue Ridge division of the Appalachian mountains; a continuation
of which skirts the boundaries of Connecticut and
Massachusetts, and pursuing a north easterly
course, passes through Vermont into Canada. The
height of the more elevated points on the banks of
the Hudson does not much exceed 1500 feet; they
are of course low in comparison of a great many of
the mountains of Scotland, but their effect in the
landscape is much more imposing than that of more
elevated masses in a hilly country.

An American mountain is in general very unlike
a Scotish one. Ours are bare craggy ridges, sharp
and angular in their outline, rearing a flinty peak
towards heaven; with perhaps a few, straggling
bushes scattered near the base, but more commonly the purple heather or yellow broom is all
that is found on the scanty patches of earth which
here and there cling to its sides. In America the

hills swell up in undulating curves, rounded gracefully off both at the base and the summit, and car-
peted completely over with dense forests of pine.
In the Highlands of the Hudson, however, there
is a partial intermingling of the Scotish character;
bare masses of rock project at intervals from among
the thick foliage, and creeping shrubs of various
kinds weave a net work round them. The mel-
lowing tints of Autumn were now spreading themselves among the forest leaves, imparting to the
scenery the richness and variety which are peculiar
to the season, and as our steam boat ploughed its
way along, the eye feasted itself on the ever-varying
landscape, or rested on the brilliant reflection in
the placid mirror below.

The ramparts of Fort Putnam now opened to
our view on the left, perched upon a natural platform about two thirds up the ridge. Events of
tragical interest, in the history of the Revolutionary
war, identify themselves with this fortress—events
which I feel no interest in recalling, but which can
never be forgotten while the name of André sur-
vives. Beyond Fort Putnam, on another elevated
flat of considerable extent, stands the Military
Academy of West Point,[9] containing 250 cadets.

---

[9] Geoffrey Crayon once more—here came down the fearful flaw of
wind from the mountains, which threw the sloop on her beam ends
in which Dolph Heyliger took his passage for Albany, and knocked
the vagrant dog into the water. On the left hand shore took place
his perilous adventure with the rattlesnake, his narrow escape from

This institution was established by the general
government a considerable time ago, but since last
war it has been fostered with assiduous care, and
now the tactics of Napoleon's school are taught in
it by men who discharged similar offices in the
polytechnic schools of France. A bare rock on
the opposite side of the river serves the young soldiers as a target, and its battered brow bears token
of their proficiency.

Nearly opposite to West Point is the Sugar Loaf
mountain, conspicuous by its regularly conical outline, and among a numerous succession of others
are the Crow's Nest, Butter Hill, [10] and New

the bullet of the Heer Antony Vander Heyden, and his subsequent
merry carousal with that jolly rover and his Indians. See the
second volume of Bracebridge Hall.

[10] A large rock which once crowned the summit of Butter hill,
1520 feet above tide water, now reposes on a sand bank in the
bed of the river nearly opposite West Point, far enough from the
shore for vessels to sail round it. An account of its transition from
its former to its present resting place is thus given by Colonel
Tucker, an officer who assisted in its removal.

" This famous rock, originally a native of the Highlands
above West Point, was situated on the extreme height of Butter
hill; when the morning fog was descending from the hill it
had a very beautiful appearance, not much unlike a horseman's
tent, or hospital marquee riding on the cloud. It was a common
amusement for the officers when off duty to roll large rocks from
the sides of those hills. These often set others agoing with them,
to the great terror of those persons who were below. One day
when this laborious amusement was over, Colonel Rufus Putnam
(in whose regiment I served as Lieutenant,) proposed going up to
take a peep of this curiously situated rock; it was found situated

Beacon. Anthony's Nose tosses high on the right
a bare peak of granite, and holds its name in virtue of the real or fancied appearance of its beetling
top.

The sun began to decline in its path as we approached the northern outposts of the Highlands.
The hills still rose on each side, like a mighty ram-
part guarding the more fertile country, but we could
descry before us the opening prospect of an extensive and diversified plain. The gigantic shadows
of the towering steeps were now stretching across
the water, and gradually rising above our heads.
We watched them climbing up the sides of the

on a flat rock of great extent and near the brink of a considerable
precipice, and hanging very much over it. Colonel P. believed
that it was moveable, and if once moved would roll over; and
falling from 20 to 50 feet, commence its route to the river. A few
days after, in the month of June, 1778, we formed a party of
officers, with our servants, who took with them axes, drag ropes,
&c. in order to procure levers for the purpose of moving the rock,
which we soon found was in our power. The levers being fixed
with ropes to the ends of them all, Colonel Putnam who headed
the party, ordered us to haul the ropes tight, and at the word CON-
GRESS, to give a long pull, a strong pull, and a pull altogether.
This we did; the levers fell, the rock rolled over, tumbled from
the precipice, and took up its line of march for the river ! The
party then had the satisfaction of seeing the most majestic oaks and
loftiest pines bowing down in homage and obedience to this mighty
traveller, which never stopped till it reached the bed of the river,
where it now lies. This party followed after in its path and were
astonished to see that rocks of many tons weight and trees of the
largest size were ground to powder. On arriving at the river the
party embarked, and landed to the number of sixty or seventy on

opposite mountains, rock and tree one after another dropping into obscurity, till at last the parting sunbeams overshot the last woody summit, and 'left the world to darkness.' Very soon, however, a bright harvest moon rose in the evening sky, and under her peaceful light we emerged from the mountainous region, and sped pleasantly onwards surrounded by the more fruitful plain.

During the night we passed on our left the Kaatskill mountains, [11] about 3000 feet high, which we had seen at a distance the evening before; we passed also many of the populous little towns which teem along the banks of the Hudson. When I went on deck next morning, a cold heavy fog rested on the surface of the water, so dense that even the banks of the river were in a great measure obscured. About nine o'clock we reached Albany, and were soon moored in safety at the wharf.

the rock, where Colonel Putnam broke a bottle of whisky, and named it ' Putnam's Rock.' "   *American Journal of Science, Vol. V. p.* 37.

[11] " Whoever has made a voyage upon the Hudson must remember the Kaatskill mountains; they are a dismembered branch of the great Appalachian family, and are seen away to the west of the river, swelling up to a noble height and lording it over the surrounding country. Every change of season, every change of weather, indeed every hour of the day, produces some change on the magical hues and shapes of these mountains, and they are regarded by all the good wives far and near as perfect barometers. When the weather is fair and settled they are clothed in blue and purple,

Albany though a small town in comparison of
New York, has been for a long time the seat of
the State legislature. It seems a remarkable feature in the domestic politics of America, that both
the Supreme and State Governments select remote towns, or more properly speaking villages,
as the scene of their legislative labours, in preference to the populous cities upon the sea coast;
notwithstanding the many inconveniences which
must necessarily result from being thus in a manner excluded from the living world, from access to
recent intelligence, and from means of ascertaining
the minds of their more intelligent fellow citizens
in sudden and difficult emergencies. We have an
annoyance at home somewhat similar in kind, although much smaller in degree, in those parts of
the country where some old decayed borough
tenaciously maintains its dignity as county town,
taking precedence of the younger commercial or
manufacturing cities, which have greatly outgrown

and print their bold outlines on the clear evening sky; but sometimes when the rest of the landscape is cloudless, they will gather
a hood of gray vapours about their summits, which in the last rays
of the setting sun, will glow and light up like a crown of glory."
The reader must have recognized the introduction to Rip Van
Winkle. The author has often regretted that the Sketch Book
did not appear until after his return to his native country; he
would otherwise have gathered more information respecting the
scenery which it has immortalized, and among the rest, about
the Kaatskill mountains, which on two other occasions he passed in
good day light, without anticipating that they were so soon to
acquire celebrity from the eventful story to which he has alluded.

it in wealth and population, but with us this is an unwished-for consequence of the gradual change which manufactures and commerce have produced in the country, and is an evil which we tolerate because it is not very easily removed. In America on the other hand it is a matter of deliberate and voluntary choice, resulting from the republican constitution and the prevalent system of universal suffrage. A jealousy exists throughout the agricultural districts of the influence of the larger cities, and no sooner do they begin to concentrate a considerable portion of the wealth and talent of the State, than the landholders take the alarm and vote the legislature away, some hundred or two of miles into the interior. In this way the Legislature of Pennsylvania was sent from Philadelphia to Lancaster, a small town sixty-two miles off, containing about six thousand inhabitants; and subsequently to Harrisburgh, thirty-five miles farther, with only between two and three thousand. It may thus travel onward till it is ultimately stopped by the State of Ohio, or the shores of Lake Erie; and for the capital of New York, it may be necessary hereafter to search somewhere about the falls of Niagara, or the lake of a Thousand Isles.

Albany was an early Dutch settlement and the streets are filled with Dutch names, of most difficult and cacophonous utterance. The town consisted originally of a single street, skirting the bank of the river, which takes a slight bend here; but it subsequently extended backwards very considerably, and some of the recent streets towards the north are spacious and well built, and as usual lined with poplars. In many places there is a singular mixture of poverty and splendour. A number of the old Dutch erections are still standing; small houses of red and yellow bricks, with the gable end to the street, having a door and window in the ground floor, a single window in the next, and above it the year of their erection embossed upon the surface in huge iron figures, and the whole surmounted with an iron weather-cock rusted upon the rod. There is an air of antiquity about these buildings, which is interesting in a country where antiquity is so rare. The modern erections exhibit the same tasteful style which prevails in New York and Philadelphia. Two or three of the public buildings are of white marble; one of them is surmounted with a very neat dome, but in another the effect of the marble wall is sadly disfigured by the untasteful addition of a red tiled roof. The Capitol, or State House has rather a neat portico, and a dome surmounted with a statue of Justice; it stands at the upper end of a very steep but wide street, running at right angles to the river. Near the Capitol is a very neat Academy with two wings, built of reddish coloured freestone.

Albany, notwithstanding its commercial and

legislative advantages, does not contain above
twelve or thirteen thousand inhabitants; the probability is, however, that a great increase of wealth
and population will take place, when the great
western canal is completed, which is to connect
Lake Erie with the Hudson, joining the latter in
the neighbourhood of this city.[12]

[12] In this stupendous undertaking New York has, to use the
words of the North American Review, "shown a spirit of enterprize, and set an example, which are above all praise. The great
canal of the Lakes is an undertaking of which the most powerful
government on earth might be proud. It is not more a glory to the
State than an honour to the country. The canal of Languedoc,
which has long been the boast of France, and perhaps we may say
of Europe, is not to be compared with this."

The western canal which was begun in 1817, and is now navigable for two-thirds of its whole length, commences at Black
Rock at the bottom of Lake Erie, runs parallel to the river Niagara till it joins the Tonawanta creek, makes use of its bed for
eleven miles and then stretches along, with but little deviation from
a straight line, till it approaches the Mohawk river, at a small town
called Rome, a few miles above Utica; thence it runs parallel to
the south side of the Mohawk, till it joins the Hudson near Albany.
Its whole length will be 363 miles, and the country through which it
passes is singularly adapted for canal navigation. After leaving
Lake Erie it rises by locks 48 feet, to the summit level, and
thence descends at intervals 601 feet, to the level of the Hudson.
In the whole extent there are 77 locks. Two levels extend severally
65 miles and 69½ miles, without locks, and between two points 240
miles apart there was not, it is said, a single yard of rock which
it was necessary to remove. Connected with this astonishing undertaking, is a corresponding branch beginning at Waterford on the
Hudson, eleven miles above Albany, and running northward to
Whitehall, formerly called Skenesborough, at the bottom of Lake
Champlain. A glance at a map of the United States will at once

In Albany is found a singular vestige of the feudal system, probably the only one that exists in the United States. A gentleman of the name of Van Rennselaer is Superior, or ' Patroon' as he is called, of the city and a great part of the surrounding country. His sway extends over a surface

show what an enormous extent of inland trade is thus laid open to the city of New York. The Champlain canal is 61 miles long; the whole length therefore of the two will be 424 miles. Each canal is 40 feet wide at the surface, 28 at the bottom, and 4 feet deep; the locks are 90 feet long, and 14 feet broad. The estimated expense of the Erie canal was five millions of dollars, and of the other, one million; in all £1,350,000 sterling; but by an unusual result in such undertakings, it is ascertained, from what is already finished, that they will be completed for probably £200,000 less. The literary journal to which I have already alluded says that the average cost of the Erie canal per mile, is 13,800 dollars, £3105 sterling, while the cost of canals in England has generally been about £5060 sterling, per mile, notwithstanding of the difference in the price of labour.

The Commissioners for completing these canals, in their Report to the legislature of the State presented 24th February 1823, which is now before me, state that boats have actually passed upon the Erie canal for a distance of more than 220 miles, and upon the Champlain canal throughout its whole extent, from Whitehall to Waterford. They do not anticipate the final completion of the works on the Erie canal till 1824, but they expect that by June 1823, it will be navigable throughout, from Rochester near the upper end, to Schenectady fourteen miles from Albany, and that by November boats may pass completely through into the Hudson. From the portion which was completed in 1821, they had anticipated a revenue in 1822 of about 40,000 dollars, but on making up the accounts it amounted to no less than 60,446 dollars, £13,600 sterling, while the whole expense of collection, attendance, and repairs, on the same portion, was but little above £1800.

X 3

about sixty miles in length, including two counties and a population of sixty or seventy thousand, of which about five thousand are his tenants. Report says that he is worth seven millions of dollars; upwards of a million and a half sterling. He is said to possess here a political influence very similar to

On the Champlain canal, during the same period, the receipts had been 3,625 dollars, £815 sterling; giving a total from the two canals of £14,415. Among the multitude of articles which passed on the Erie canal, were, 184,522 barrels of flour, 17,665 barrels of salt, 9,495 barrels of provisions, 4,872 barrels of ashes, 93,174 bushels of wheat, 46,822 bushels of water lime; the total weight merchandize transported was 35,444 tons. The market price of wheat in the upper part of the State had been raised fifty per cent., solely by the facility of transportation which had been already afforded.

The contemplation of this astonishing canal, leaves us at a loss whether most to admire the felicity of the first conception, the boldness of the undertaking, the skill and success with which it has been carried into effect, or the almost boundless prospect of commercial productiveness which it opens to view. To whom the merit of first projecting the work belongs, has now become a matter of animated controversy in America, but from the statements of various claimants, as noticed in the North American Review, it seems probable that no one individual is entitled to this honour; the proposals by two or three persons of water communications through portions of that district, resulted at last in the magnificent idea of one great canal, and Mr. De Witt Clinton, then governor of the State, was undoubtedly the most efficient instrument of promoting the undertaking. The legislature of New York by undertaking a work on their own responsibility to cost more than a million sterling, while the State revenue was under £140,000, the annual expenditure very nearly as much, and the population no more than 959,220 persons—carrying forward the work with such vigour that there is every certainty of its being finished within seven years from its commencement—have shown what LIBERTY is, and what free institutions can

9

that of the great landed proprietors at home; he does not indeed now interfere with politics, but he can if he so chooses command a great number of votes. This, however much some may deprecate the result, is the natural influence of property in a representative government, and more especially

do, to stimulate the enterprise and strengthen the energies of mankind. Of the ultimate effects of this canal, and the spirit for such undertakings which it has diffused throughout the whole country, it is impossible to form any adequate conception. The reviewer contemplating future improvements, says, that "by an artificial navigation of sixteen miles, the voyage from Buffalo to Pittsburgh would be uninterrupted. The communications between the Ohio and Lake Erie, are numerous and not difficult. A short cut would join the Muskingum, which discharges itself a hundred and seventy miles below Pittsburgh, with the Cayahoga. The junction of the Scioto with the Sandusky, and the Miami of the Lake, with the Miami of the Ohio, is practicable. Lakes Michigan and Erie may unite their waters by means of the river Raisin, while by the Chicago river which runs into the former, and a branch of the river Plein, a passage might be secured into the Illinois, and thence into the Mississipi.——The time must soon arrive, when that extensive territory from the Ohio to the Great Lakes, and from the Missouri to the borders of Pennsylvania, a country fertile and healthful, inhabited by a race of hardy and vigorous men, capable of supporting a population of enormous magnitude,—a country in comparison with which the fairest kingdom in Europe is almost sterile, will hereafter receive all that may supply its wants or add to its luxuries through New York, and will in turn transmit by the same channel, the rich fruits of an exuberant soil, owned and cultivated by a free population.——The imagination is startled by its own reveries, as it surveys the coasts of Erie, Huron, and Michigan, and traverses the rich prairies of Indiana, or the gloomy forests of Ohio. But we firmly believe that these bright anticipations will be converted into facts, and that our country will

of landed property. An independent freeholder,
however small his patrimonial inheritance, may in
general please himself as to his vote, but a tenant
will in almost every instance find it his interest to
please his landlord.   Were the pestilent system of
universal suffrage, therefore, introduced into Great
Britain, it is not in the agricultural, but in the commercial and manufacturing districts of the country,
that its destructive effects would be first visible.
The landed proprietor would bring forward his
tenants to the poll, as easily as the highland chief-
tain of old mustered his clan for the battle, and
Knockdunder's remark to old David Deans, respect-

---

hereafter exhibit an inland trade, unrivalled for its activity, its
value, and its extent." See an interesting article on the New
York canals, in the North American Review, No. XXXIV. p.
230.

There is not a doubt that these canals will also carry off a
large amount of trade which would otherwise have found its way
down the St. Lawrence to Canada.   When the country on the
Canadian side of Erie, and the lakes above it, is settled, the
farmers will find a much nearer market for their grain by the
smooth navigation of the canal, than by the *portage* at the Falls of
Niagara, and down the furious rapids of the St. Lawrence, besides
gaining nearly two months in the year of those which they now
lose by the ice,   The Champlain canal has already begun to bring
down to New York a lucrative trade, from the banks of that lake,
which heretofore went northward to Montreal.   In fact much of the
moral and political, as well as commercial aspect of this vast continent, will, in the course probably of a few years, undergo a very
great revolution.   The Erie canal has done more to endanger to
the British crown the loss of Upper Canada, than all that warlike
operations could ever have effected.

ing the call of the congregation to Mr. Butler, would exactly apply—" I believe the best end of it was, ' Long live M'Callummore and Knockdunder.' —And as to its being a unanimous call, I would pe glad to ken fat business the carles have to call ony thing or ony body but what the Duke and mysell likes." The Patroon's residence is in a pleasant situation a little to the northward of the city.

Albany, although not reputed unhealthy, is in the summer months a very warm and uncomfortable residence. While I was here for a few days in the latter end of June, the thermometer ranged from 85° to 92°, and on sabbath several persons took off their coats in church.[15] In the evening of the same day there was a great deal of lightning in the west and north west. This brilliant phenomenon is exceedingly common in America, but I never saw it so abundant or so vivid as on this occasion. The horizon was overspread with thickly gathered clouds, undefined and obscure in the intervals between the flashes, but instantly and powerfully lighted up, and the figure and density of every rolling mass exhibited in the most beautiful gradations of shade and colour. The arrowy streams of electric fluid darted along with very little intermis-

---

[15] It must not be supposed that this is a customary practice in America; I never met with it elsewhere but on one occasion at Boston when the thermometer was about 95°. When I mentioned the circumstance in New York my friends assured me that they had never before heard of such an occurrence.

7

sion till after midnight, sometimes descending towards the earth, more frequently shooting upwards to the heavens, and again across the sky from one mountain of clouds to another. At one time the storm seemed to approach us, if storm it could be called; a few heavy drops of rain fell, and I heard the deep toned murmuring of the distant thunder. I lay in bed with the window open, gazing at the splendid scene till midnight, after which it gradually died away. There is seldom a fine summer evening, in this country, without less or more lightning.

There is a fall of some celebrity on the Mohawk river, called the Cohoes. The Mohawk has its source near the Oneyda lake, in the upper part of the State, and flowing from west to east, nearly at right angles to the Hudson, unites with it nine or ten miles above Albany. The Cohoes fall is between two and three miles from their junction; it is seventy feet high, and according to Weld about three hundred yards broad. The banks below the fall are quite precipitous and are chiefly composed of slate rock and limestone. The precipice over which the water descends crosses the channel at right angles to the banks, not unlike an immense dam dyke, and the brow of it is as steep and nearly as smooth as the Palisades near New York. There was not nearly enough of water, when I visited it, to cover the rock, but while it rushed in pretty copious streams over some parts of it, others were left quite dry. This circumstance and the great breadth of the fall, in proportion to its height, materially weaken the effect, and altogether my expectations were somewhat disappointed. At the deepest part of the stream however the water broke into foam at the verge, and a cloud of light spray rose gracefully over it, in which the prismatic colours went and came. In returning I crossed the Mohawk a short way below, by a wooden bridge, from the centre of which there is a finer view of the cascade, than can be obtained close by it.

Passing through the village of Waterford, I crossed the Hudson by another wooden bridge and went through Lansingburgh and Troy. At Lansingburgh, nine miles above Albany, terminates the sloop navigation of the Hudson. This was for some time a thriving town, but is now on the decline, in consequence of sand having accumulated in the bed of the river, which obstructs the passage of sloops. 'Jetties' have been built at various places to reduce the bank, but hitherto without adequate effect. Troy is nearly three miles below, and seems to increase in population and wealth as its neighbour falls off. One bank was formerly sufficient for the commercial transactions of both towns, now Lansingburgh has one, and Troy two. I crossed from Troy in a ferry boat; and in returning to Albany, passed by the way two Government magazines.

There are in Albany eleven places of worship,[14]

[14] These are, 3 Presbyterian, 2 Dutch Reformed, 1 Dutch Lutheran, 1 Baptist, 1 Episcopalian, 1 Methodist, 1 Quaker, and 1 Romish.

and two Sabbath schools were instituted about
a year and a half ago. I have spent only one
Sabbath in Albany. In the forenoon I heard a
communion sermon in one of the Presbyterian
churches, from the words, ' Christ our Passover is
sacrificed for us.' The discourse was judicious
and strictly evangelical; the speaker's manner animated and interesting. After finishing his discourse, he came down from the pulpit and presided
at the communion table, according to the customary form in Presbyterian churches. His auditory
was numerous and attentive. In the afternoon I
heard an Episcopalian minister, from the passage,
' The sting of death is sin.' Though by no means
a very eloquent discourse, it contained an explicit
statement of the doctrine of original sin, the ina-
bility of man to effect his own deliverance, the
perfection of Christ's atonement, and salvation
through belief of the truth, and renewal of the
Holy Spirit. In the evening I heard another minister in the same church, but his discourse was
confused and inaccurate.

I had occasion to remark in the churches of Albany, as well as every where else in this country,
the jealous separation which takes place on all occasions between the whites and the blacks. None
in whom a tinge is detected of African blood are
permitted to mingle with white men ; they are all
restricted to pews in the farther end of the gallery,
conspicuously apart from the rest of the congrega-

tion. How reprehensible is such a scene, in the house and presence of Him who hath said, ' Look not on his countenance—for the Lord seeth not as man seeth ; for man looketh on the outward appearance, but the Lord looketh on the heart.' But, alas !

> " He finds his brother guilty—of a skin
> Not coloured like his own !"

and even in the worship of the Most High he must manifest his horror at such an enormity.

END OF VOLUME FIRST.

Printed in the United States
79550LV00004B/125